CW01497547

Venezuela's Collapse:

The Long Story of How Things Fell Apart

Carlos Lizarralde

CODEX NOVELLUS

First Edition, 2024.
ISBN 979-8-88-403385-6
Library of of Congress Cataloging-in-Publication Data has been applied for.
Offset and ebook editions of this book are also available.
codexnovellus.com

Contents

La Guaira y el Concorde by Tony Vázquez

Preface

"*The past is never dead. It's not even past.*"
William Faulkner

Breaking the sound barrier on every flight, the Concorde supersonic jet had a way of pushing the imaginary limits of time and space. During the plane's inaugural flight of the Paris-Caracas route on April 10 of 1976, the cream of Venezuela's elite fantasized about their country's imminent leap to first-world status. If such an innovation could transport them from Paris to Caracas in a miraculous six hours, almost half the time of a regular flight, they were now certain their oil dollars could buy them a brand-new nation. Sitting at Maiquetía Airport every Sunday after that flight, the airplane became a totem of a perfect future.

Four decades later, with Venezuela in ruins, exiled artist Tony Vazquez Figueroa found an anonymous photograph of two boys contemplating the wonder of French engineering at Maiquetía. He outlined and then filled the airplane's image with an oil-based resin. Black and shiny as the heaviest of crude oils, the plane's new surface and the way it compulsively calls for our attention speaks to a reality few could have articulated back then.

The innocent boys stand in for an entire country, transfixed by a vision of peaceful and seemingly endless prosperity. A dozen airport workers gawk in unison at the marvel of streamlined metal. Oil had not only purchased the best products found all over the world, but it had also seemingly mended a social rift by endowing a modern nation and its liberal state with magical powers.

The Concorde, bathed in oil, is a perfect metaphor for how 20th-century Venezuela dedicated itself to building a glossy, impossibly attractive façade to try to make the nation forget its fractured past.

The reflective layer captures everyone's attention, inside and outside the photograph, while hiding the more disturbing possibilities. What if the country had always been, save for the few oil decades, poor in resources, divided along ethnic and racial lines, and simmering with deadly violence? In that case, the "Venezuela question" is no longer about why such wealth, consensus, and peace disappeared so suddenly in the 21st century. Instead, we should ask why we ever thought the 20th century bubble of prosperity and possibility was anything but a rare exception. Almost a fluke.

For those of us who were born in the golden years, in Vazquez Figueroa's Concorde Age, it has been difficult to shake the belief that Venezuela had been rich and peaceful from the very beginning and would be forever. A place where everyone understood each other, just like the boys on the tarmac, best friends, brothers, accomplices without contradictions, gawking at an aircraft that seemed to symbolize perfect social peace. A moment that, like the supersonic jet and its mirage of progress, is now gone.

By 2014 the country had descended into a crisis of hunger, violence, ethnic conflict, and circus-like politics that mirrored Venezuela's past. Be it the bloody, all-out war over the founding of Caracas in the 1580s, the violent slave rebellions that freed the entire Valle de Yaracuy from Spanish rule by 1732, the genocidal Race War of 1814, the vicious Federal War of the 1850s and 1860s, or the desperate rural poverty of the early 1900s. It now seems the oil boom, and the country it created to forget that fraught history, already contained the seeds of the economic self-destruction that has come to pass.

Probing the country's past, looking underneath the layer of resin, is the only way to tackle another question that has yet to be answered: why did vast majorities at first, and significant minorities later, continued supporting the Chavista dismantling of the 20th-century liberal state even as hunger and murder gripped the country? Why was the opposition to Chavismo unable to prevail over more than twenty years, even during a humanitarian crisis? It is hard to think of a government letting year-to-year inflation go from fifty to one million percent, over half a decade, and remain in power by year six.

This book was written over the years the country I knew as a child self-destructed. In that sense, it is a personal search. Not everyone gets to see their country of birth literally vanish without a clear sense of how or why it happened.

I found my answers in the broad historical structures that converged in the Venezuela of the early 21st century. Instead of dwelling on the daily politics, the colorful personalities, or the fleeting circumstances of this or that event, this book is grounded in cultural, economic, political, and social patterns taking place over centuries. The trends focus on peoples' living conditions over time, which choices and opportunities have been available to some, denied others, who lost and who gained resources, and how political narratives shaped daily life. While leading historians have interpreted the country's long-term history before, the impulse not to look for the roots of current events gives this approach urgency.

Most explanations about Venezuela today come from the intuitive feelings of those who have suffered the consequences of a collapse. Their immediate situation and that of their families and friends, tragic as it is, cannot give a good account of the bigger picture—or of centuries-old trend lines that continue to shape the country.

The first chapter in this book tells the story of Venezuela between 1999 and 2019 in relation to the country's social and political history; the second one probes the self-destructive nature of an economy built with oil revenues in the 20th century; the third chapter examines the country's history of ethnic and racial conflict between the arrival of the Spanish and the Wars of Independence.[1] The concluding chapter details Chavismo's deliberate dismantling of the state, the economy, and civil society starting in 2004.

The short essay at the end is the book's epilogue. It tells a story about General José Antonio Páez in the 1830s—years when the aftermath of the Wars of Independence saw ravaged territories and the beginnings of a nation—a time resembling our own.

I
Implosion,
1999–2019

By 2019 Caracas's airport was empty. Few remembered the long-ago Concorde flights. Most world airlines had ceased Venezuelan operations altogether. Many around the world still think about their last walk through those terminals on their way to exile with a mixture of bitterness and nostalgia. Yet few ever consider that their plight is not unique in Venezuela's long history, nor the most tragic.

The Venezuela of 2019 bore an eerie resemblance to that of 1819, which saw the beginning of the end of the Wars of Independence from Spain.[1] The conflicts started in 1810, engulfing the territories in a bloody decade that left a trail of death and destruction. The wars had turned Caracas into a ghost city, empty and somber. Throughout the countryside, fields lay burned to the ground. Nothing was left of the trading company that had managed the colony's exports for decades, save an empty building in ruins. Most colonial functionaries had been hunted down and killed unless they had been lucky enough to flee. The territories had no recognizable civil administration. Hundreds, perhaps thousands, of small traders who ran the country stores feeding the territories had been killed by both sides.

A third of the country's population died in the long and vicious conflicts.[2] When they ended, the population of Caracas was half of what it had been in 1810.[3] Survivors and their descendants would not forget the acts of plunder, torture, rape, and senseless killing by royalist and independence forces for 150 years, or until the oil boom reinvented the country and its story.

There is a broad consensus the devastation left by the Venezuelan independence wars was unique.[4] A military historian has written that "Venezuela saw the fiercest battles, witnessed the worst atrocities, and suffered the greatest losses" of the Spanish-American wars.[5]

After the Battle of Carabobo in 1821, the territories were almost entirely under republican control, but hunger and disease ravaged a virtually stateless country overrun by banditry.

Fast-forward 200 years. By 2019 Venezuela was again gripped by death and catastrophe: a four-year-old humanitarian crisis had left starvation and epidemics across the land. The average citizen had lost twenty-four pounds between 2016 and 2017.[6] Infant mortality increased a hundredfold between 2012 and 2016.[7] Factories, oil facilities, tractor production lines, steel mills, food depots stood abandoned and rotting.[8] Inflation had reached almost a million percent in 2018, the power grid had nearly collapsed, and the oil industry lay ransacked.[9] The state had lost control of its own jails. Vast swaths of territory were in the hands of freelance miners. The country had become a highway of drug shipments between the Andes region and the world.[10] It is impossible to find actual murder rates in the country after 2005 because the government stopped releasing comprehensive data. The direst independent estimates pegged the 2017 homicide rate in Caracas at 100 deaths per 100,000 people. If accurate, the city would be the most dangerous among large urban centers in the world during that year.[11] Beyond citizen's safety, many of the government's infrastructure and service functions had been dismantled by then.

While a few in city bubbles enjoyed a middle-class life, the choice for others had been to flee or die. Instagram snaps of cute birthday parties in manicured gardens conveyed a strange sense of normalcy, but millions were walking away from their old lives to reach uncertain refuge in Colombia, Brazil, Peru, Ecuador, and Chile. They set off on this trip, thousands of miles away, wearing flip-flops and carrying small bundles of possessions. Four-and-a-half million refugees had left by 2019. The United Nations called it the largest human mobilization in Latin America's history.[12]

There is an obvious question about the events of 200 years ago and those spanning the twenty years between 1999 and 2019: why would a group of individuals, or a social class, or even a single leader, destroy a state, and an entire economy, right after taking control of both?

In Mexico and Peru, the 19th-century Wars of Independence from Spain were about gaining control over, never destroying, colonial government. President Benito Juárez, the indigenous lawyer who transformed Mexico a few decades later, forged a new state out of surviving administrative structures created by the Crown.

Simón Bolívar led the Venezuelan armies to victory over Spanish rule, but by 1819 the economy and the colonial government his own family had helped establish were burned to the ground. Both sides in the war were vicious, with Bolívar himself having a direct hand in the country's destruction. The unleashed furies must have been triggered by something much deeper than a conflict over political sovereignty.

The self-destruction would be even more puzzling in the 21st century. Hugo Chávez peacefully assumed the reins of power through several significant electoral victories. He had every imaginable incentive not to dismantle a state he headed, and even less of a reason to ruin the widely profitable state oil enterprises. Overlapping Chávez's own years in power, strongmen like Vladimir Putin in Russia harnessed the state bureaucracies to profit from his country's energy resources. A decade later, General el-Sisi would do the same in Egypt. In contrast, by 2014, the year after Chávez died, the Venezuelan state and its oil company had started its self-destructive decline, while the country descended into a humanitarian crisis.[13]

Most people tend to think that Chávez was either an evil fool or a romantic one. For his part, Bolívar is thought to have been brilliant but helpless in a storm he could not control. But without understanding the massive social and economic changes that took place in the Venezuela of the 1800s, and then again in the 2000s, the impact of their oversized personalities makes little sense.

In the 1800s and the 2000s major demographic shifts transformed the dynamics of both societies. The Spanish colony had been consumed for decades by a struggle between those castes of Spanish origin and their descendants on one side, and those of African and mixed-race origin. By 1800 mixed-race free Pardos became 45% of the population. Along with the free population of African descent, non-indigenous free people of color made up 49% of the colony.[14]

The ethnic conflict in the colonial territories reached a boiling point by 1810, the year independence from Spain was declared in Caracas. The decade started with declarations of fraternity and would end in an orgy of death.

The firestorm of ethnic passion and acrimony during the 1810s would be reignited 200 years later. By 1998 a political system broken by two decades of low oil prices witnessed the rise of a long-simmering ethnic divide. The welfare democracy could no longer deliver for the descendants of the mixed-raced Pardo caste living in the informal settlements of every major city. A reckoning became inevitable.

Once again, the tectonic plates of Venezuelan society gave in to pressures that had been building for a long time. The resulting earthquake of December 3, 1998 delivered dashing Lieutenant Colonel Hugo Chávez. He promised his country the moon while ushering in an era that turned, twenty years later, into an unimaginable catastrophe.

The destructive choices made by Venezuelans and their leaders during the Wars of Independence and the Chavista Revolution only make sense by going back to the country's rocky foundations. The answers lie in the tangled intersections of race and caste, cocoa, coffee and oil, and the distribution of power over several centuries.

Venezuela's Beginnings

The Spanish first arrived in 1498. Almost immediately they attempted to conquer over half a million indigenous people scattered over seemingly endless territory.[15] Venezuela was no island bound by coasts, like Hispaniola, and there was no single seat of empire to occupy, as in Tenochtitlan. Fragmented culturally and geographically over a vast expanse, indigenous nations resisted, coexisted with the newcomers, were reduced to forced labor, or fled. Sometimes they did all of these, at different times.

A few decades later, kidnapped Africans were brought to work as slaves. Amerindian women and those enslaved in

West Central Africa were raped or entered into relationships with different levels of coercion with thousands of southern Spanish men. The first children of mixed-race were born.

Unlike the imaginary that gave rise to an American world of distinctly Black, white, and indigenous individuals, the culture of Iberia blurred racial and ethnic lines from the very beginning of the conquest. The children of a West Central African mother and a Spanish father were not automatically considered Black, as would happen in the British colonies. They would have a unique identity, sometimes with distinct rights.

In 1503, the Spanish Queen Isabella issued a provision that would have been unthinkable for any Tudor royal to contemplate. Marriages between Spanish settlers and Amerindians, proclaimed the Queen, were "legitimate and desirable."[16]

Before the conquest of the Americas, Spain had been a conflicted yet functional multi-ethnic society. A Muslim Caliphate had occupied significant parts of the country for the better part of seven centuries. In those possessions populations of different ethnic ancestry and religious heritage coexisted within a caste system. Arab elites, Berbers, Mozarabs (Christians under Muslim rule), Muladies (those of mixed Arab, Berber, and Mozarab descent), Jews, Black Africans, and Slavic mercenaries were each assigned specific neighborhoods, rights, and privileges. Since the ninth century, those who could demonstrate true Arab and Syrian ancestry had a higher social position than other Muslims.[17]

Unlike England, Spain in the 1490s was a place of many colors. In the colonies, this worldview meant that Spanish men held power and physically and sexually subjugated everyone at will, women and men, but in a society that recognized itself as ethnically diverse.

As in Granada, the last Muslim Emirate in Spain, distinct castes in the Spanish-American colonies were at the center of colonial life from the beginning. The difference between the Americas and the Andalusian city lay in who was on top, and who was at the bottom of the pyramid. Those born in Spain had the highest rank in the Americas—if they were noble, more so. Until the mid-1600s, nobles of indigenous nations who had been allies of the Spanish also had many rights and privileges.

Further down in the caste hierarchies were Amerindians who fought on the Spanish side. Then came the Mestizo offspring of Spanish and Amerindian women. Someone's position within the scheme determined both unspoken and legislated privileges and rights. These determined who could work as a free artisan or join a specific guild, who could own land, and who could serve the Crown. At the bottom of the caste system were those Amerindians in evolving forms of bondage and slavery. They included most of the indigenous population within the colonial system.

Others at the top of the caste universe included Creoles, direct descendants of the Spanish-born conquerors. They were the landowning and slaveholding class, often in political conflict with the Spanish-born colonial administrators. For them, the Spanish-born were intruders without roots or a future in the colony. By law, Creoles could not hold most positions with the Crown. However, they managed many municipal and local affairs through parliamentary bodies resembling those found in Spanish cities.

Alongside the caste system, enslaved West Central Africans who were originally kidnapped, and their descendants, were at the center of a plantation economy. Their work sustained the country starting in the middle of the 1600s. On the plantations, a regime of terror enforced multi-generational slavery for tens of thousands of people. Surviving 1767 documents from a slave plantation in the valley of Chuao detail the prison-like rules and regulations that kept people living wholly isolated from the outside.[18]

Yet, anyone visiting the former plantation today can see the impenetrable rain forest of the steep Cordillera de la Costa rising a few hundred yards from the original site. The geography lent itself to escape, and not just in Chuao. The military means to control the territories were often slender, given the relative poverty of the colonies. Thousands of enslaved workers would escape plantations every year to join free communities established deep in the jungle, or the faraway plains. These "cumbes" or "rochelas" were beyond the reach of colonial power. Historian Brito Figueroa estimates that by the end of the 1700s there were as many as 40,000 former slaves living in rebellious communities in the jungles, forests, and mountains away from Spanish control.[19] This figure would constitute about 25% of the entire kidnapped workforce from Africa.[20]

Unlike their even more unfortunate counterparts in the American South, those enslaved in the Spanish colonies had more varied and acceptable legal mechanisms to gain their freedom. As the 1600s ended, an increasing number of free Blacks founded communities in every town. They established trading links with the mutinous communities in the countryside.[21] Surreptitiously, the rebellious communities started trading with those legally free in towns, connecting the "official" African colony with the renegade one.

All these factors created cities and towns of considerable social and economic complexity. People of different races and ethnic backgrounds lived side by side, with rights and obligations of a feudal nature, and with varying degrees of freedom. During the first 200 years of colonization, or until the early 1700s, the Muslim-infused culture associated with Queen Isabella, Charles V, and Philip II organized colonial life and sought to manage its internal conflicts. Everything would soon change.

The War of Spanish Succession that ended in 1714 brought significant changes around the world and Phillip V, a French-born king, to Madrid. A new royal ideology wanted more central control throughout the empire in the Americas, less power for Creoles, and a stricter social order. A French-influenced bureaucracy also responded to their century's obsession with organizing and classifying every aspect of society. In Spanish America, they would find a unique challenge. Most societies there had been aggressively jumping ethnic and racial lines for two centuries. This was especially evident in the Venezuelan territories. The population of New Spain—current-day Mexico—had always been primarily indigenous, and those of Cuba and Hispaniola were already mainly African. By the early 1700s sparsely populated Venezuela enjoyed more numerical balance between those of Spanish origin or descent, African origin or descent, and Amerindians, than other colonies.[22]

Influenced by the new winds from Madrid, both Spanish-born inhabitants and Creoles in every Spanish colony became obsessed throughout the 1700s by the classification of every person's ethnic descent. Those of African and Spanish descent had always been called Mulattos. Mestizos were those of Indian and Spanish origin. The classification became more formal, and especially in New Spain, more complex. In a 1763 painting, the offspring of Spanish and Mulatta were called Morisco. Children of Spanish and Morisca descent were called Albinos. The children of Spanish and Albina were labelled *Torna atrás*, or "go back," presumably because the physical features of grandparents would visibly return by the third generation.[23]

Fascinated by everyone's ethnic descent, and charged with imposing greater social control, Spanish colonial administrators tightened the regulations of freedom, rights, and privileges for different groups. There were many caste-based restrictions on who could work where; who was allowed to rise within the army, the church, the world of commerce, colonial government; who could worship in particular churches and not others; who could wear certain clothes; who could travel with what permits and where could they go; who could own what and how much of it; or who could get what kind of education.

While an intricate classification dominated the Spanish Americas' imagination, the civil administration of the marginal colonies in the Venezuelan territories lacked the resources to replicate much complexity. In practical terms, the Venezuelan caste system concerned seven groups of non-slaved people: 1) the Spanish-born; 2) those born in

the Americas of Spanish origin or Creoles; 3) those born
in the Canary Islands; 4) indigenous people integrated
into colonial society; 5) those indigenous in some form of
bondage; 6) those formerly enslaved and now free Africans
or their descendants; and finally, 7) those of mixed-race, be
they Mestizos, Zambos, or Mulattos and their descendants.[24]
The latter were increasingly known as Pardos.

Colloquially, the word "Pardo" designates anyone not
of pure Spanish, Indigenous, or African descent, but rather
a mixture of them. In a more literal sense, Pardos simply have
brown skin.[25]

Often enough, documents from the time group every
person of mixed-race as a Pardo. The imaginary castes that
divided everyone of mixed-race into dozens of categories
became, in practice, mute. The regulations and restrictions
regarding those of mixed-race increasingly focused on Pardos.

The 1700s were also years of relative plenty in the
Venezuelan territories. The prices of cocoa and sugar, indigo,
and other plantation-economy products were booming on
a global scale. While Venezuela never had the extensive or
ideal lands for cultivating sugar that made Haiti, and later
Cuba, spectacularly wealthy, the economy grew significantly
compared to the hard times of the 1600s. As cities and
towns across the country prospered, the population grew, and
Pardos specifically grew as a share of the population. Little
noticed at the time and barely mentioned by contemporary
historians, the increasing percentage of the Pardo population
would change everything.

Those of mixed-race were already a significant part of
the population. According to calculations by Rosenblat, cited

by Brito, in the mid-1600s those of mixed-race numbered 30,000, compared to 30,000 Spanish-born and of Spanish descent, within a total population of 370,000.[26]

By 1800, the Venezuelan territories' population had exploded to 898,000. Mixed-race Pardos made up 407,000 inhabitants within the colony by 1800. By contrast, the Spanish-born and Creoles of Spanish descent had been reduced to a mere 20% of the population integrated into colonial life, or 184,000. Free subjects of African descent amounted to 33,000, while those of Indigenous descent integrated in colonial life amounted to 76,000. The rest were escaped slaves and those of indigenous descent living beyond the reach of colonial power.[27]

Pardos were already a near majority a decade before the independence wars. Along with legally free Blacks they made up almost half of the population. If those of indigenous descent living in colonial parishes were included, the free people of color already made up a super-majority among those not enslaved in the colony of 1800.[28]

Pardos were explicitly barred from most commercial and professional activities, key army posts, colonial government positions, and, most importantly, holding specific kinds of property. Despite these obstacles, Pardos' demographic ascendancy forced the issue of liberalizing the caste system's restrictions into public debate.

The political intrigues over the rights of Pardos in the 1700s remain unresearched and mostly unknown. Although historians have yet to pore over royal archives and explore this history in detail, it is clear the conflict dominated public life for over half a century.

Either because the Crown wanted to leverage the Pardo issue in its never-ending political battle with Creoles, or due to the political pressures of a new social reality that could no longer be ignored, or both, a ferocious debate ensued. The Crown moved to loosen up many restrictions.

The slaveholding Creoles opposed these changes. In Venezuela, Creoles were called Mantuanos after the exclusive privilege of Creole women to wear shawls (*mantas* in Spanish, therefore Mantuanos) over their heads on Sunday. This was something no other caste was permitted to do. Their defense of their entitlements and privileges, and their insistence on maintaining restrictions for everyone else, was ferocious. Creoles pushed back against the liberalization of the caste system by addressing the King, getting involved in specific judicial cases in the colony, and publicly shaming any Pardos who tried to move beyond the restrictions against them.

By 1790 the Cabildo de Caracas, a body that functioned both as a Creole guild and a municipal authority, petitioned the King regarding efforts to liberalize the caste system. The formal letter accused Spanish-born colonial magistrates of "the open protection that is shamelessly afforded to Mulattos or Pardos and all kinds of vile people to undermine the high esteem held by the old, distinguished and honorable families."[29] These words are so incredible in the context of Venezuelan society's current idealization of Creole or Mantuano society that the original Spanish text is reproduced here: *"la abierta protección que escandalosamente prestan a los Mulatos o Pardos y toda gente vil para menoscabar la estimación de las familias antiguas, distinguidas y honradas."* The document goes on to decry royal efforts "to level Pardos and Mulattos by making an exception of their low quality in order to provide the instruction that so far they've lacked and should lack in the future."[30] In the original Spanish: *"franquear a los Pardos y facilitarles por medio de la dispensación de su baxa calidad la instrucción de que hasta ahora han carecido y deben carecer en lo adelante."*

The small minority of Creoles were clearly nervous about the power of ascendant Pardos. As recounted in the third chapter of this book, Creoles left no stone unturned. They fought judicial cases in which individuals classified as Pardos petitioned for university admission or economic rights. And they publicly shamed those who tried to overstep their caste.[31]

Creole power was threatened on every front. If the Pardo demographic tsunami was not enough, the world was undergoing a human rights revolution that would overturn their plantation economy. By 1789 the French National Assembly had declared that "all men are born free." By 1791 enslaved workers in Saint-Domingue (soon to be called Haiti) rose in arms to make the claim come true. The wealthiest colony in the Americas became free of slavery, igniting an already precarious social order in Venezuela. The 1794 slave rebellion in Coro, and one in Maracaibo in 1799, explicitly called for freedom in the name of the "French laws."[32]

Civil Wars over Independence

Venezuelan children of the Concorde generation were taught a particular story of Venezuelan independence. It all started, according to the narrative, in a sleepy colonial outpost known as the Royal Captaincy General of Venezuela that was peacefully plodding along at the end of the 1700s. By 1808 Napoleon had invaded Spain, imprisoned the King, and imposed a puppet government over the empire in the Americas. Venezuelan Creoles, using the Cabildo de Caracas, seized the opportunity in 1810 to break away from a now-illegitimate monarchy, proclaimed sovereignty, wrote brilliant declarations, and led the first independence armies.

Yet, the Creole independent forces were, to their surprise, systematically defeated between 1810 and 1817. They seized Caracas twice, and declared and established independent Republics both times, only to be crushed. Their most famous representative and eventual leader, Simón Bolívar, commanded the country's most important garrison during the first uprising, only to end up in exile in Cartagena. Years later he led the failed Second Republic before fleeing again.

What the elementary school stories never mention is that with the Spanish King imprisoned, and nearly every Spanish soldier on the planet fighting the French on Iberian soil, the so-called "royal" soldiers defeating the First and the Second Republics were mostly locals. The conflict was never one between newly self-conscious Venezuelans and royal Spaniards, but rather one between castes. The war of the First Republic was one of Pardos against Creole-led armies. Those of mixed-race felt no allegiance to the King, had no interest in the monarchy, and did not feel Spanish in any way. They flew the King's standards, but they were fighting against Creole rule.

The battles had been previewed in court rooms and petitions for years. Creoles had fought for keeping Pardos illiterate and without any meaningful access to the economy, the army, or government. A growing Pardo population had been pushing back.

This is why the population took sides in the early war along ethnic lines, a fact well known to Caracas elites for at least 150 years after the conflict. Laureano Vallenilla Lanz, one of the best-known establishment intellectuals of his time, wrote in 1919 that, "Until 1815, the vast majority of the Venezuelan people were royalists, or godos, that is to say, enemies of the patriots…"[33] While, by the 1970s, schoolchildren were told about the fierceness of the 1814 battles between Spanish and Patriot armies over the Second Republic, writer Juan Uslar, in 1952, had already called the conflict "a popular rebellion" against Creoles. For Uslar, the early conflict had been a civil war between future Venezuelans.[34]

Pardos, free Africans, mutinous slaves, and many others of indigenous descent, destroyed Creole-led pro-independence governments twice in four long years. They battled Creole-led armies that sought to preserve the caste system and slavery in a newly independent republic. As the third chapter of this book chronicles in detail, the social and military dynamics had changed by 1816. Still, the first half of the independence wars remains critical to understanding what happened by the 1820s.

The violence and destruction of the civil war escalated during its first four years to a point of no return, reaching a bloody climax in 1814. As chronicled by Juan Uslar, an Asturian-born ex-convict named José Tomás Boves led a mixed-race army that emerged from the central plains to loot, torture, and kill every Spanish-born inhabitant and their descendants crossing their path. Boves' rag-tag army burned all plantations and many towns as they traversed the country on their way from Calabozo in The Plains, to Cumana on the far eastern coast, all the while flying the Spanish King's flag.[35]

By the conflict's end, the unleashed tribal furies had a clear result: a third of the country's population died over the course of the wars, the same proportion who had perished in Europe during the Black Death of the 14th century. The economy was ransacked, the countryside burned down, and the Spanish colonial administration decimated by slaughter or forced exile.[36]

This havoc in the 1810s led directly to the terrible poverty and lawlessness Venezuela experienced throughout the 19th century. This dark period witnessed episodes of human suffering and death unmatched in subsequent Venezuelan history, not even by the recent tragedy of the Chávez era.

While the Venezuelan ethnic and racial wars had little to do with the experience of independence in Mexico or Peru, the similarities with the Spanish and French Caribbean colonies are apparent. Eighteenth-century Caribbean colonies, with societies built on rigid ethnic castes and supported by slave plantation economies, could mainly expect tragic futures.

Saint-Domingue, as Haiti was known, had already experienced this. The colony was one of the wealthiest places in the world off its sugarcane and coffee plantations, until the slave mutiny of 1791.[37] The conflict pitted former African-born slaves, Haitian-born ones, those who had been free before the mutiny, and tens of thousands of Mulattos (free and of mixed-race), against each other and against white French planters, Spanish, British, and French troops. The vicious

wars included several campaigns of racial and ethnic extermination and ended fifteen years later in a stalemate between
two factions. In the north a former slave of pure African
descent, King Henri Cristophe, led a plantation society based
on forced labor. In the west and south, Alexander Pétion,
a Mulatto, abandoned sugar production in favor of small
plot cultivation.[38]

By then half the population had died in the long wars.[39]
The consequences of the furious conflicts fueled by ethnic
acrimony, and their violent aftermath, still plague the
island today.

As in Haiti, the result of Venezuela's vicious civil conflict
in the 1810s produced cycles of turmoil, violence, deep
poverty, and brief periods of a fleeting renaissance throughout
the 1800s. Then the oil boom changed everything, and this
history was forgotten, and then rewritten.

Fast-Forward 200 Years

Hugo Chávez became president in 1999 after an
overwhelming electoral victory that most commentators
had imagined impossible a few years before. The formidable
political machines of traditional parties Acción Democrática
and Copei that had stood for sixty years, vanished into
thin air. Venevisión and RCTV, the television conglom-
erates that had shaped consumer behavior for decades,
discovered they could no longer sway voters either way. They
maintained an uneasy neutrality in the election. These were
unprecedented times.

Why did things change? A long-simmering demographic
shift after twenty years of low oil prices had blown apart the

20th-century order. The conditions for this explosion were laid down several decades previously.

Venezuela's transformation into the world's number one exporter of oil by the late 1930s turned the country into a magnet for migrants after the Second World War. While the 1961 census only records 541,000 foreigners in the country, a closer look at arrivals intending to stay more than six months, those who entered without registration, and unregistered children, yields a much higher figure. It is estimated that between 1948 and 1961, 800,000 people emigrated to the still-rural country, making up about 10% of its population in 1961.[40]

The real influence of this immigration wave was felt in Caracas, where the new future was being built. It is estimated that by 1961 one out of four people within the city had been born in a foreign country.[41] Many of the city's neighborhoods would retain a distinctly southern European flavor through the 1980s. The Italian-language daily *La Voce d'Italia* would be published starting in 1950.

By the 1940s it was clear the world would run on oil in the future. At the same time, news was spreading that Venezuela had as much of it as could be extracted from the ground. The coming oil bonanza acted as a gigantic draw for the kind of driven, hungry immigrants who seek to make their fortune in countries more blessed than their own. They came from the 1940s and through the 1960s to escape poverty in Italy, the post-Holocaust in central Europe, scarcity in post-war Spain and Portugal, upheaval in Syria and Lebanon, pogroms in Morocco, the Soviet occupations of eastern Europe, violence in Colombia, and economic stagnation in Peru, Argentina, Chile, and Cuba.

These newcomers shared their outlook with two groups already in the country: the few remaining descendants of colonial Creoles that had survived the Wars of Independence and had not left the country, and immigrants who had arrived throughout the 19th century. The latter had initially gone to Venezuela as traders, adventurers, and technicians from France, Corsica, central Europe, the UK, and the United States. They had prospered into the wealthiest families not directly tied to the government. On the other hand, the sons of the provincial Creole elites, educated in Caracas, had stayed in the capital city to become the backbone of an oil-financed new governmental and professional middle class.

It is hard to believe that Caracas was still a small town of barely 200,000 people in 1936.[42] Yet, a very modern country was about to be built from the capital.

The immigrant wave very quickly filled a huge knowledge vacuum in the infant country with their professional expertise and their entrepreneurial spirit. They accelerated the building of many of the institutions of state and the nascent private sector. As the century progressed, their children and grandchildren enjoyed the built-in advantages of their intellectual and family equity, as well as the financial pole position acquired at the beginning of the oil years.

The Rural Poor in the City

The foreign immigration boom of the 1930s to 1960s was mirrored by another demographic development: the growth in numbers of poor Venezuelans moving from the countryside to the big cities near the coast. In the sixty years between 1941 and 2001, the country's urban population rose from 31% to 88%.[43]

The migrants in this rural exodus were the poorest Venezuelans. They represented a country with 80% illiteracy by 1935.[44] They were suffering a centuries-old malaria epidemic that had infected nearly one in four Venezuelans, or 800,000 people, by 1940.[45] They were fleeing a countryside condemned to poverty by low-yield soils. They were direct descendants of the mixed-race poor population from colonial times.

After the Spanish left in 1821, the formal caste system was abolished for all mixed-race, indigenous, and free African peoples, and civil and economic rights were widely extended throughout the population except for those enslaved. But flowery constitutions and well-written laws could do little or nothing for most people. The ideology and the culture of the caste system was translated into an informal code. In effect, a societal hierarchy loosely based on shades of dark skin, in addition to hair texture, accent, and education, became standardized. The lighter the skin and straighter the hair, the more urbane the Spanish spoken, the higher societal standing would accrue. These were the new de facto social markers of privilege, or marginality, in the post-independence country.

For most Pardos, as those of mixed-race were known in colonial times, the issue was sheer poverty and illness. The peasant conditions of the 1700s had likely been worsened by the disastrous consequences of the independence wars. Without a strong state, most Venezuelans remained dirt poor, hungry, and sick, in the vast countryside. Caracas managed to grow during the coffee boom of the 1830s, then again during the three presidencies of Guzmán Blanco in the 1870s and 1880s. So did the lighter-skinned social classes that managed the Atlantic trade of coffee and cocoa. Still, other than a few exceptional mixed-race individuals, the old Pardos continued at the margins of society.

Beyond a few blocks in Caracas, the entire country was stuck in time. By 1881 the United States was being industrialized, connected, and would soon be electrified, but Venezuela only had twelve towns of over 4,000 people.[46]

All this would change in the new century as the oil boom and new political leaders enabled massive social spending that transformed the country: mortality rates dropped from twenty-five to thirty per 1,000 people in 1936 to 7.4 per 1,000 in 1961. Malaria was eradicated, transforming average life expectancy from thirty-eight years in 1936 to forty-three in 1941, fifty-four in 1950, and sixty-one in 1961. These trend lines continued for years so the population would double between 1950 and 1960 to reach eight million, and then maintained Latin America's fastest growth rate at close to 3% per year, until 1995.[47]

Spending on education, health, water, and sanitation, which in the early years of the 20th century had reached 5.3% of government budgets, came to surpass 30% by the 1970s.[48] The life and the world of the rural peasant, still in the countryside or already in the city, was transformed with massive investments in infrastructure, food supply, and sanitation.

But as the 1970s gave way to the 1980s, one thing became clear: the oil welfare state delivered on a long overdue social debt, but it could not erase in a few decades the conditions underlying 350 years of poverty.

Ultimately, no one had a direct or short-term way to erase the deficit in education, justice, and equity created by a ruthless conquest, a lopsided colonial government, a slave-plantation economy, and the predatory rule of local chieftains, known as *"caudillos"*, throughout the 1800s. Nominally all Venezuelans were equal by the 1960s, and the floor of physical subsistence and health was radically raised over several decades. But the chasm between those with darker skin who had come from the countryside and their descendants, and those with lighter skin who had emigrated from wealthier countries with long institutional histories, continued to be enormous.

For reasons already alluded to, racial and ethnic issues in Venezuela are not as clearly defined as they are in today's United States. Whereas the racialist strictures of plantation culture define the American experience, the Spanish Crown's caste system continues to drive Venezuela's social imaginary.

The legacy of colonial-era castes has kept alive a connection between skin shade, cultural affinities, and parental provenance, among other elements, as markers of social identity, but in a country where an overwhelming majority of the population is of mixed-race. Racial and ethnic lines separating groups can often be ambiguous, while social hierarchies do not run along clearly visible lines.

How society has forgotten the origins and continuing influence of the colonial-era caste system becomes evident in some Venezuelans' reactions to descriptions of their own lighter skin and cultural legacy in ethnic terms. Yet, they forget that not long ago, the Criollo caste was defined by language and accent, education, place of birth, shared values, as well as by skin shade and hair texture. Criollos' defense of what made their caste culturally and physically unique was as ferocious as their listing of the qualities they felt differentiated them from Pardos.

Today, ethnicity is described as the "identification of a group based on perceived cultural distinctiveness that makes a group into a people. This distinctiveness is believed to be expressed in language, music, values …"[49] Much as the ideology of 18th-century castes would have done, our world can add visual cues such as facial features, skin tone, and hair texture to the elements making up an ethnicity. The origin of parents and older ancestors is sometimes considered part of the mix.

The ambiguities of such a contemporary definition encourage the arguments of those for whom this does not help explain Venezuelan society. In this context, they point out those individuals of lighter skin who cross the supposed ethnic divide. Under the influence of American ideas that racialize identity by giving skin color a preeminent role, doubters fail to grasp how many factors, including language, accent, manners, and other cultural markers, determined the assignation of colonial castes. Back in 1819, Simón Bolívar and José Antonio Páez were perceived by their contemporaries, and probably by themselves, to have very different identities, regardless of similarities in their facial features and skin color. By 2019, President Nicolas Maduro's identity had less to do with his lighter-skin and European facial features than with other cultural markers. The latter set him apart from his main opponents, whose language, accent, outlook, and mannerisms gave them a distinct social identity. This is undoubtedly related to class differences between Maduro and the most prominent opposition politicians. But in Venezuela, it is impossible to speak about class as something isolated from the history and legacy of castes. Henrique Capriles, Leopoldo López, and María Corina Machado descend from recent Eastern European immigrants, 18th-century land-owning Creoles, and 18th-century Spanish hidalgos and aristocrats, respectively. The profound cultural and social impact of these legacies cannot be ignored.

Those who follow quantitative social sciences also find this reasoning too imprecise. Strides in statistics, and the insights provided by sociological models, have persuaded many that, unless a social reality can be clearly defined and quantified, it does not exist. Just because the Venezuelan racial and ethnic landscape does not conform to the social models of the more easily quantifiable American experience, it does not mean the issues are not real. Few would dispute the historically documented ethnic difference between Bolívar and Páez, which cannot be assessed in simple black-and-white terms. Nearly all would agree that culturally, Nicolás Maduro and opposition politician María Corina Machado come from very different places.

Beyond the imprecisions, a mountain of documentary evidence beginning in the XVI century shows the issue of identity obsessed the Spanish, the Creoles, those of mixed-race, those of African descent, and those of indigenous descent, as every group tried to define itself in relation to others and later, in relation to the idea of a "Venezuelan" nation. Many records make clear that ethnic and racial struggles drove the founding of the modern country (the third chapter expands the argument). And there are plenty of clues that these issues resurfaced in the public discourse at the cusp of the last century.

A New Social Reality

By the 1990s, the original welfare state had faltered, precipitating an acute social split. The accelerating inequality between those who had migrated from the ravaged countryside and their descendants, and those who had come from other countries with the tools of commerce, enterprise, and intellectual production in their national legacies, became irreversible by 1998. If immigration had been a critical factor in the changing cities of the 1950s and 1960s, from then onwards, the growth belonged to the original poor migrants from the countryside.

By 1998 the foreign-born and their descendants had become a smaller group as a percentage of the population. Yet they continued receiving an overwhelming share of the country's wealth. At the same time, the majorities in the favelas were growing in numbers and becoming increasingly more impoverished as oil prices faltered. This argument does not have better data because no 20th-century study seems to have attempted a classification of the population in terms of national origin and descent, and relationship to the original Spanish castes. But the development of the Caracas urban grid is as good a predictor of the sharp divide being described here.

Architects Alfredo Brillembourg and Hubert Klumpner, professors at the Swiss Institute of Technology, have been the most exhaustive researchers of Venezuela's urban footprint. They estimate that by the beginning of the 21st century,

55% of the Caracas population lived in informal settlements or favelas, occupying 34% of the city's area.[50] That is to say, more than half of the population lived in some of the densest informal settlements in Latin America, mainly built on the hillsides encircling existing fixtures of city infrastructure, with difficult access and constructed in often-hazardous sites. The majority of Caraqueños lived in rudimentary hillside shacks, often with dirt floors, no water, and no direct access to the city other than endless stairways leading to the urban grid below.[51]

The differences between the two Venezuelas, in the formal and the informal urban grid, became ever sharper by 1998 against the backdrop of a profound economic and political crisis.

The price of oil had been dropping since its record high in 1980. Rafael Caldera, the then eighty-four-year-old president, symbolized an exhausted system. Healthcare was faltering, government jobs ceased to be engines of opportunity as real incomes dropped, and a crack epidemic overtook the poorly policed city as gangs fought over valuable markets, and the murder rate skyrocketed. According to the Central Bank models, extreme poverty doubled between 1990 and 1996.[52] Everyone in the favela knew someone in jail, as Venezuela became one of the top countries in the world in terms of inmates per 100,000 of the population, at 136.[53]

On the other side of the city, the orderly one, something entirely different was taking place.

The federalizing reforms of the early 1990s that were intended to bring more democracy to the country had had the opposite effect. Citizens now voted for their local representatives, but the new political system promoted massive inequality within the country. Local and state governments were allocated money directly from the federal government and were given an enhanced infrastructure to collect taxes. Overnight, affluent districts were flooded with new revenues. While the central state welfare functions were financially starved because of sharp declines in oil revenues and ever higher foreign debt service payments, the federalizing reforms had created islands of prosperity in otherwise blighted cities.

The super-rich municipalities in Caracas and every other large city where the foreign-born immigrants and their descendants lived acquired shiny, new, and respectable police forces. They had brand-new roads and sidewalks, responsive local officials, even toll-free numbers to register complaints.

The development of strong local governments created a vast divide in the quality and quantity of services delivered to each part of the city. For many people, the central government's importance in their lives was replaced by the private sphere. The lighter-skinned middle classes sent their children to private, likely bilingual, schools and never, ever visited a public hospital.

Those in the formal city did not (or would not) understand how the drop in oil revenues had decimated the government services to the more than half of the population living in the favelas. They could not, or would not, see how the standard of living of the majorities in urban informal settlements and rural enclaves had been gutted. Because informal settlements continued to grow outward from existing favelas, it was impossible to grasp their size from the city's highways. This is

why, even today, there is such a misunderstanding about the
state of the country when Chávez took over.

What united everyone in late 20th-century Venezuela was
the realization that earning money in the new environment
of low oil prices was quite different than it had been in the
good old days of plenty.

And in that newly contentious world, it is clear who had
better access to the best jobs in government and the private
sector; who had a better chance of understanding how to
take advantage of the increasingly erratic economy and its
ever-changing foreign currency rules; who was more likely
to be elected to run the newly rich municipal governments;
and who was better prepared to rise in the state-controlled
oil industry.

The answer was simple: the children whose parents,
grandparents, and great-grandparents had college degrees,
who spoke English and might have a master's degree from
the oil program at Oklahoma State, or even Harvard's
Kennedy School of Government. Those with no family legacy
in commerce or politics, growing up at the edge of a favela or
up the hill in one, who had taught themselves English or did
not speak it at all, and had never left the country, did not
stand a chance in a world of diminishing wealth.

The lighter-skinned descendants of immigrants had every
advantage, even though there were many well-known stories
of individuals who had defied those odds. People were sorted
in a universe of real, if informal, castes.

The lower middle classes who were caught in between
the newly bilingual upper middle classes and those in the
informal settlements turned angry. Their standard of living

dropped precipitously as devaluations and inflation gutted their salaries. Their traditional privileges associated with patronage and government favors had vanished, and they became particularly vulnerable to rising violent crime. Then the crack epidemic destroyed many of their families. This hopelessness fueled their grievances, which were soon twisted into an ethnic hatred that had not been openly discussed in Venezuela for a century.

The same year Chávez was first elected, journalist and author Alejandro Rebolledo published *Pin Pan Pun*, a novel that exposed the raw nerves of an ethnic time bomb.

The protagonist gives voice to the troubled, racist view of that lower middle class who could not come to terms with the fact that their country was in a deep dive, "All of a sudden you turn around to realize that what's around you doesn't look like the movies you watch on TV, that this is not California, this is just a bunch of shantytowns, people listening to merengue and having cats for breakfast...."[54]

Chávez

Hugo Chávez saw his moment and seized it. He was young, born in a rural area, from an indigenous and Afro-Venezuelan family legacy, and the product of an entirely public education. His military career path, his accent from the rural Plains, and brown skin, identified him as the voice of the new majorities living in the informal settlements. No one understood the times better than him.

At the beginning of his presidential campaign for the 1998 election he was widely ignored. He would stand on Caracas' streets speaking to a few supporters, more like a lonely preacher than a future president. Except for a few American correspondents, the media dismissed his message as out of synch with the country.[55] No one attacked him then.

But he saw a nation divided and articulated a cause that started to resonate with those living in the city's informal settlements. He campaigned tirelessly for years in the areas traditional politicians no longer visited. Eventually, his personal charisma, his persistence, and his conviction broke through to a base of mixed-race voters that wanted to hear what he had to say. No one had voiced their pain and anger as Chávez had. His emotional empathy was real, and his story-telling made sense out of an uncertain world. His polling breakthrough sometime in the early summer of 1998 was propelled by his unique ability to see the moment.[56]

Chávez became a symbol for a group of Venezuelans shut out of the best jobs, economic opportunities, and the global world emerging in the late 20th century. As the campaign progressed and election day neared, he moderated his language to broaden his base. Yet, his initial breakthrough came from a base of supporters he had gained over years of door-to-door campaigning in the poorest areas of the country.[57]

By contrast, Chávez's fellow contenders for the presidency in the election came to stand for precisely the ethnic difference he had hoped to exploit.

The campaign's early front-runner was Irene Sáez, mayor of the country's richest municipality, and a light-skinned former Miss Universe. Her national recognition had come from claiming success in the country's most visible program to bring beauty and cleanliness to any city. She supervised the outfitting of traffic police officers with crisp white gloves and safari hats. "Her" sidewalks were scrubbed clean every single day. Entire local government teams were dedicated to the maintenance of flowerpots on every corner, and the installation of Christmas lights every season. This happened as favelas were caught in a spiral of gun violence, drug dealing, faltering health services, and a broken welfare state that could no longer deliver much well-being.

Her electoral promise was that she would bring the beauty and cleanliness of her small municipality to the entire country. But she had no tangible solution for poverty other than her earnest and sincere desire to end it. Chávez, on the other hand, had for years been providing a crisp description that was self-evident: the nicer, cleaner, and better policed neighborhoods of every city belonged to light-skinned, affluent Venezuelans. And a seemingly intuitive solution: it was time the money reached the places where the majority lived.

The mayor's initial high polling numbers, partly based on her celebrity status as a former Miss Universe, crumbled. Chávez's support started to show up in polls, and to expand.

Soon Irene Sáez's campaign imploded, and the traditional opposition closed ranks behind an older businessman who had gone to prep school at Lawrenceville and college at Yale. Carabobo Governor Henrique Salas-Römer, who spelled his name with an umlaut to emphasize his German origins, pitched the country on the virtues of patrician, principled leadership. Instead of rallies, he preferred leading hundreds of wealthy supporters on horse-rides through the former slave plantations of the central valleys. His purebred white horse,

Frijolito, or Little Bean, became a character his campaign hoped would humanize the candidate.

The dissonance between Salas-Römer's persona and the urban realities of densely packed informal settlements could not be stronger. His message was no match for Chávez's direct, personal empathy, or his realistic descriptions of the country.

Given the candidates and their messages, it is difficult to argue that ethnicity, and its role in Venezuela's cultural history, were not central to Chávez's electoral breakthrough months before the election.

The overwhelming force with which Chávez's electoral juggernaut routed all opponents, despite their considerable financial and media resources, leaves no doubt whose message connected with the new country of the 21st century.

Racism

When many Venezuelans hear this essay's argument about the centrality of ethnic politics in the country's history, they take a step back. The idea that Chávez's first election had an ethnic dimension, for example, is often contested, despite Chávez's building of an electoral base in informal settlements years before the election, or the clear ethnic contrast between him and his two main opponents. For some, there is always an anecdote about a light-skinned uncle who voted for Chávez in that election. As if the clear ethnic divide in every major city, and the overwhelming Chávez margins in informal settlements compared with affluent neighborhoods, were not enough to prove the divisions within the country.

This is why I was not at all surprised when in November 2016, at a symposium on Revolution at New York University's King Juan Carlos Center, a big argument broke out over this subject.[58]

The audience included famous, even legendary, journalists who had covered Latin America for decades, as well as the new Venezuelan exiles. They were an amalgam of graduate students, academics, professionals, and retirees eager for any chance to hear their own story.

On the podium were a group of journalists and politicians who were from Venezuela or had worked there. Richard Gott, a former *Guardian* newspaper correspondent, definitely stood out. He was decidedly in favor of what Chávez had done, if not so clearly in support of the Chavismo that came afterward.

At some point, the British journalist waited for a break in the discussion, and then said, "The Venezuelan situation is akin to that of South Africa."[59] A white minority, he continued while relishing the way he had everyone's attention, had oppressed a Black majority for years. Chávez had finally given voice to that majority. And perhaps, he seemed to imply, everyone on the panel, as well as the audience, were part and parcel of that "white" cabal that Chávez had fought against.

The audience erupted into a collective cry of moral outrage, seething at the idea their country and their plight could ever be compared to that of South Africa, drowning out the journalist's final words. The furor no doubt confirmed for the speaker that Venezuela was like Zimbabwe, and the exiled audience was a contemporary version of the white Rhodesians who had roamed the world in the early

1980s after Mugabe had kicked them out of "his" country. From that point on, the argument turned into an all or nothing fight.

Tamara Adrián, a Venezuelan congresswoman in New York for the event, attempted a rebuttal. She was defiant: "There is no race issue in Venezuela." Our "DNA," she proceeded to explain, is so mixed that race has never been a political issue in the country.[60] In her view all attempts by her fellow panelist or by Chavismo itself to raise race as an issue were nothing other than a distraction. Worse still, injecting race into the discussion was about legitimizing a dictatorship with a lie.

The differences between Anglo-American racial histories and those of Iberian Latin America are so obvious that comparing South Africa and Venezuela would never make sense. Yet 500 years of castes, slavery, and the reassertion of ethnic identity in the Chávez years, were not something that could be suddenly ignored.

No wonder Venezuelans are confused about their own history: in an audience with dozens of specialists in Venezuela and Latin America, no one had an alternative rebuttal for the accusation that Venezuela had endured South African-style apartheid. The discussion started and ended with recriminations about false or accurate comparisons between two completely different countries. Either Venezuela was exactly like South Africa, or it was not like South Africa at all.

Since the middle of the 20th century, Venezuelan intellectuals and politicians had stopped talking about race and ethnicity. The truth, that day in New York City, is that few had given the matter much thought.

To understand why and how the ethnic and racial fractures of the past were put aside it is necessary to go back to the 1930s. The fierce political debates that shaped a national project then were about both the country's identity, and its social debt to the descendants of the Pardo population.

A Race-Blind Venezuela

Rómulo Betancourt was the architect of a Venezuela in which race and ethnicity were eradicated from the public discourse. An early 20th-century pro-democracy leader, he laid down the basis for the country's race-neutral ideology as Venezuela's president first in 1945, and then again in 1959. Adecos, as Betancourt's followers were called, would go on to become the political reference point in the life of the country, until Chávez and the new demographic wave destroyed their social project. Their vision's successes and failures are virtual keys to understanding contemporary Venezuela.

By 1940 the thirty-three-year-old Betancourt was already a promising political leader, but one in the very middle of a unique moment in history. Behind him lay a poor, provincial country with a vast countryside still recovering from the deep social fractures Laureano Valle-nilla had described in 1919. Ahead of him was a nation with a once-in-a-lifetime chance to start over again. He imagined that properly distributed, oil money would create a brand-new country to be filled, like a vast empty canvas, with great ideas and institutions. The young Betancourt knew he could shape an entirely new political imaginary. He was convinced he could solve the underlying issues of the country's ethnic fracture.

His political program for change was clear: the state would charge a 50% tax on all profits obtained by American and British oil companies to underwrite a welfare state that would wipe out poverty, and level all Venezuelans. An enormous investment in education would transform people into informed citizens, and an influx of migrants would bring their legacies to form a new society made up of equals.

His political party, Acción Democrática, would organize workers, peasants, students, professionals, and industrialists around the unifying idea of a new Venezuela that left behind castes, ethnicities, and places of birth. The party's manifesto called the organization "multi-class" and was purposely silent on matters of race, ethnicity, castes, or regional origin.[61] Oil would fuel the country's development and well-being, and act as a social glue linking everything together.

In 1925, Mexican intellectual and former Secretary of Education José Vasconcelos had promoted the idea of a "cosmic race" made up of Indians, Spanish, and Africans.[62] This brand-new identity, unique to Latin America, would bury the legacies and grievances of three ethnic and racial groups. It would be a bridge over enormous social chasms. Venezuela's ethnic makeup already looked "cosmic," at least compared to other South American countries. The number of enslaved Africans brought to Venezuela over the centuries had been roughly the same as the number of Amerindians who had survived war and illness into the 19th century. Compared to overwhelmingly African Cuba or Jamaica, or the majority indigenous Mexico or Peru, Venezuela was more diverse ethnically. Most important of all, those of mixed-race had been a majority for over 100 years. Betancourt would pick up where Vasconcelos, writing in the heyday of a cultural revolution in Mexico, had left off.

The ideology of the "cosmic race" legitimized the idea of a mixed-race John Doe, or Juan Bimba, already the "Venezuelan everyman" in the popular imagination. Betancourt's push toward a post-ethnic country was based on giving power to that average Venezuelan. If the majority descendants of Pardos embodied the country, and ran it, and those who would soon come from Europe and South America would mix in, ethnicity and national origin would never become political currencies. The fracture closed, a new country would be born.

Betancourt had to embody that majority to sell this project. He emphasized his mother's African descent. His hometown was on the western edge of the Afro-Caribbean Barlovento coast. His accent lacked the upper-class singsong of Creoles, and he would occasionally refer to himself as a "mulatto from Guatire." His Spanish was laced with provincial colloquialisms.[63]

But most importantly, Betancourt's public persona embraced the mannerisms, language, and humor of ethnic Pardos. Ethnicity is an ambiguous combination of perceptions, far from the clearer lines that can define race. By embracing and claiming to be a Pardo, Betancourt became the perfect spokesperson for a project that someone with a Creole accent, a more formal manner, or wearing starched shirts with cufflinks could never sell.

Betancourt's ethnic-neutral vision of a new social compact would be crystallized through several paperbacks written by fellow party member and future president Rómulo Gallegos.

The novel's role in politics is a uniquely Venezuelan trait. The country's rulers had, over the prior forty-six years, been four generals from the same small state in the profoundly conservative Andean highlands. Their reactionary view of the world had suffocated all channels of meaningful political debate by concentrating all power at the very top, forcing most advocacy into the realm of literature.

As the general's powers waned, novelists and poets would take turns as ministers, presidents, senators, and even hard-knuckled political operators. Even if the country was essentially illiterate, Gallego's novels were embraced by those producing radio and later television.

A Country in a Novel

Two novels describe the crux between the past and the imaginary future proposed by Betancourt: *Las Lanzas Coloradas*[64] (*The Red Spears*) by Arturo Uslar Pietri, and *Doña Barbara*[65], by Rómulo Gallegos. The novels were published in 1931 and 1929, respectively, and both seek nothing less than to explain the country and its prospects. Naturally, both stage their dramas in the countryside.

Uslar Pietri's *Las Lanzas Coloradas* tells the story of a slave plantation owned by the descendants of the original Spanish founders at the time of the Wars of Independence. *Doña Barbara* takes place at a cattle ranch worked by free peons rather than slaves.

Gallegos' *Doña Barbara* is the story of a college graduate who returns to modernize his father's land only to find himself opposed by a vicious, uneducated woman with near-magical powers. Barbara, standing in for the country's dark past, will stop at nothing to derail the civilizing ideals of the protagonist, whose name is Santo, Spanish for Saint. The widely popular soap opera plot in Gallego's novel ends, predictably, with the triumph of noble civilization over barbarism.

Uslar Pietri's novel, on the other hand, ends with the Creole family's plantation burned and reduced to ashes, the last female descendant of the founder graphically raped and murdered by the Pardo foreman, and the white male heir half-crazed and wandering through the countryside.

Several books on the gender politics of Venezuela's twin foundational novels still have to be written, but reading their racial and ethnic postures sheds much light on the country's history.

The young Uslar Pietri was the last writer of a generation obsessed with the country's ethnic divides, the savagery of the 19th-century wars, and what some have called the pessimistic view of Venezuelan history.[66] *Las Lanzas Coloradas* is packed with impressionistic descriptions of the brutality of life for enslaved workers at the plantation, the psychological effects of human submission, and the fury mixed-race Pardos felt toward their Creole masters. Uslar Pietri's novel also offers an alternative and radical view of the independence wars' early years.

The text imagines the Creole plantation owner's boredom and sense of entitlement leading him straight into the romantic folly of an independence war against Spain. He, and presumably his entire social class, cannot grasp the reality of the slave society they have built. They cannot understand the cataclysm they are about to unleash with their push for an independent nation. The Pardo foreman, Presentación

Campos, who later rapes the owner's sister, burns down the plantation, commands the enslaved workers to join the war on the King's side, and becomes the voice of this critique: "He knew him [the plantation's male owner] to be indecisive and timid ... He believed himself strong, but he was not; he believed himself a revolutionary, and he was not. He believed himself intelligent and he was not; he believed himself master, and he was not."[67] By the end of the novel, every character has been killed or has lost their mind.

The novel's main theme is the hopelessness of the racial and ethnic caste system, in place since colonial times. This reality drives the story and determines the fate of every character; there is no way to avoid or escape it. The story's unrelenting message is that slavery and the caste system can only end in a violent, pointless war, or in the country's utter destruction.

By contrast, Gallego's novel cleverly changes the conversation by placing the action in cattle ranch country, far south from the coastal valleys where slave plantations flourished. While slave-picked cocoa and sugar cane, never cattle, sustained the economy, it is in the vast empty Plains with fewer enslaved Africans and a more diffused sense of castes that Gallegos sets up his mythical battle between good and evil. The story's conflict does not come from the built-in contradictions of a structural system without an exit, as in *Las Lanzas Coloradas*. Instead, the book shows two opposing cultures, either of which can prevail over the other. The source of evil for Gallegos is ignorance, rooted in what at the time Latin American intellectuals called "barbarism." In this view, Venezuela would see progress as soon as the primitive brutality of the local warlord, or *caudillo*, the ignorance of the sorcerer, and the self-defeating folk tales and practices that reduced the population to hunger and misery could be eradicated.

Reshaping History

In *Doña Barbara*, the dilemma of Venezuela's society neatly fits Betancourt's social democratic program: bring rational and technical solutions to a newly educated population of equal citizens, and "barbarism" would vanish from the face of the earth.

By purposely burying the ethnic fractures and attributing the pervasive violence and poverty to a mere lack of education, rather than to the more intractable social legacies of slavery and the caste system, it would be possible to pay for a fully developed country with oil revenues. If race and ethnicity could be erased and never mentioned again, and oil continued to fetch good prices, Betancourt's vision would be realized.

If Betancourt was successful in reshaping the country's public debate, then plenty of credit for the cultural shift goes to Gallegos for his compulsively readable novels, which relentlessly pushed the "civilization vs. barbarism" message that is still present in today's political debates. But it is easy to lose sight of how the Venezuelan establishment of the 1930s was much more on the side of Uslar Pietri than of Betancourt and Gallegos. Those in power, particularly the old generals, had vivid memories of how difficult it had been to pacify the country. To them, the endemic violence, regardless of its historical origin, was an ever-present reality if their iron fist was ever loosened. They were the first military generation since Spanish colonial times that had seen the countryside at relative peace and were determined to keep it that way.

Uslar Pietri came from a family that had agricultural interests. The stories of burning and looting—which had taken place until the 1890s—were genuinely terrifying to him, and to the rest of the moneyed class who likewise had agricultural roots. They grew up on their parents' and grandparents' stories of surviving the Federal War of the late 1850s and early 1860s. Fifty years after independence, the conflict had killed 10% of the country's population and destroyed its economy.[68]

Betancourt and his closest collaborator, Raúl Leoni, along with Gallegos and the rest of the Acción Democrática leadership, fought a tireless battle for full democracy. Their adversary was the overwhelming sense of doom that supported the old Andean generals' iron-fisted regimes from the 1910s through the 1940s.

Rómulo Betancourt became interim president in 1945 after a coup d'état by young officers who wanted to break free of the old stodgy generals. He started implementing parts of his liberal program right away. National elections were called for in 1948, which were handily won by the Acción Democrática ticket. Rómulo Gallegos of *Doña Barbara* fame became the first popularly elected president in Venezuela's history. Having a full mandate, Gallegos and Betancourt accelerated and deepened their reform program, but it was not to be.

Eight months later, in November of 1948, the same young officers struck again with another coup d'état, this time so they themselves could rule. They had likely been supported by oil companies worried about Acción Democrática's taxation policies, as well as a US State Department then pushing for military anti-communist regimes around the world.

By 1950 General Pérez Jiménez became the sole head of state, instituting a sometimes-vicious dictatorship that lasted until 1958. Betancourt then returned from exile and was elected president in December of 1958, to be followed by another overwhelming Acción Democrática electoral victory resulting in Raúl Leoni becoming president in 1964. In that straight decade of AD power, most of Betancourt's ideas from the 1930s and 1940s were given their due. An almost miraculous level of shared prosperity sprouted across Venezuela.

For the first time in the country's entire history, the health, habitat, nourishment, and literacy of every poor Venezuelan was transformed in a matter of years. All talk of racial or ethnic issues vanished. However, by the early 1980s Betancourt's project of a seamless Venezuela without racial or ethnic differences was already showing strains. The unspoken question was, "What would happen when the money ran out, growth stopped, and the distribution mechanisms that had kept an easy peace gave in?" Few ever considered the possibility that after all this time the ethnic and racial cracks running through the country's foundation would come back to haunt and bury Betancourt's project.

The early 20th-century intellectual debates over the country's racial history contextualize congresswoman Adrián's comments on the South Africa-Venezuela comparison at New York University in 2016. She was on Betancourt's side, and very much against a young Uslar Pietri's structuralist view of race and ethnicity. Her position is widely shared by most opposition figures, and many Venezuelans in exile, to this day. In their minds, all Venezuelans are mixed and there are no ethnic distinctions worth considering. Their refusal to see ethnicity as a hazy marker of language, mannerisms and culture superimposed on people's descent, typically leads to an anecdotal argument. The darker skin color of some opposition leaders, and the lighter skin of some pro-government figures, is offered as proof that there are no real differences. To them, the structural and historical issue of ethnic differences in Venezuela is a form of political manipulation by a few figures to grab and sustain power.

To make matters more confusing, by the 1980s a mature Uslar Pietri would become far less interested in social issues. Instead of developing his 1930s insights on the ethnic conflicts underlying the country's history, his views turned more conventional.[69] He sided with those historians who, while recognizing the violence that has always plagued Venezuela, emphasize the coherent sense of nation progressively articulated by intellectuals of different generations.[70]

Yet Venezuela's social explosion in the 21st century proved the young Uslar Pietri right. His initial structural thinking about the racial and ethnic chasm the country had been founded on, and his first writings on the doomsday that would follow the oil bonanza, can only be seen as prophetic.

Few things can be more helpful to understand the present times than connecting the history of the intellectual debate between young Uslar Pietri and Betancourt, to the rise of Chávez. Betancourt won the debate, but his magical welfare state started to falter in the 1980s and 1990s. That turned out to be Chávez's moment in the sun.

Chávez from the Plains

The slow collapse of the Adeco project started in the early 1980s, as oil prices fell and did not rise again, except for the Gulf War hiccup in 1990, until 2004.[71] In 1998, when Chávez won his first election with 56% of the votes, the price of oil had just dropped in real dollars to its lowest levels since 1972.[72, 73] Venezuela's population was then twelve million people, as opposed to the twenty-three million inhabitants of 1998.[74]

If the country's oil prospects had helped Betancourt dream of erasing, and then burying, any sense of racial and ethnic identity from the country at the beginning of the 20th century, 1998 presented a different landscape. The return of ethnic difference in the nation's consciousness was already in the air.

As explained, Chávez broadened his base toward the end of the electoral campaign and eventually won the 1998 election with support from lighter-skinned middle-class voters. He campaigned hard for those votes by tapping into the desire for a powerful military figure at a time of uncertainty. He said the country and the state were broke only because someone, an "evil group," had stolen all the wealth. By then his speeches lacked any mention of redistribution, and merely mentioned theft. If he stopped "them" from stealing, there would be plenty of money for all. But this was campaign rhetoric. It was clear to anyone who looked at the numbers that Chávez would not be able to do anything once in power.

Oil prices had hit rock bottom, and there was only so much revenue to go around. There were not even enough resources to satisfy Chávez's core base in the favelas, much less reconstruct the state that had glued the country together for so many decades. Chávez's short-term economic options were almost non-existent, but it is also clear he did not even have a plan.

What Chávez had was a prescient understanding of power: he realized the color-blind society built over the prior fifty years was broken and ready to die. Despite his one-nation pitch in the final months of the campaign, Chávez was aware that his powerbase could only be nourished by deepening, not bridging, the ethnic gap. He intuitively understood 19th-century Venezuelan politics, specifically the 100-plus years during which rulers had to grab and retain power in a country with vast swaths of extreme poverty, a weak state at best, and very little money.

The young Chávez vividly understood everything the young Uslar Pietri had described in his novel *Las Lanzas Coloradas*, which most of the country had forgotten. His encyclopedic knowledge of the songs, legends, heroes, and language of bygone times became a political currency of incalculable value. His humble origins in the rural Plains and his self-proclaimed Zambo identity (the original caste designating those of mixed African and Amerindian descent) made him a different kind of politician. The memory of his great-great-grandfather Maisanta, a renegade warlord whose guerrilla actions had killed former President Crespo in 1898, helped him understand the new politics that were to come.

He saw the power vacuum in front of him, as had been the case for ambitious would-be-rulers throughout the 1800s. Back in that century, a sudden drop in coffee prices, a shift in population, or a palace revolt in faraway Caracas, were always seen as golden opportunities for men of war to march with a few peons and take over the trophy capital while advocating the grievances of Pardo peasants.

In the middle of Chávez's inaugural address, he called for a countrywide referendum on whether the 1961 consti-tution should be abolished. He wanted the vote to take place in a matter of weeks. It was his first move in a realignment of Venezuelan politics around the concept of an ethnic tribe. Naturally, he would be the chief, or in the old parlance, the *caudillo*. Because constitutions are weighted with symbolism in Venezuela, he quickly proposed a brand-new magna carta. He hastily rebranded the preceding years of 1959-99 as the Fourth Republic, and in the French style, declared himself the founder of a new republic, the glorious Fifth Republic, his own creation.

The new constitution turned into a political manifesto: it decreed a massive expansion of presidential power, an extension of the presidential term with a new option of reelection, and an alternative structure of governance to bypass modern party machines. Every 19th- and early 20th-century *caudillo* had done more or less the same by passing twenty brand-new constitutions over the 120 years from 1811 to 1931. Little if any of what those constitutions said made any difference to the *caudillos* that promoted them, but the pomp and circumstance of their passage served as potent political tools.

The referendum that followed Chávez's February 1999 inaugural speech asked the electorate if the current constitution should be rescinded, and a new one written. More than 80% of those voting in April 1999 said yes. In July of 1999, a new nationwide election was held to elect the members of the constitutional convention that would rewrite the document. Chávez's slate won with 66% of the vote.[75]

The convention's constitutional draft created the most powerful presidency since the days of dictator General Pérez Jiménez, and a new referendum was called on its merits. The president's term would be extended to six years, with a new option of reelection, while many aspects of the federalizing reforms that had been brewing over the prior twenty years were eliminated. By December, all citizens were asked to vote to approve or reject the new constitution. An overwhelming 70% of those voting turned the draft into law, even if many people stayed home and did not bother to vote. Ominously the price of oil in real dollars remained at 1972 levels.[76]

Chávez's early electoral successes were not solely the result of a honeymoon with voters. There was more to them than a charismatic leader with persuasive communication skills. He was briefly supported by television channels and newspapers. However, by mid-1999, and especially by early 2000, most private media outlets had become viciously and personally anti-Chávez.

By 2000 new presidential elections were mandated by the newly approved constitution. Chávez was elected as the Fifth Republic's first president with 56.93% of the votes.[77] He kept increasing his victory margins by mobilizing a base of strong supporters while others tuned out of politics and stayed home. The symbolic meaning of the *caudillo*, practically enshrined in the new constitution, seemed to hold more force than the government's actions. For all intents and purposes, taxation, patterns of expenditure, the central bank's laws, exchange rates, welfare rules, customs, and import policies were not being meaningfully changed in any way. And the result was that daily life for all Venezuelans in July of 2000 remained exactly where it had been two years before. This was true for the destitute as well as the industrialists, the middle-class government employees, and those in the private sector. Which means that for Chávez's supporters, and for those who now despised him, everything had to do with what he represented, what and how he said it, what he looked like, and ultimately, what he made of that fact.

What Chávez understood better than anyone was that he could reshape the country's power structure through the politics of identity. He gave a voice to his tribe by harkening back to the cries against conservative white elites during the Federal War of 1859. Chávez's constant and ferocious speeches against oligarchs were actually quite old.

The word "oligarchy" had been used in the 1830s to identify all those in favor of free trade. Over the years the word came to stand for the light-skinned ruling elite almost entirely based in Caracas. "Oligarchy" appears over and over again in the war cries of Commander Ezequiel Zamora's Federalist troops. Their slogan was *"Respeto a los campesinos, horror a la oligarquía"* ("Respect for the peasants, horror to the oligarchy"), while troops sang, *"Oligarcas, temblad"* ("Oligarchs, tremble") as they marched into battle.[78] The words vaguely connected Boves' 1814 path of torture and systematic killing of whites through Calabozo, Valencia, Puerto La Cruz, and much of the countryside between those cities, with the renewed sense of identity of the mixed-race peasants of 1859. The author Lisandro Alvarado, in his history of the Federal War, records fighters joining Zamora in the states of Cojedes and Barinas to the cry of "Death to the whites."[79] Chávez appropriated this powerful political legacy, until then abandoned, to shape his own political base.

The New-Old Politics

Chávez gave the old 19th-century discourse against oligarchy a new edge to fight a modern enemy. For Zamora the stark differences between peasants and landowners, city bankers and peons, were a sufficiently clear political argument. But Chávez not only had to fight against the upper classes that, at least in his mind, controlled the country. He had to push back against the vast machine Betancourt had built to erase the idea of tribes, ethnicities, and racial difference.

The Adeco project had spawned unions, public schools, free universities, a welfare state, a system of justice, and many other structures that sought to empower all citizens. They were predicated on the respect every equal person had to have for the institutions of government, and its vision of a color-blind society where ethnic identities had no role.

Chávez had called the period between the fall of Dictator Pérez Jiménez in 1958 and his own first election in 1998 the Fourth Republic. By this count, the short-lived First and Second republics happened during the Wars of Independence, one in 1810 and the other in 1813. Chávez's formulation imagined a Third Republic where no historian had ever seen one: the 128-year period of nearly uninterrupted military regimes between 1831 and 1958. His creation allowed him to name a Fourth Republic: the civilian democracy of the 20th century which his rule had demolished. And a solution, his own glorious Fifth Republic.

What made the Fourth Republic unique in history, and evil in Chávez's discourse, was the vast liberal state and its duplicitous rules and codes. Chávez mocked notions of color-blind statutes and a sense of respect for a plurality of viewpoints. He railed against the empire of the law, and the supposedly abstract, impersonal nature of good government. Portraying the state and its representatives as a cabal of thieves and identifying the ethnic identity of those in power ("the oligarchy"), versus those out of power ("the people," or *"el pueblo"* in Spanish), he undermined the idea of justice for all. In his explanation of what ailed the country, impartial, color-blind liberal justice had been the instrument of oppression of an ethnic group rather than an attempt at leveling all of society.

Against the abstract nature of the liberal state, Chávez offered his personal story as a claim of legitimacy. His emotions, fears, life-story, childhood memories, even his anger and confusion at the complexity of the modern world became a comprehensive political claim. His feelings, which reflected those of his tribe, would become his politics. Nothing would be more helpful to him in this effort than live television.

The informality of live television allowed him to speak directly to his people, and to infuse every decision with the immediacy of his instincts. He bypassed regular party structures and state bureaucracies, as well as traditional media filters. He used the language, imagery, and culture of the informal settlements and that of the countryside to explain himself and everything else.

In 2002 Chávez started a weekly television show broadcast live every Sunday and extending for several hours without a fixed endpoint. He would typically sit at a desk which was fully fitted with pencils and rulers, a cross between a bureaucrat's place of work and a child's desk at school. In the audience, in front of and a few steps down from his desk, sat his entire cabinet. The leaders of his different initiatives, top military brass, and assorted guests sat a few rows behind.

Aló Presidente

Aló Presidente was a variety/talk show produced to communicate that Chávez was not an appropriately dressed president who belonged, or wanted to belong, to the formal world of European manners and legalistic thought.

Chávez hosted the show while singing acapella or twirling an audience member around in an impromptu demonstration of his salsa skills. He raged, he cried. He retold old folk stories from the countryside and recited popular poetry from memory. He talked about his life in the most personal, even intimate ways. The audience felt they knew him.

After a marathon four- or five-hour-long show, he would sit sweating under the lights, all notion of formal, Western decorum out the window.

Month after month Chávez's performance grew more informal. Eventually he started cursing on daytime national television. His behavior mimicked a 19th-century *caudillo* from the countryside, unafraid to show he ruled, or to share his ancient notions of culture, sexuality, and gender. The show became proof that he came from a different world than any of the presidents that had governed during the Fourth Republic. The rural poor, those in the urban informal settlements, anyone who felt excluded by the propriety and pretense of the prior governments, could see themselves in that studio.

The cabinet, a few steps down from him, were not there to advise him, but rather to serve as his audience. The seating arrangements signaled something new. Decisions would not be made from precedent, based on regulations or administrative procedures, or after listening to the advice of experts. Government action would be freed from lengthy processes. The president would not govern, he would rule from his gut, immediately, in real time.

It was as if Chávez had taken Donald Trump's television show *The Apprentice* to the next level. That American show defied the idea of formal and modern business practices in favor of street wisdom and emotional intuition. For reality TV star Trump, feelings were much more meaningful than thought. The premise was that marketing, operations, product, or legal experts with the experience and credentials necessary to deliver results in business were irrelevant. Instead, celebrity apprentices guided and judged by an all-knowing billionaire could achieve anything they set out to do. They only needed sufficient passion and good instincts. The right feeling would trump decades of experience every time. For Chávez, *Aló Presidente* set aside laws and legal procedures, the contributions of experts, and rational thought, in favor of the patriarch's country wisdom.

In early 2008, an hour into one of his shows, Chávez started to talk about a news item from that day.[80] The Colombian army had bombed a guerrilla camp on the Ecuador side of the Colombia-Ecuador border. He spoke of having met a leader who had died in the raid, and slowly, but with increasing vigor, praised him as a hero of freedom. Before long, Chávez was overwhelmed by a furious rage, apparently prompted by the memories of the fallen comrade. He described the president of Colombia, whom he had met many times before in formal settings, as a "criminal," a "low-life," and an "assassin." Four minutes later, he pointed to the Minister of Defense, sitting in the audience, and ordered him to move ten army battalions to the Colombian border, immediately. All on live television, fueled by his anger, and apparently unprompted.

This is exactly what a favela gangster, later known as a *pran* in Chávez's Venezuela, would have done to show his colors and uphold his pride against a rival gang that had overstepped another's territory. If President Uribe was going to order a hit on the Ecuadorian side of his border, "we better tell him and show him who we are, lest he gets any ideas about crossing our own line." Chávez's political base was entirely in tune with the dynamics at play. His opponents were appalled at what they considered impulsive, nonsensical behavior, but more importantly, were convinced that what they saw as a "madman gone rogue" was obvious to all.

Chávez would reenact the "Ten battalions to Colombia at once" episode countless times. He knew exactly how to get his political opponents to say or do something that would betray them as bona-fide members of a different social group, and a distinct tribe bent on imposing its will. The more these earnest, graduate-school educated, perfectly polite and rightly accented young women and men from the main opposition parties argued for rational policies, order, efficiency, transparency, cleanliness, and the rule of law, the easier it was for Chávez to box them into an ethnic category.

A majority of Venezuelans did not hear the opposition's critique of Chávez. Voters could not get past the opponent's accents, their endless adjectives, their lack of colloquialisms, their perfectly pronounced English words, or the way they were dressed. For the regular person on the street, everything opposition politicians said, did, or wore confirmed they belonged to the "oligarchy" Chávez pinpointed as the origin of all evil.

Consider the fight over the word "socialism." For Chávez, who would quote from the Bible and invoke Christ more often than anyone else in the political scene, "socialism" was a way of saying the wealth from oil should reach every corner of the country. After all, oil was treasure, and the government controlled all of it. When Chávez said "socialism," his non-college educated base understood the dream of cheap and plentiful gasoline, no taxes, public housing, large and free public concerts, jobs, and everything else the government might provide.

Yet, every time Chávez's opposition heard "socialism," they instantly invoked Karl Marx, Friedrich Engels, Vladimir Lenin, and Joseph Stalin, devoting hours of television time and thousands of printed words to rehashing rebuttals to Marxism from the 1960s and 1970s. Businesspeople at fancy dinner parties quoted the University of Chicago's Friedrich von Hayek to one another. Meanwhile, Chávez kept talking about his ideal of a Venezuela with social services, housing, and almost free gasoline.

As Chávez's opponents used obscure arguments against socialism, or denounced the idea of the government distributing an oil wealth that belonged to all citizens, it became obvious they were not "true Venezuelans." Chávez gained the upper hand politically by boxing his minority opponents into their own ethnic group, a foreign minority who meant harm and pain to the country's majority. He did this regardless of the underlying rationale for the government's policies, independent of who benefited and who did not, or what their specific effects on the economy might be.

New political formulas in Latin America have rarely succeeded without their model being tested somewhere else. Juan Domingo Perón, who invented modern populism in the region, had been at Mussolini's rallies in Rome before ever giving one of his rousing speeches in Buenos Aires. Simón Bolívar, whose continental conquests of Spanish-held territory from the Caribbean coast to the current Chilean border briefly made him a near-absolute monarch, had been in Paris the day Napoleon declared himself Emperor.

Yet, more than a decade before Donald Trump's presidency, and in a much more radical way than Silvio Berlusconi ever governed Italy, Chávez led his country as if on a reality TV show, performing without equal to this day. Perhaps because it was so novel in its time, or due to its fleeting, real-time nature, few understood the power and reach of what he was doing.

Coup d'état

Between his swearing-in at the beginning of 1999 and the spring of 2002, Chávez's revolution changed the conversation in the country. Over thirty months the lines of a broad cultural conflict between two Venezuelas were drawn. Chávez was able to craft his message of identity, and to convey through a variety of means the ways in which he was advocating for his tribe.

The reaction to Chávez was equally fierce, particularly by all those who felt excluded and directly attacked. Chávez became demonized by opponents in the still private and mostly opposition media. On both sides of this conflict, attacks were charged with hatred and became very personal.

Yet, the actual effects of Chávez's revolution in the government itself were incipient, even timid, at that point. Military personnel were being slowly inserted into all levels of state, and an early version of a parallel government structure was barely getting started. The first quasi-governmental organizations called Misiones had already appeared, and the idea of a neighborhood-level political organization was already in the air. But it almost seemed to be window-dressing to support the rhetoric rather than any attempt to actually change anything.

For the public at large, egged on by a media frenzy of opposition and pro-government politics, things were increasingly based on social identity and feelings, rather than on ideologies, or even ideas. All of this, while the price of oil rose—but not enough, or fast enough, to still make a real difference to the economy.

The upper middle and upper classes throughout the country had become virulently anti-Chávez. The middle classes continued to see their standard of living deteriorate as the terrible economic trends of the 1990s persisted. Together, the three distinct social classes formed an energized opposition movement that felt entitled to demand change. For the more radical among them, the urgency of their claims, and their ability to mobilize millions of opponents for street demonstrations, was enough to start planning a violent coup. Chávez's words and actions, in their view, justified his removal by any means.

Everything came to a head on April 11, 2002, when hundreds of thousands of opponents congregated to protest the administration in the eastern part of Caracas. Either because a small group of conspirators had planned to divert the march, or as an organic expression of prevalent anger against the president, many of those participating walked directly toward the presidential palace to demand Chávez's resignation.

As marchers approached the palace, mayhem broke out. Sharpshooters (still unidentified to this day), anti-government municipal police, and armed Chavista cadres started firing at each other, while the marchers were caught in between. Hundreds of people were wounded and nineteen died, all on live television across the country.

Chávez decided to address the nation there and then, but private broadcasters split the screen in two. On half of every TV set, the president spoke from his office at the presidential palace to claim everything was under control. On the other half of the screen, live scenes of street violence, death, and mutilation were being broadcast from outside the palace.

Chávez ordered the army and the National Guard to leave their bases, take over the city, and take back power for his government. The generals refused. It became evident that a full-fledged coup d'état was underway. The generals eventually went to the palace to ask Chávez for his resignation. Disarmed, he was removed from power and detained.

Soon after that, military officers and a committee of luminaries from the old establishment backed Chávez's nemesis Pedro Carmona, the head of the Venezuelan Chamber of Commerce, as the country's new president. He swore himself in, and then addressed the nation.[81]

It did not go well. As the new president spoke, the contrast with the people's president was clear. His face was too carefully groomed. His dark suit and starched white shirt, a dark silk tie crisscrossed by a discreet white pattern, did not fit in a tropical country. Too European. His features lacked even a hint of Indian or African ancestry, and his deep, arrogant voice reminded viewers of the imperious leaders from bygone times. Most importantly, the new president had a stiff delivery devoid of any emotion after everything that had just happened. It was as if the still unburied dead had not died, or that their deaths did not matter.

In the same televised speech, he went on to declare the dissolution of a democratically elected Congress, and the imminent signing of a decree giving him power to dissolve all state assemblies, even those where he could have hoped to find political support. With a few words and a few old-time power brokers from the previous century in the audience, he had assumed all earthly powers in the country.

If Chávez himself, master of live television theatrics, had written the script and selected the cast of characters, he could not have staged a better event to bolster his case. The Chavista movement was numerous and well organized across government and the country at large, making the response to the coup almost immediate. But the surreal speech, and an evident lack of operational organization by the plotters, ensured that failure was imminent.

Though a few generals had been able to exploit a moment of chaos and bloodshed to grab power and had maintained either the loyalty or the neutrality of most troops, the coup lacked any in-depth support in the armed forces. The original plotters had secured the complicity of a few older generals but had not attempted to persuade anyone among the middle ranks. They seemed unaware of and uninterested in the political dynamics within the military. The president's long-standing ally, Commander Raúl Baduel, had remained at the head of the very mobile parachute unit Chávez himself had once commanded. None of the organizers seemed to know anything about the well-documented connection between Baduel and Chávez, or of the danger this military unit posed to their *putsch*.

Those behind the coup seemed to think the military's middle and lower ranks were not a critical factor in Venezuelan politics. To them, merely taking over the presidential palace of Miraflores and going on national television with plenty of pomp and circumstance would suffice to control the country. Even back in 2002 no mixed-race middle-ranking army officer, after years of direct and often personal appeals of support by Chávez for his identity project, could take Carmona or his coup seriously.

In twenty-four hours, Baduel's commandos swung into action, along with tens of thousands of Chávez supporters mobilized to flood the areas around the presidential palace. It did not take much to kick Carmona out of power and detain him on his way to an eventual exile. Chávez was brought back from an island where he had been detained, now stronger than ever.

While the coup had been defeated, the opposition forces that had supported the military takeover were in the same place, and in the same mood, as they had been on the evening of April 10: they felt Chávez had to be driven out of power at any cost.

With or without a failed coup, there was still an enormous political base that could be mobilized against the president. A few months before, more than a million people, or 4% of the entire country's population, had gathered in one place at a given time to voice their discontent of the government. The aerial photographs of the opposition mobilizations in Caracas are still impressive, and without parallel in Venezuelan politics.

Over the next few weeks, the opposition started to push for an oil strike that would choke the country's economy. Suddenly the country's center of gravity, the state oil company and its middle and upper middle-class managers, became the best hope for the anti-Chávez movement.

The old guard, chattering at dinner parties, political soirees, and restaurants all over Caracas, were convinced they could predict the outcome: PDVSA, the state-owned oil and natural gas company, would come to a complete halt without its US-educated managers. It was taken for granted that as soon as the company's cash flow stopped, Chávez would be done. And if a general strike could be called to help the PDVSA strike, nothing could stop the opposition from gaining power again. At least that is what was assumed in Caracas's more affluent neighborhoods.

The role of the military's middle ranks in the April events, or the prior 500 years of history over the Venezuelan territories, was simply not part of that conversation. The fact that Chávez commanded the loyalty of millions of followers who would not follow the call for a national strike was also ignored.

Critically, the vast balance sheet of assets and resources at Chávez's command was also ignored. Oil flows might be stopped, but it would take years to truly choke the power of the oil state and its global resources. The people master-minding the opposition's moves did not consider these factors. As happened repeatedly during the political struggles between Chavismo and its opponents, the latter always assumed they had more leverage than they did.

When oil industry staffers and managers finally went on strike in December 2002, Chávez promptly fired them all. Then, he went after the remaining employees who looked as if they might be against his "revolution," but had not walked out, and fired them as well.

The upshot of the strike was that, while the long-term viability of the company was put at risk, and eventually most of the oil infrastructure in Venezuela collapsed, the short- and mid-term effects of the strike on the ability of the state to exercise power were negligible.

The general strike was even more of a failure. The lighter-skinned half of Caracas, in the east, was paralyzed.

This meant the lives of those radically opposed to Chávez underwent great suffering. The other, poorer, and deeply Chavista part of the city continued operating as if nothing was happening. Downtown, the stores were open and business went on as usual.

If tax collection mattered to the Venezuelan government, or if the state had less of a role in everyday life, and banks, insurance companies, and large and small businesses had more of an impact on the economy, the strike might have achieved something.

In a country entirely sustained by oil revenues, and therefore entirely dependent on a wealthy state, the strike could only bring misery to those in the opposition. The ethnic geography of the strike, the allegiances of those leaving and staying at PDVSA, the forced blocking of entrances to middle-class neighborhoods so no one could go to or from work, encapsulated a hopeless situation for the opposition. The fire-bombing of businesses that stayed open in the eastern part of the city spoke of the rising light-skinned ethnic rage.

The List

The broader cultural context of Chávez's offensive was a new emphasis on the notion of being a "real" Venezuelan. Building on 19th-century tropes, Chávez kept talking about a connection to the land, the music, food, and customs that were thought to be "pure." These were the opposite of the culture espoused by the "cosmopolitan" classes with roots elsewhere. One of Chávez's favorite words came to be "endogenous," or that which comes from the inside, to refer to everything he and his movement stood for: endogenous development, endogenous economy, endogenous culture and film, and by direct implication, endogenous power. Those who had come from somewhere else, and descended from them, or looked to those countries for their inspiration or education, were in this sense not true Venezuelans. Their blood was not tied to the land.

As in prior purges based on ethnicity and religion throughout history, the most important thing was to have a list: a piece of paper with the names of those who were not "real" Venezuelans.

The opportunity to create such a comprehensive classification came about when 1.5 million signatures were collected to force a recall vote against the president in early 2004. While people signed the petition in the hope of bringing about political change by removing the president, the electoral authority leaked the data file containing the names, national ID numbers, and addresses of every single person opposed to Chávez who had signed. A ruling party congressman then uploaded every record to a public website. That is when the ethnic purge went fully digital.[82] Many on the list did not descend from Creoles, or 19th-century German families, or 20th-century immigrants. No existing database can empirically determine the precise ancestry of those signing the petition, but it seems clear that a vast majority had parents and grandparents who came from somewhere else.

The infamous "Tascón List," with its millions of names, was a classic example of political persecution. It became a virtual and universally accessible blacklist. Entire government agencies and ministries were purged, as were employees of government-owned banks, insurance companies, and other enterprises. Government contractors, scientists, college professors, people in highly technical positions, beneficiaries of government services, and anyone who had a connection to the state, was summarily dismissed, cut off, and otherwise vanished from access to government funds.[83] The systematic persecution and disfranchisement of those who wanted Chávez out simply added to the growing number of those who, not wanted in their own country, would choose to migrate.

The 1.5 million signatures triggered a full recall referendum, which Chávez would win with 58% of the vote.[84] The election's fairness was questioned by some, but the elections were deemed impartial by former US President Carter, who personally oversaw the process.[85]

Between strong political and electoral victories, the wholesale firings from the oil company, systematic purges from all state functions, and the beginning of an exodus of Chávez's most educated opponents, the Chavista ethnic identity project was beginning to change the political landscape, and perhaps the electoral one as well.

Nearly a Trillion Dollars

Then one day in late 2004 something almost unimaginable happened. After decades below its 1980 peak, the price of oil started to shatter price ceilings not seen in years. The price spike was not driven by a threat of war, a war itself, or a weather event.[86] By all accounts, the new oil prices were related to a structural supply and demand imbalance that would remain in place for years.

Fate rewarded Hugo Chávez with close to a trillion dollars in oil sales for what remained of his lifetime, or until 2013.[87] He probably had not given even a few hours of serious thought to the economy during four hard-fought years of political battles to preserve his hold on power, and possibly his life, until then. Yet here he was, presiding over a fantastic, overnight, lottery-like bonanza.

The period between late 2004 and the death of Chávez at the beginning of 2013 is by far the most baroque in the country's history. Hopefully somewhere in a faraway exile someone is writing a novel worthy of the era.

The almost ten-year-long oil bonanza—in all its excess, contradiction, and surrealism—holds the keys to Chávez's legacy, the humanitarian crisis, and probably everything that will happen in the country until at least the 2050s.

The ethnic conflict between mixed-race Venezuelans and those of lighter skin was superficially tamed, and simultaneously put on steroids by the oil cash inflows. Serious opposition protests to Chavismo subsided, but the ethnic identity divide deepened as the new money financed the final burial of Rómulo Betancourt's liberal state. In its place, a vast amorphous world with its politics, culture, and the self-conscious belief that it represented the best aspirations of an ethnic identity, arose to replace the old model of state.

The rise in oil revenues immediately impacted the ability of the government to spend more money internally, and also, critically, to allow more businesses to access dollars through new exchange controls. The result was a sharp rise in imports. As had been the case in every oil boom reaching back to the 1930s, it became cheaper to import a product than to make it;

more efficient to import than to farm, fish, or mine. This had already been the case, but now the money to make it possible was plentiful. The result was a flood of imported goods and a payday for those servicing those making money importing. Luxury restaurants, luxury buildings, luxury everything could now be found for businesspeople and government officials. People in all corners of the country began to spend, creating an orgy of personal consumption.

Suddenly many wanted, and could afford, a car. Traffic on the streets of every city exploded with both cheap and luxury vehicles. When they were not driving, the newly wealthy Venezuelans were shopping. There was never enough supply to satisfy what seemed like a supernatural demand for every product and service.

Chávez and Chavismo's political agenda was based on a massive transfer of wealth to the poorer parts of the country. This was accomplished through direct payments, as well as many health, environmental, food, and educational projects spawned by new, rising organizations loosely tied to the state. Health workers visited informal settlements that had not received that type of help in decades. Universities were created overnight to provide instant degrees for people from families that had never reached college. In a short time, the standards measuring poverty started to reflect the trans-formation in the living of millions.[88]

The amount of money at stake created a distinct aesthetic, a new social class, a generation entirely devoted to exchange control schemes, and a few billion-dollar fortunes. The portmanteau label "bolibourgeois," after the expensive tastes of a political movement inspired by Bolívar, was born to

name the era and its protagonists. The times also revealed the
true nature of foreign-educated elites that plunged without
shame, or sense of place, into the bacchanal of money to gain
anything from a few thousand to several hundred million
dollars. The invention of the iPhone, YouTube and Instagram
during those same years accelerated the madness while
recording it for posterity.

Meanwhile Chávez started to believe he was an old
sorcerer from his native Los Llanos. His alchemy seemed too
real. He called the spell "21st-Century Socialism," and the
gold it generated came in the form of a grossly overvalued
new currency officially christened the bolivar fuerte, or
strong bolivar.

The rhetoric of messianic socialism, paired with real
money seemingly falling from the sky, unified people from
different walks of life within Chavismo, each cashing in their
set of grievances for a few or many magical bolivar fuertes.
The poor in the informal settlements could see it. The rural
poor could see it too. For the working middle classes who
had never been part of the Caracas elites, or who came
from the provinces and had not attended the legacy universities, the Chávez miracle was real. They would displace the
legacy elites and would eventually run everything from the
oil company to new film studios churning out nationalist
cinema. The Chavista party, the upper layers of government,
and the myriad new organizations being born by the minute
were now captained by those who just a few years before felt
there was no future for them.

Jonathan Jakubowicz captured the way in which the
newly famous and the anonymous parroted the Bolivarian

line in his satirical pop novel, *Las Aventuras de Juan Planchard*.[89] The narrative's anti-hero, a former Procter & Gamble executive who gives up marketing toothpaste to join Chávez and his cause, is the perfect metaphor for those who felt left out of all prior oil bonanzas. His fellow travelers in Chavismo had never made it as far as getting a marketing job at an American consumer company; most had been stuck in dead-end positions. But Juan Planchard spoke for all.

The protagonist becomes an overnight millionaire and joins the ranks of those with substantial fortunes made through state schemes. Thinking about Che Guevara in a Las Vegas elevator on the way to an invitation-only swingers party, Planchard muses on what "socialism" has done for him:

> "We owe everything to Che. Without Che, we would still be working for gringos, getting shit salaries, making some Portuguese or Jewish capitalist rich, all without a chance of social mobility. Che gave us freedom, and whatever happens, we must remember that. Fatherland or death, we will prevail!"[90]

In a culture and a country not created by oil, the idea that socialism would be linked to social mobility would be out of place. In Venezuela, where people of all classes had lined up to get everything from the government for the previous 100 years, it made perfect sense. In the protagonist's mind Chavismo has righteously delivered his slice of treasure ahead of those of Portuguese and Jewish descent. As a true Venezuelan, it is what he deserved and had never received.

The pop novel articulates the nature of the ethno-nationalist cocktail Chávez and his supporters in the cultural sphere were perfecting. Immigrants and their descendants would not only be sent to the back of the line in favor of real Venezuelans, they would be demonized, and eventually exiled. The oil treasure would finally be properly distributed.

Two Forces

The years of the oil bonanza, the bolibourgeois era, are difficult to decode. The signals were contradictory then and looking back on the period remain so today.

Consumer consumption was king, yet most embraced the concept of socialism. The poor's standard of living rose for the first time in thirty years, yet a new business class added many hundred-million-dollar fortunes. Despite an unprecedented amount of money and political capital at his disposal, Chávez started to dismantle the governmental structures and assets already under his control. A collective imaginary privileging "real" Venezuelans over those with roots and outlooks elsewhere fueled an ethno-nationalist political agenda. Yet, the light-skinned middle classes enjoyed the highest disposable income of their lifetimes, until a decline in oil prices accelerated the logic of these contradictions to deliver a perfect storm.

Those contradictory years only make sense by exploring the details of a radical political and social revolution starting in 2004. Chapter Four chronicles the Chavista dismantling of the liberal state during the era of plenty and the ensuing whirlwind of violence, hunger, and illness. But before turning to those events, it is necessary to search for their historical context.

The nature of the country's self-destruction lies in the intersection of the two forces shaping modern Venezuela: mineral resources and ethnic identity.

Next, we turn to the oil story of the magical 20th century and the economic culture spawned by fossil fuels. Then, in the third chapter, we explore the much longer and painful history of racial and ethnic strife.

II
Economics in the Magical Century, 1922-1998

«And yet some of our soldiers were saying that they were seeing a dream, and it is not to marvel that I would write here in this manner, because there is much to ponder in that I don't know how to tell it: to see things never heard of, or even dreamed, as we were seeing.»
Bernal Diaz del Castillo,
The True History of the Conquest of New Spain

It was dawn in the tiny fishing village of Cabimas when the earth started to shake on December 14, 1922. A roaring explosion followed the tremor, and a furious rainstorm of thick oil fell over the straw-roof shacks and dirt roads. The black rain went on for days.

The Barroso II oil field's spectacular blowout spewed one million barrels of oil in a little over a week.[1] It was then the world's biggest known oil field, tapped just in time to feed a global economy fast converting from coal to fuel oil. The black rainstorm signaled a new era for one of South America's poorest countries. Exploration and production would spread throughout the sparsely populated country as American roughnecks turned *"béisbol"* into a national pastime and pound cake into a local delight, *"ponqué."* Everything from the most trivial to the most consequential would be transformed, starting with the economy.

Ever since Barroso II, three numbers have dominated many conversations seeking to explain the country's destiny: barrels produced per day, their price in the global market, divided by the country's population.

During the heyday of 1974, oil production reached 3.4 million barrels per day, the global price of crude oil stood at US$48 in 2019 dollars, and the country had thirteen million people. By 2019, the price of crude stood at US$50, production had bottomed out at 877,000 barrels per day, and the population had reached 28 million. By this somewhat arbitrary measure, the per capita production value in 1974 was US$4,582 for every Venezuelan. By 2019, it was US$572.[2]

For many, this simple math tells their country's story, a kabbala of its miseries and triumphs. The Chavista leadership of the late 2010s prayed the accelerating emigration would tilt the simple formula, or at least its trendline, in their favor. If enough people left the country, there would be fewer mouths to feed and able bodies to revolt, even on declining oil revenue. No one imagined, much less understood, the extent to which millions and millions of Venezuelans walking away from their country would answer the wildest wishes of those in power.

And yet, the long history of social and geographical conflict means that even a positive balance between oil production, international prices, and population cannot always guarantee peace.

The revolt leading to the coup d'état against General Pérez Jiménez in 1958, and Commander Chávez's attempted coup in 1992, both took place when the global price of oil, and production capabilities, had not suffered significant downward pressures. Chavez's coup came weeks after the end of 1991 when the economy had clocked the world's fastest growth at 9.73%.[3]

The dynamics behind the 1958 coup are illuminating. Three decades after Barroso II, the country was experiencing massive urban migration of the rural poor to the cities and unprecedented European and South American immigration. A new professional middle class and rising prosperity in many regional capitals had contributed much complexity to the country's politics. General Pérez Jiménez never understood that the way he was brokering the oil wealth was out of step with a fast-changing Venezuela. The emerging actors demanded a new accommodation. By January 1958, a broad coalition overthrew the last general to rule the country in the 20th century.

Eleven months later, Acción Democrática's Rómulo Betancourt set out to build a novel liberal state designed to broaden the oil treasure's distribution. The new democracy would ensure the old rural poor, in the countryside or the big cities, received a much higher share of the bounty. The far from perfect but more independent unions, courtrooms, congressional chambers, political parties, and professional and trade associations allowed for a deeper and broader distribution of resources across constituencies throughout the country. Betancourt was determined to erase old ethnic and racial fractures but also paid attention to the growing expectations of more assertive regions, a nascent immigrant commercial class, and new industrial and financial interests. A more sophisticated accommodation to manage the oil bounty made sense for a country that had become too complex for the iron hand of a highland general and the machinations and prejudices of his conservative cronies.

While the construction of Betancourt's gigantic new state would be very visible, a key component underpinning the country's society since the 1930s would remain unmentioned: the currency's value.

The bolivar's high value relative to the dollar had been a political and cultural demand of economic elites and the nascent middle class as far back as the late 1920s. As oil revenues increased in the aftermath of President Franklin Roosevelt's 1934 dollar devaluation, the bolivar emerged as one of the strongest currencies in the world. The country's unique history and the realities of an oil economy developed on the back of a poor and virtually empty geography had turned the overvalued currency into a true religion.

The generals and their conservative allies, and later Betancourt along with his socialist and liberal supporters, both built societies on the foundation of a strong bolivar. Their very different answers to the social, ethnic, and racial fractures that had torn the country apart for four hundred years had a shared, if silent, premise in the long-running currency consensus.

However, as often happens to societies whose good (and bad) fortunes depend on a single commodity, oil and its ability to prop up the currency became a fixed reference in the nation's identity and a conveniently forgotten factor in its destiny. The connections tying modern universities, great theater, sophisticated newspapers, vibrant public debate, and transformational strides in nutrition, health, and education to the price of oil and the overvalued bolivar were always fuzzy.

By the 1970s, the Middle East wars and the rise of OPEC, drove crude prices higher than ever. The country's GDP more than doubled from 1970 to 1975.[4] An orgy of infrastructure investment projects meant Venezuelans began to hope their country would soon have a first-world economy (in addition to the first-world cuisine and fashion the strong bolivar had already brought to Caracas). But the wishful thinking would not last long.

While prosperity was not enough for peace, only high oil prices could sustain the currency consensus and the liberal state's vast apparatus.

The population had continued growing, but the price of a barrel of oil and the country's ability to produce and sell more of them needed to be higher to sustain the status quo. Oil prices dropped and stayed low, save for a significant blip during the First Gulf War, for twenty-four years after 1980.[5] The growth orgy of the 1970s had generated a debt binge with crushing interest payments, forcing a radical devaluation of the currency in what came to be known as Black Friday on February 18, 1983. It was the first real devaluation after decades in which the country had lived off overvalued bolivars. By the late 1980s, the government—the state itself—was broke. Betancourt's dream of consensus, and the peace it had maintained, were mortally ill.

By December 1988, Carlos Andrés Pérez, Betancourt's protege, was elected president for a second time. He gambled everything he had helped create to save it by betting that an economy and a society independent of oil could and would thrive. His administration wanted to eliminate much of machinery of oil-revenue distribution laid out over decades: patronage networks that functioned as welfare systems, subsidies and incentives that protected and fed entire industries; fixed prices meant to guarantee consumption by the poor, protectionist tariffs established to preserve jobs and entire companies; and myriad regulations privileging professions, regions, and numerous institutions. Even more critical, Pérez struck down the cornerstone of a social consensus that had lasted for most of his own life by freeing the bolivar-dollar parity to the whims of the market. The bolivar's value dropped immediately as a reflection of the economy's real prospects.

While Pérez and his ministers can be seen as mere messengers of ill tidings, they would pay dearly for the tone-deafness with which they pierced modern Venezuelans' identity.

What happened next went against the original plan but confirmed an age-old reality of Venezuelan politics. Fate had Iraq's dictator Saddam Hussein invade Kuwait's oil fields just as the Pérez administration thought it was curing Venezuela of its oil addiction. The First Gulf War of 1990 sent crude prices up and kept them there long enough for a fortune to flood the country's coffers. Then, the government went on a new debt binge. By December 31, 1991, year-to-year GDP growth had surpassed even China's growth. [6]

Thirty-six days later, Commander Chávez led his troops out of their garrison. Despite spectacular macroeconomic results, the Perez administration's refusal to address the political, social, and cultural arrangements that had maintained peace for decades created a massive vacuum. Breaking the social contract behind a strong bolivar and undermining Betancourt's wealth distribution mechanisms brought back long-buried ghosts in the country's history.

On the fateful February 4, 1992, the rhetoric and the violence of the 19th century made a grand televised entrance on the national scene. An old nightmare was just getting started, again.

Coup d'état

It was already dark when hundreds of paratroopers in full combat gear started boarding a fleet of rented buses on February 3, 1992. Their base was about fifty miles from Caracas, and traffic was expected to be light past ten o'clock PM. As the buses rolled out onto the highway, yet another in a long history of military takeovers in Venezuela had gotten underway. As the night progressed, commanders in several bases throughout the country would successfully take over their respective cities. But the entire enterprise would succeed or fail in Caracas. It was all in the paratroopers' hands, and in those of their charismatic commander, Lieutenant Colonel Hugo Chávez.

The coup d'état needed to grab the president, and control at least one national television network in order to persuade the rest of the armed forces to join in.

Chávez's ear was tuned to the national mood. He understood the sense of dislocation that the radical changes had brought about. The more the Pérez government tried to convince citizens of the importance of shattering the seventy-year-old benevolent oil state: its rules, borders, social mores, even its language, the more anxiety it created.

Commander Chávez could see how these poorly explained, "too much, too fast" changes had affected people in every social class. He also sensed the universal desire for a strong military leader to end the uncertainty. This longing ran through the most miserable informal settlements, the middle-class gatherings in the suburbs south of the Guaire River in Caracas, and the poshest drawing rooms at the Country Club. At that point, President Pérez was universally distrusted and reviled, and Chávez meant to put him on trial for treason, that very night if possible.

But first, he had to capture the president and control at least one television network, and outrun the minister of defense and several actively pro-government forces who had become aware of the coup.

Hugo Chávez and his paratroopers comfortably traversed the highway to Caracas in a fleet of rented buses with cabins likely plastered with images of Che, Jesus, Legba, happy faces, peace signs, and broken hearts. They already had a clear order of battle. A unit would take over a major private television network, and another would control the government's Channel 8. Another unit would storm the presidential residence in the east side of the city, and a fourth one, the presidential palace in the west side of the city. Chávez himself would oversee all operations from a military museum on a mountaintop near the presidential palace. Surrounded by the vast informal settlements of eastern Caracas and the glories and amulets of his army, Chávez would wait to take his turn in a long list of military heroes who had shaped Venezuela over 200 years. But amidst the soaring dreams of grandeur, the plan's operational details and its actual military aspects had taken a back seat.

To begin with, the troops could not be sure where the president was. He had been traveling to Davos, in the Swiss Alps, to sell Venezuela's "Great Turn" to free enterprise, but upon landing, had been alerted to the coup's existence. Rapidly adjusting to the new reality, Pérez went into survival mode. He dashed off to the presidential residence in the east but left either before or just as it was coming under attack by Chávez's units. The presidential guard, along with the secret police, fiercely defended the residence, where the first lady and the president's family spent hours hiding from the battle raging outside.[7]

Right away, Chávez had lost his ability to surprise. The initiative was no longer his.

Pérez fled to the presidential palace in the west, unknowingly running toward Chavez's command post at the museum and straight into one of his strongest units. Despite this extraordinary piece of good luck for the rebels, Pérez and his loyal followers managed to enter the palace and barricade themselves inside it.

In the meantime, the paratrooper units tasked with taking over the country's oldest television network had gotten lost in the big city. Apparently, they had the wrong address for the TV studios and, for some reason, were unable to make their way to one of the most visible and public buildings in Caracas.

The unit tasked with taking over the government television network was confronting problems of their own. They reached the right location and quickly subdued the guards on duty. But when they produced the videotape with a pre-recorded message, they were told the technical format did not work and that it could not be broadcast.[8] Chávez had recorded his message with a low-quality consumer camcorder. Someone in charge explained to the soldiers that only broadcast-quality material could be broadcast. The mainly rural troops trained for jungle warfare were out of their depth and took the technical issues at face value. The coup would never get on television, in low- or high-res.

Meanwhile, the president was encircled in his palace and the battle raged all around. Even without television, the rebellion was getting close to grabbing or even killing President Carlos Andrés Pérez on the spot. That would be a game-changer. Commander Chávez stayed at his museum directing operations from afar, even though he had worked at the presidential palace as a military aide and presumably had a good grasp of its layout.[9]

While the rebellion's troops naively, or symbolically, focused their firepower on the palace's front door, the president fled through a back tunnel to reach the eerily silent parking lot underneath the government towers of El Silencio. While Chávez waited for news surrounded by Bolívar's uniforms, swords, and other relics, Carlos Andrés got in the trunk of a Caprice Classic and fled the scene. The car sped straight to the studios of the largest television network in the country, a bunker-like concrete structure on top of a mountain that could only be accessed along a single lane narrow road.[10] It was the perfect place from where to fight a coup without a single soldier, and the one media outlet that had been entirely left out of Chávez's military plans.

Within minutes a composed and sharply suited president was on the air declaring the coup had been defeated, and everything was under control. This was far from the truth, except that in 1992 there was no web, barely any cell phones, and no private national radio network. The image spoke a thousand words even though the country's second and third largest cities, as well as the presidential palace in Caracas, were under the full control of the rebellion. As in most coup attempts, many army officers throughout the country were waiting to see which way the wind would blow before committing to a side. The powerful image of the president addressing the nation was enough. Without access to a television or even a broadcast radio signal, Chávez was militarily lost.

The night had shown who had what it takes to win in battle: extraordinary physical courage, situational awareness, creative and relentless initiative, and the hunger to survive under the most extreme circumstances. Yet the long day was just getting started.

By dawn the situation was at a standstill. Paratroopers controlled television stations but had no content to broadcast. They occupied the government's seat of power but had let the president flee. They had even managed to capture several governors and garrisons in key provincial capitals, but hardly anyone knew this. Neither camp had any public support as people slept or hid at home, fearing for their lives. The minister of defense, who had been loyal to the president from the very beginning, started to negotiate a surrender.

After a series of phone calls in which it has been reported that Chávez only asked that his rights be respected, he abandoned the military museum and turned himself in. This was a critical first step for the government. The coup's ringleader had given himself up well before key garrisons controlled by the rebellion had made any moves to surrender. The defense minister had no ability to retake these garrisons by force and knew that any further delays in resolving the situation could make it worse. He authorized a nationally televised surrender by Chávez. It seems that in exchange, Chávez would plead with his comrades to give up arms.

The Commander would finally get what he had been dreaming of in his long night at the museum: a big loudspeaker. Either because there were officers sympathetic to him who helped out, or because the minister's people thought the others would surrender faster if their leader looked well taken care of, Chávez was able to shave and put on a pressed uniform and an unruffled beret before addressing the nation. While on YouTube the video looks snowy, squarish, and almost black and white, the impact that morning was impressive. A young, dashing-looking officer gave the shortest, most effective speech in Venezuela's history. Two phrases within the 177 words that Chávez spoke that morning would stay in people's minds for years, and probably forever: "Our objectives haven't been fulfilled, for now," and, "I take full responsibility."[11]

By one o'clock PM on February 4, 1992, the rebellion was officially over. Chávez, along with his fellow officers and about 1,000 rank-and-file soldiers who had left their bases in different cities, were under military arrest. The streets of Caracas were deserted. The government declared a state of emergency and a night curfew, adding to an unsettling sense of foreboding. While a few figureheads went on television to declare their support for democracy, there were no daytime street demonstrations in support of the system, not to say the government. The president set out to create a coalition government, but he too seemed stunned.

In the informal settlements in Caracas and all the major cities, the apartment buildings of the small but influential middle class, and in the opulent houses of the country's wealthiest families, feelings ranged from open admiration to restrained respect for the young officer who had had the "cojones" to take responsibility for what had just happened. "I take full responsibility," he had said. The very words the country wanted to hear.

Pérez, the politician, had won militarily while Commander Chávez had proven careless in planning, clueless about intelligence, and inept in battle. Yet the military man proved to be the cannier politician, clutching the most important victory of his life with a deceptively simple, short speech. Twenty million Venezuelans had been desperate for an explanation for the uncertainty into which the government had apparently plunged their lives. The affirmation of responsibility became both an explanation and a solution: everything is broken because no one is in control. With me, Chávez was saying, the buck stops here.

Across social classes, regions, and ethnicities, Venezuelans finally had a clear vision of what they wanted and had been missing: a strong man, a strong state, and preferably both. After two years of deregulation and liberalization, the "foreign voodoo" widely held responsible for inflation and uncertainty in jobs, pensions, and entitlements, here was something different. People wanted someone who would take full control and face them directly. On the morning of February 4, on television screens across the country, a young Lieutenant Colonel stepped up to the role. But the dynamics at play that night had begun hundreds of years before.

The Geography of Poverty

Venezuela has always been extremely poor, at least until global oil demand changed everything. In different periods cocoa and coffee created some wealth, but never enough to fundamentally change the dynamics of poverty for most people or to launch a modern nation-state.

Resources were scarce in Venezuela. It was a problem in colonial times and during its first ninety years as an independent republic. To begin with, the country had always lacked people. As the original settlers of the Americas crossed the Bering Strait to establish themselves from Alaska to the

North American plains, Mexico, and the Andean region, their civilizations lined the North–South axis across the western coast. Venezuela's geographical position more than 1,000 miles from the Pacific corridor kept it largely unpopulated relative to its size. Just as Europe was settled along the East–West axis that nurtured Mediterranean civilization, the Americas thrived along the North–South axis straddling the west, away from the Atlantic and the Caribbean.

When Columbus sighted modern-day Venezuela in 1498, the local indigenous populations were worlds away from the culture and sophistication of Machu Picchu or Tenochtitlan. The Spanish Conquistadors found almost no gold or silver, and soon the territory's unsuitability for agriculture, fishing, and even cattle-raising became all too evident.

By 1612 the Spanish Governor of Caracas Province wrote the king as much:

"I have found the affairs of this Province in such bad shape that I cannot refrain from pleading that your majesty grieve for it. Because it is so poor and so far gone, and the locals so few, that I am assured, and I have seen it, that three-thirds of six years have gone missing, and this is the reason the mines have been abandoned. There is not a Crown in the entire Province, and your majesty is owed ninety thousand ducats, without any existing means of collecting them."[12]

With not many exceptions, the Venezuelan coastline lacks the kinds of shallow seas and bays that promote seafaring nations. Instead, for hundreds of miles, the mountains descend directly into a deep, treacherous sea. This northern mountain range is a tropical forest with very thin soil which later would turn out to be great for cocoa and coffee but never enough to feed, much less launch, a great metropolis. To the south of the mountains, there are patches of lands fertile enough for wheat, sugar, and indigo, which were cultivated from the very beginning of colonial rule. But there was not nearly enough fertile land because much of the country is riddled by thin soil. Ultimately, its proximity to the equator means it lacks even mild winters to fight the numerous crop-destroying plagues which go on year-round.

The enormous plains, Los Llanos, rise south of the coastal ranges and valleys. Monsoon-like rainy seasons flood tens of millions of acres every year, but it remains one of the most difficult places in the world for organized, modern cattle ranching, or for sustained agriculture. When the rainy months give way to the dry season, The Plains become a huge dustbowl. The cycles of floods and drylands condemn the Venezuelan Llanos to a difficult and often miserable life. Tens of thousands of wild horses and cattle roamed there for years, and cattle-raising has been a mainstay of Los Llanos for centuries. However, in economic terms, it bears little resemblance to the plains of Texas and Patagonia that fed the world with meat in the 19th and early 20th centuries. Without floods, mosquitoes, and malaria, with yearly winters naturally checking plagues, and a temperate spring giving rise to grasslands rather than dusty fields, the Texan and Argentinean plains stand in stark contrast to the challenged Venezuelan plains.

In the bottom third of the country, its deep south, the Amazon tropical forest has the thinnest of soil. It is easy to be fooled by the endless green landscape and the supernatural abundance of fresh water, but the Amazon landscape is among the planet's least hospitable to humankind. The shallow soil is so devoid of nutrients that trees have been fighting each other for millions of years by going upwards in a mad dash for sunlight. Underneath the canopy, a parasitic battle rages to sap the trees of life. The eternal shadow under the canopy is one of the world's most biodiverse environments, but one where only a few mammals have ever survived.

Less than 100 miles from the equator at its most southern point, Venezuela's Amazon is scorching hot. Even where elevation turns the jungle temperate, in the Canaima region, the rocky soil has yielded little for the Pemón People in the 1,000 years they have inhabited the place. The one valuable thing modern society has found there are diamonds, which can be scavenged on ancient riverbeds that flow down from the high plains. Gold is found deeper down. Yet the gold never, even to this day, amounted to the reserves of precious minerals found in Mexico, Bolivia, or Peru. It was the same for diamond mining.

Throughout the 19th century and up until the 1920s, pre-oil Venezuelan economics was about a few agricultural products that could be farmed, like cacao and coffee, to be sold abroad, and the few products that were imported to satisfy a small and impoverished nation. The global cocoa boom of the 18th century changed the dynamics of the colony, and later the European coffee craze helped create a semblance of government, but neither commodity was able to fully finance a modern state, or lift the majority from abject poverty.

The population in 1830, the year after the country ended its association with Colombia to become an independent republic, was 880,059. By 1873 the First Republic's first official census counted 1,420,889 people.[13] Caracas had all of 30,000 inhabitants.[14]

But all of this changed on December 14, 1922, when the Barroso II oil well had its spectacular blowout. The well alone would start producing 100,000 barrels of oil a day almost from the beginning, sealing the sudden novelty of Venezuela as a new promised land. In a few years, the thinly populated, barren country would become the world's number one exporter of oil and the second largest producer on the planet after the United States. Nothing was ever the same again.

Paradise on Earth

Venezuelans' perceptions about their own country changed fast. In the late 1890s, Caracas was a backward, small city; Los Llanos an inhospitable and insurmountable landscape; the jungles of the Amazon a dark, malaria-infested region; and the coastal valleys scarcely populated and dangerous. Everyone was poor, extremely poor.

In a few years, cars, airplanes, paved roads, and air conditioning paid for by oil transformed this view. By the late 1930s and 1940s Rómulo Gallegos was writing novels that turned Los Llanos into a sublime expanse, and the Amazon into a mythical place of unsurpassed beauty. The coastal valleys reclaimed a colonial grandeur it is not clear they had ever had. Alfredo Boulton's photographs transformed Margarita from a barren and hard island into a Garden of Eden. These authors implicitly claimed that Venezuela was not rich because of oil; rather, the country had always been a paradise.

The revisionist optimism spread. You could throw a mango on the side of the road and a tree would surely sprout from it. The sudden new fertility of the land—at least in prose, poetry, and photography—conveniently erased the thin soil year-around plagues, and torrential floods that had caused so much pain and hunger for centuries.

Before oil revenues started to finance the rise of an intellectual middle class, there was little romanticism in the descriptions of the Venezuelan landscape. But a rapid transformation changed the way Venezuelans saw themselves and their country.

German explorer Alexander Von Humboldt's extensive narrative of his 18th-century travels finds him intoxicated by his scientific observations of the specific plants and animals he is collecting, even marveling at the sight of the Avila mountain in Caracas. But he never fails to return to the challenges of the landscape: hunger, mosquitoes, ant armies, voracious crocodiles, caribe-infested rivers, and air so humid he cannot even see the sky at night. His near-fatal passage through the scorching hot Llanos, or his and his comrade Bonpland's recurring bouts of fever and dysentery, are essential to his chronicle.[15] The many British, French, Irish, and Spanish officers who fought in the Wars of Independence left thousands of pages describing the unexpected hardships of a land riddled by heat and plagues.

Even when Bolívar, the Great Liberator, writes to evoke a nation few others could see, he marshals a spirit of the people, the forces of history, or the destiny of a new race. Those are the only metaphors he can find to build his idea of the national identity. He seldom, if ever, speaks of beauty, or of the rich and plentiful land which would obsess 20th-century writers.

The national anthem, written in 1814, does not contain a single word describing a natural feature of the country, its beautiful mountains, coastline, jungles, or what would later be considered its magnificent Plains. Instead, the lyrics sing of a raging battle between good and evil. An oppressed people, located in a geographic vacuum, yearning to break the chains that will not let them be free.

If the late 1800s American Hudson School painters focused on the upstate New York landscape and the supernatural vistas at Yellowstone, their Venezuelan counterparts of the time seldom stepped out of their studios. It seemed the equatorial light and lush tropical colors were not that interesting to them. Instead, Tovar y Tovar, Michelena, and Cristóbal Rojas spent years painstakingly recreating cruel battles, imprisoned or dying heroes, and people on their death beds. Michelena painted a beautiful sunset on the horizon in *Vuelvan Caras*, but natural beauty is not the protagonist of his work.

The oil bonanza changed people's perceptions of their country, and of nature. Manuel Cabré's paintings offer a great example of the new interest in the landscape as oil revenues grew. Cabré's canvases hung in every self-respecting wealthy home of the 20th century. They are single-mindedly obsessed with the beauty of the Avila mountain. The mountain-totem is seen from many angles but always away from the buildings, people, and informal settlements that defined Caracas. For Cabré, the city was just a beautiful mountain. It is remarkable that he could only capture its soul, its inner wealth, by turning his back on the city's inhabitants, its politics, its theater, and its buzzing, noisy, urban ways. In those paintings, prosperity is represented by nature. As democracy took root in the 1960s, Cabré's paintings became more and more valuable. And today, with the dream utterly shattered, they are just as popular as the nostalgia for something that has been lost rises. The Avila is the same mountain that Von Humboldt first explored in the 1790s and which, he claims in his writings, no Spanish or Creole had ever climbed all the way to the top. If this is true, for 200 years the slave-owning Creoles could not be bothered to walk up 3,000 feet and see their spectacular valley from above. The beauty of nature was not yet something that mattered to them.

Cabré was twenty-four years old when the first formal oil well was drilled in 1914: a time when his work would have been disregarded by the Caracas elites. By 1950, well into the bonanza, the mountain paintings had captured the zeitgeist and would not stop growing in popularity for decades. By then nature equaled wealth.

Cabré's contemporary, the painter Pedro Centeno Vallenilla, experienced an opposite trajectory in the late 1920s. Like Bolívar, he ignored the landscape, its depth, and its beauty to concentrate on the symbolic legacy of history: idealized tribal chiefs, impossibly chiseled Conquistadors, noble and beautiful kidnapped Africans. His flat paintings and murals depicting mythical icons enthroned Vallenilla as a leading artist just before oil transformed the national culture. His work remained in favor with the military rulers of the 1950s, but more because of nostalgia for bygone eras than anything else. A famous photograph of Vallenilla painting in a khaki uniform, the artist as heir to a 19th-century army, seemed incomprehensible to artists that by then saw themselves living in paradise, far away from any battlefield.

As Cabré's landscapes became more recognized, Centeno Vallenilla's early fame faded, and his work was relegated to the dustbin of history for almost 100 years.

Later, in the Chávez years, a prescient interpretation of Centeno Vallenilla by artist Alexander Apostol would provoke a reappraisal of the painter-soldier. Apostol's *Rehearsing the National Posture* (*Ensayando la Postura Nacional*, 2010) is a series of videos and photographs reenacting Centeno Vallenilla's view of the nation's identity. The work portrays contemporary individuals in current-day settings attempting poses already perfected by the chiseled warriors in Centeno's canvases.

Apostol zeroes in on the painter's obsession with masculine beauty. Before then few had noticed that, for Centeno Vallenilla, the country's ancestral identity lay in the erotized and racialized bodies of Indians and Africans. The mystery of Venezuela's strength, despite its poverty, lay in exotic, sexually charged warriors. Their African and Amerindian origins supposedly endowed them with supernatural qualities that explained the country's ancestral inner fires.

The prolific oil gushers would dispense with this origin myth for the nation. Now that the earth itself was alive with a liquid gold bursting out into the sky, the source of the country's spirit changed. After centuries of pain and violence, Venezuela turned out to have been touched by divine grace all along. Centeno Vallenilla's neo-colonial dream of ancient sexual energies would be quickly replaced by the myth of a naturally endowed country.

Apostol's insight on the rise, fall, and revival of Centeno Vallenilla is critical to appreciate the later Chavista imaginary. When the poverty, chaos, and violence of the 19th century returned in the 21st, the country could no longer explain itself as the recipient of a divine touch. Amidst the growing chaos, Chávez placed himself in the symbolic place Centeno Valle-nilla's warriors had occupied. He spoke of his body in highly symbolic terms, claiming his Zambo identity, a mixture of Amerindian and African descent, placed him at the very core of the nation's origin. The Comandante's endless sexual innuendo reaffirmed Centeno Vallenilla's most important theme.

At the very least, Apostol's work suggests that, in the ransacked Venezuelan landscape of the late 2010s, the metaphors of natural plenty could no longer sustain a national myth.

Medieval Magic

The 1930s idea of Venezuela as resource-rich was inspired by the worldview of the first Spanish Conquistadors of the 1490s. When they arrived at the shores of today's Dominican Republic, Haiti, and Cuba, the medieval men of the 15th century only saw a Garden of Eden, a place full of magic.

Columbus's journal entries of his expedition to the Americas were written to seduce and capture the imagination of Spain's warrior Queen Isabella. His experiences would mirror those of writers in the 1940s. On October 13, 1492, Columbus writes of the landscape as "completely covered with verdure and delightful to behold."[16] A few days later he describes fish "so beautiful that no one beholding them could fail to express the highest wonder and admiration."[17] Later he writes of Cuba: "This island even exceeds the others in beauty and fertility."[18]

Columbus was a well-traveled Genoese who had already seen early capitalism at work, but he cleverly omitted what he must have known about the nature of wealth. The audience for his letters still held the medieval Christian and Muslim concept of value. For the Spanish conquerors from Andalusia and Extremadura, beauty, not banking, was inextricably linked to wealth. For them, riches could not be reproduced: they could only be found. They believed that wealth was static and could only be captured in conquest, as spoils of war, or conveyed from fathers to sons through inheritance. This was an article of faith throughout the south of Spain in the early 1500s.

Basque merchants had already revolutionized the cod trade and many Castilians were profiting from global wool demand, but the Queen of Spain and the men of 1492 were warriors who had fought against Muslims in the *Reconquista* war. The Spanish saw the "beauty" of the islands, and the mountains of gold and silver in Mexico and Peru, as confirmation of what they already believed: wealth was found, not created.

The local populations were enslaved to extract this newly discovered wealth. Africans were kidnapped and transported to the Americas to continue extracting and moving resources to Spain. Unlike a majority of North American settlers, who traveled to the future United States to create a religious utopia where they wanted to stay and prosper, the Spanish colonist in the 1500s and 1600s wanted to get rich and get back to his hometown as soon as possible. The garish 17th- and 18th-century homes still lining the main street of Cáceres, Spain, say plenty about the adventure.

For those left behind in the colonies—the descendants of slaves, native populations, poor Spanish who had never made it back, and the few rich ones who had decided to stay—the original conquerors' foundational idea of wealth had stayed true. While the exuberant beauty the men of Extremadura had seen and spoken of was not heard of again, their view of wealth was evident in the 19th-century Venezuelan struggles. In the extremely poor cities and even poorer countryside, wealth was given or taken, and usually it was taken.

And then, as if by magic, oil appeared. It was a lottery, an act of God, something as supernatural as the out-of-control gushers around Lake Maracaibo. It was Columbus "finding" a "verdant fertility," Cortes "discovering" Mexican gold, Pizarro "uncovering" Andean silver all over again.

The mining mindset would cement itself in Venezuelan consciousness during the 20th century. The oil boom would confirm the idea that riches can only be found and extracted, never reproduced or grown. That the country was beautiful, and that beauty lay remarkably close to wealth, neatly encircled the idea. What is fascinating, and little explored, is how the mining mindset, and the myth of the magical country, ended up shaping both an idea of wealth and the actual structure of Venezuela's modern economy.

Oil Economy

The accepted wisdom among many Venezuelans as late as the 2010s was that their country's oil dependency was a factor in the country's tragedies during those years. What few ever entertained was that whatever economic activity existed in the 20th century was entirely dependent on oil exports. This leads to a question that is seldom asked in Venezuela: what is a modern economy?.

By the year of the big oil blowout in 1922, Western economists had a clear idea of how industrial economies came to be. Throughout the prior 150 years, the world had seen how the deployment of capital to industrialize the United States, the United Kingdom, and Germany had delivered never-dreamed-of growth.

By 1776 pioneer economist Adam Smith had explained how industrial economies came into existence. It started with individuals, industries, towns, and entire countries focusing on producing what they could make better and more cost-effectively than anyone else. The exchange of those goods for others manufactured in different towns or countries created the profits that would add up to form capital. The investment of that capital to make the process bigger, faster, and more efficient became capitalism.

Less than a century later, Karl Marx argued that profit, or, in his language, surplus value, could not belong to a single individual, the capitalist, but rather to all the workers who had created it. Where Marx saw an inherently evil appropriation of the worker's toil transformed into profit and then capital, Smith described a seamless circle of specialization and exchange generating privately owned wealth.

Yet both agreed that the industrial production of goods for commercial exchange and the ensuing accumulation of profits as investment capital, regardless of who enjoyed the benefits, had transformed humanity's ability to generate wealth.

In hindsight it is easy to appreciate the confusion, or delusion, affecting the Venezuelan business and political elites of the 1930s. The preindustrial peasant country of the 1910s had vast amounts of capital by the 1930s, having skipped industrialization. An incredible pile of wealth was accumulating without a local productive base. The local elites assumed that all money worked the same in a nascent economy. They believed, or chose to believe, that the capital coming in from oil was the same and worked in the same manner as if they had worked to create a productive economy.

The fact was that a handful of American companies had arrived with their own capital, their own specialized and manual workers, had tapped the largest oil fields in the world, had shipped out the crude, and then sent the government and a few cronies of the ruling dictator, General Gómez, royalties for their drilling rights.

The economies of Europe and the United States, and much later China, had been forged by tens of millions of workers toiling in Dickensian conditions: inhumane factories in polluted cities, tens of thousands of clerks and accountants scribbling in ledgers, armies of tax collectors at ports and railroads, and a capitalist and then a banking class amassing and reinvesting the profits. Meanwhile, the Venezuelan government and the business elites were getting a check in the mail.

Twentieth-century Venezuela started with those royalties. While they did not finance a modern economy, they did pay for the infrastructure of the state. Before the 1920s there had never been enough money to pay for a real government over the entire territory: a standing, mobile army that could be sent anywhere to assert the state's power; good roads for that army to have real reach; enough functionaries across the land to administer justice; a national system of education that could reach at least a few children in every region to assure a standard language; and a shared identity among the elites across the country. The Spanish colonial system had, in its time, managed to achieve remarkably uniform control over the territory, but no 19th-century government had been able to replicate it. Even President Guzmán Blanco, who dreamed of such a state in the 1880s, built its monuments all over Caracas, and passed endless laws to create the apparatus of governance, did not have enough money to make it come true. In the end, apparently frustrated by the fact that fancy buildings, mausoleums, and paper ministries by themselves would not give him authority over the land, he left for Paris to live out the rest of his days.

General Gómez (who had come to power in 1908) was, by contrast, both lucky in the size of the windfall, and methodical in his build-out of a state. He skipped the grand symbols of power others had dreamed about. Instead, he dedicated himself to building a modern army, a network of roads, and hiring enough policemen and functionaries to enforce the kind of peace the country had never enjoyed before. Compared to Gómez's oil-financed iron-fist rule, even the Spanish had been constantly challenged by permanent slave and indigenous rebellions.

Two markets emerged early in Gómez's brand-new nation. The first was the government, and particularly the army, which became an avid consumer of all kinds of technology, goods, and services. The bigger and more efficient it became, the more it needed, and because nothing was manufactured in Venezuela, the middleman between a foreign vendor and the government buyer was born. This enduring character, typically from one of the few educated, bilingual families from Caracas, would become a key protagonist in the country's modern history.

The second market, now that every corner of the nation was at peace and would soon have a road leading to it, was made up of oil exploration and production facilities popping up east and west of the country. While oil companies directly imported everything that was critical to them, their sprawling camps would buy all the goods and services that could be found locally.

As the government grew, so did its purchasing power and the array of companies importing and sometimes assembling goods for it. As the oil camps became small cities and the scope of the industry grew, and the big cities themselves became bigger and wealthier, a small consumer market was born as well.

The foreign oil industry continued to expand along with the state, and by the 1930s there was economic activity everywhere. A growing middle class working directly or indirectly for the government or the oil companies could now afford better housing, education, food, and health services. The working classes employed by oil, construction, and services were economically a world away from the poor peasants of the early 1900s. The wealthier state started to deliver more services, particularly in education and infrastructure, which in turn expanded both its own purchases, and the nascent consumer market.

For a modern economy to emerge in such a scenario, the marketplace would eventually generate its own supply of goods, some form of specialization would appear, and in such a small country, exports would necessarily follow. Companies would be started to supply the local market, and necessarily grow around the world to maintain their original competitive advantages, increase their scale, and grow their productivity. In other words, the country's business class would take what their factories could create better and cheaper than anyone else to other markets abroad.

Because by the 1930s there were some factories and plenty of construction, as well as more and more cars in the streets and radio sets in homes, it appeared that a modern economy was on its way. The reality is that royalties sent by the foreign oil industry were coming into the country and were going right out to buy consumer, military, and infrastructure goods. There were a lot of imported shiny products and buildings in Caracas, and a lot of commercial activity, but no trace of the early industry that would characterize a modern economy.

Adam Smith described the nature of this paradox as far back as the 18th century:

"It is not by augmenting the capital of the country, but by rendering a greater part of that capital active and productive than would otherwise be so, that the most judicious operations of banking can increase the industry of the country."[19]

By "banking operations" Smith is referring to the state's treasury, which in the Venezuelan story is even more critical because it sets the bolivar's value against the dollar. Because most wealth came into the country from royalties paid out of international sales of crude oil, the value of the bolivar in relation to the dollar defined all economic activity.

Typically the value of the currency reflects how rich a country is, as happens with the contemporary Swiss franc, for example. However, because the value of the currency affects the economic choices of individuals and companies, policymakers often intervene to set more arbitrary values. China is the contemporary example of a country that chose to devalue its currency to discourage its citizens and businesses from buying products abroad. An expensive dollar made anything purchased outside China more costly, and anything locally produced and purchased with yuan more competitive throughout the world. China grew at near 10% annual rates for decades due to the building of the world's largest export economy. The devalued yuan was the financial cornerstone of that growth.

The debate over exchange rates in Venezuela briefly flared in 1934. Future Minister of the Treasury Alberto Adriani argued for devaluation of the bolivar as the only way to save the viability of an export economy. Vicente Lecuna, businessman and former president of the Central Bank, argued for revaluation: the more expensive the bolivar in relation to the dollar, the more dollars oil companies would have to bring to pay for their royalty obligations to the state.[20] In other words, the higher the value of the bolivar vis-à-vis the dollar, the richer the country would be in the short term.

The option of devaluing the bolivar was never really on the table. Soon the business and political elites were united in forging a century-long consensus around the need for a strong bolivar. It is true this flew in the face of any viable, long-term strategy to create a sustainable economy. It also went against the interests of agricultural businesses that wanted to export their goods. But culturally, people now believed they lived in a magical, beautiful country with an inherently wealthy landscape. The old belief would not go away: true riches were always found, never created. The mining mindset had a strong cultural pull, going back hundreds of years to the Spanish Conquistadors' medieval belief systems which had shaped Venezuela's culture.

An inflated local currency offered plenty of easy profits using overvalued bolivars to buy goods and reselling them to the two nascent markets: the government and its army on the one hand, and the local consumer economy that started around the oil camps.

As the country grew, the strong bolivar became an article of faith for the elites. Their assets in Venezuela: their land, their real estate, their import companies, would always be worth more in dollars when the bolivar was strong. Conversely, they would be as good as worthless if the currency lost its value.

Creating an export economy was not a priority for the business elites. In their eyes, the incredible profits they were reaping from the 1930s all the way through 2015 amounted to something real. Even businesspeople who had earned economics degrees at America's most famous universities thought they were developing the country's economy. They considered the ability to profit in the lopsided commerce of an overvalued currency to be the same thing as participating in a productive economy. In the minds of many, extracting capital became capitalism itself.

Adam Smith would have recognized a modern version of something he had already seen: the Spanish Crown's mismanagement of the gold and silver fortune extracted from America and shipped directly to Spain in the 1500s and 1600s.

The similarities between 20th-century Venezuela and late 16th-century Spain are sobering. Charles V and his son, Philip II, received the biggest mining payoff in history. Yet, within the fifty years of Philip's reign, Spain had gone from being the world's wealthiest country to a nation in clear decline. The extraordinary amounts of gold and silver from Mexico and Peru had revalued the Spanish currency, created rampant inflation, and effectively diverted the Peninsula's economic efforts from nascent industries with global potential—like wool—or established ones—like fishing and trade—toward rent-seeking behavior. The Crown directed almost all its resources to expensive military adventures abroad. On several occasions, Philip II defaulted on the foreign debt generated by the Eighty Years' War and the endless battles against the Turks in the Mediterranean.

Port cities like Hamburg and Amsterdam leveraged their nascent fleets, trading knowledge and financial acumen to become powerful in the 17th century. In Spain, trading cities like San Sebastian and Barcelona missed their chance to do the same, as the country's collective energies were distracted by the mirage of gold and silver riches, and military projects that promised international prestige.

Two hundred years later, Venezuela's companies and their celebrated leaders were in the same situation that the Spanish elites of the early 19th century found themselves in. By the 1770s, as Smith was describing the birth of industrial capitalism, Spain was poor, underdeveloped, and in many places hungry; in no way prepared to join the upcoming industrial leap in European history.

The flood of gold into the Spain of the late 1500s had a profound impact on the domestic economy and the Crown's ambitions. The Hapsburg kings spent their fortune buying soldiers and guns to fight two losing wars. In Venezuela, the most important impact of the oil boom was how the flood of dollars revalued the bolivar. Most historians gloss over how much the strong currency would determine the course of Venezuelan history: they seldom write about the scope of a national consensus around this issue, the cornerstone of the magical country.

The Bolivar

The modern overvalued bolivar was born in the aftermath of the Great Depression of 1929. The initial American response to the collapse of industrial production and the spectacular rise of unemployment had been to further slow down the economy. The dollar was revalued against all other currencies and liquidity was sapped from the domestic market. The result of such a strong dollar was more unemployment and suffering. As soon as Franklin Delano Roosevelt assumed the presidency in 1933 he reversed course by following the advice of British economist John Maynard Keynes. The revolutionary recipe to combat economic stagnation called for devaluing the dollar and flooding the domestic economy with cash, which eventually got the economy moving again.

In Venezuela the effects of a new weak dollar were radical. The bolivar's exchange rate went from 7.75 per dollar in 1932, to 3.04 per dollar after the passage of Roosevelt's Gold Reserve Act of 1934.[21] The new rate killed the export-based coffee and cacao industries.[22]

Caracas became so notoriously expensive to foreigners that in 1939 Franklin Roosevelt found time, even at the beginning of World War II, to ask for an explanation in a note to Harry Hopkins, then Secretary of Commerce. The exchange found by journalist Raúl Gallegos tells a powerful story: "Will you get me a memorandum on the relative cost of living in Caracas, Venezuela, as compared to Washington DC—in terms of American dollars?" The president continued, "The State Department tells me that for a given income of say $2,000 in Washington, the same person would have to be paid about $5,000 in American money in order to live in the same way in Caracas. I don't believe it."[23]

The explanation of the overvalued bolivar by a New Deal staffer would stand for decades: "Venezuela is one of most expensive places in which to live in the world (...) there is a housing shortage at the present time and many Americans are obliged to wait from two to three months to find a suitable home." Further on, it is explained that "automobiles, an essential in Caracas, cost from 90 to 110 percent above the list price in the United States" while "toilet articles, soaps, medicines, and pharmaceuticals cost from 75 to 200 times more than in the United States."[24]

This overvalued bolivar created a bubble that defined economic activity in Venezuela, and schooled generations of upper- and middle-class Venezuelans about business in their country. There was no easier money to be made than buying cars in the US, bringing them to Venezuela, and selling them for large markups. As early as the 1930s, it was easier to make money in the import business, in construction for the government, and the nascent consumer market. Later, enormous benefits would flow into the financial sector, as long as the bolivar remained strong.

Ultimately, the profitability of the Venezuelan private sector relied on the strength of the currency vis-à-vis the dollar, and the ability to cash in on that difference. But no one then thought much about currency values, as few do now. The idea that Venezuela and its resource strength were almost magical had engulfed everyone, even those openly critical of the government as far back as the 1930s.

Chief among them was the promising politician Rómulo Betancourt. In his writings and fiery speeches, he would repeat a single economic demand: renegotiate terms with the foreign oil companies so they would be forced to leave a larger share of the profits in Venezuela. Just as the business community was convinced their commercial activity was productive, Betancourt was certain that investing massive amounts of money on infrastructure and social projects would create a nation.

His argument made sense. Why should a small country of three million people that was the largest exporter of oil on the planet have to endure endemic malaria, illiteracy, and hunger?

Yet 100 years later, it is clear Betancourt confused the vital social projects the country needed with the creation of a real economy. For the Betancourt of the 1930s and 1940s the economy was, and should be, oil. For him, the problem was that the oil was in the wrong hands. He felt the wealth should be going to public works instead of Swiss bank accounts.

Both conservatives and socialists believed that if the new, powerful Venezuela was going to amount to anything, it needed to project its power through a mighty bolivar. This idea permeated government thinking for at least eighty years and reached its apex when President Chávez himself took off some zeros from the currency and officially renamed it the "bolivar fuerte," or strong bolivar.

Sowing Oil

The notion that resource-rich societies end up ruining existing economies was developed when academics started writing about Dutch disease. But tracing the precise ways in which windfalls from commodities cripple nations has always been a difficult task for economists and, later, for those focusing on political economy.[25]

The first theories were simple. If the selling of a single commodity flooded an economy with profits, all existing capital would flow to the one sector generating spectacular returns, like fire chasing an oxygen source. The rest of the economy would suffocate from lack of resources, and eventually die.

Yet, the Venezuelan story involves much more than a question of available capital and its destination. The early theorists of Dutch disease studied how real economies, including those with robust consumer markets, reacted to a commodity boom. These writers did not consider what might happen to a small, barely functioning country, which did not even have a modern state in place when the first oil gusher blew out. The existing capital in Venezuela was negligible, which means that other, less measurable, factors came into play.

Arturo Uslar Pietri was the first person to pick up on the cultural strands of Dutch disease well before American academics started modeling the phenomenon. He was a descendant of landowners and had seen first-hand the death of the cocoa and coffee industry upon oil's arrival. More importantly, he could see what oil was doing to the country as far back as the 1930s and 1940s. In a feat of uncanny prediction, he also foresaw the tragedy of the 2010s.

His brief analysis of the new economy was offered in a now-famous op-ed piece, "Sowing Oil," published in 1936. For him, conditions were such that the newfound riches "could make Venezuela into an unproductive and lazy country, a giant oil parasite, swimming in a temporary and corrupting abundance, and driven toward an inevitable and imminent catastrophe."[26]

The main issue, he feared, was that either oil would run out, or that something synthetic would replace it, as had happened to other commodities familiar to South

Americans, such as rubber or indigo. His thesis mirrors what the early theorists of Dutch disease would later acknowledge. What the academics ignored but Uslar could sense all around him were the broader, less tangible ways in which oil would permeate and dull Venezuelan society.

Uslar wrote his op-ed to counter the increasingly influential views of Rómulo Betancourt, who thought that oil was, and should be, everything. Alluding to Betancourt, he writes in "Sowing Oil" that having the state focus exclusively on the rent from oil was the "suicidal dream of naive men."[27] He believed the oil money should be used to develop a vigorous national industry, including modern agriculture.

The terms of this late 1930s debate were clear. Betancourt with his more leftist views wanted to redirect resources to address poverty. Uslar Pietri's conservative vision meant financing what would hopefully turn into a real economy by "taking the maximum possible rent from the mining sector to invest it entirely in aid, privileges, and stimulus funds for agriculture, husbandry, and the national industries."[28]

But the battles of these years would be left behind as the country's oil-financed growth continued decade after decade. When Betancourt became president for a second time after the overthrow of General Pérez Jiménez in 1958, his political objective was to get everyone behind him. He moderated his oil views as he fashioned the broad coalition, and the ideology of consensus, that would let him finally govern once in power.

In his second term, Betancourt's first order of business was to renegotiate the royalty payments oil companies made to the government for the oil they were extracting. The windfall permitted both the infrastructure for his vast welfare state and the attempt to create a state-financed private industrial base.

Betancourt's Mining and Hydrocarbon Minister, Juan Pablo Pérez Alfonso, was, after Uslar Pietri, the country's best-known proponent of "sowing oil" by directly investing in domestic industry. His position in government signaled that the early Uslar-Betancourt rift over how to build an economy had been solved by the late 1950s. Everyone was on the same page, and the private sector would receive every possible form of "aid, privileges, and stimulus funds."

Economic activity around the country increased and diversified. Those businesses that had started importing on a small scale to sell to expatriates and oil services companies with massive markups now had before them a wealthy state ready to help. And those who sold to the government could now count on huge state contracts for dams, roads, water treatment plants across the country, thousands of new schools, public housing, and all kinds of welfare projects. And because the consensus around the strong currency was as solid and widely shared as ever, there was no suggestion of creating an export economy.

The national consensus was that Venezuela was comparable to Mexico or Brazil; therefore, it should follow those countries' development paths. This would require a strong domestic industry to serve the needs of the national market. Government subsidies might have been able to create a sustainable industry to service a domestic market the size of Brazil, for example, with eighty-five million people by 1965. But the fantasy of a Venezuelan national economy was unrealistic because the country did not even have ten million inhabitants by then. No matter how well financed, national industries serving such a small market would never reach enough scale to be truly productive and sustainable by themselves.

And that was the optimistic view. Although it was not Uslar Pietri's intention, "sowing oil" through "aid, privileges, and stimulus funds" became shorthand for the slice of oil revenues demanded by the business elites to prop up any business, no matter how absurd its prospects. And that is how generating profits, for most companies, became a matter of figuring out how available privileges, subsidies, and intentional loopholes could make a venture viable. The creation of a sustainable and competitive export economy was simply not in the cards.

It is useful to read more recent academic research on Dutch disease to make sense of how this mindset took root across society and continued to hold the Venezuelan imagination until recently.

There are few controversies among economists who have studied what happens to societies hit by sudden discoveries of precious natural resources, or by sudden price spikes in existing crops or previously ignored commodities. It is almost universally true that "suddenly rich" countries end up experiencing lower GDP growth rates. They might get rich at one point in time, but they almost always end up poor, often even poorer than when they started. And the story of how this happens is almost always the same one.

The situation has been succinctly summarized by two leading economists: "oil exporters that suffer from an appreciated exchange rate, a narrow industrial base, and a skewed distribution of productive capacity in favor of non-tradable sectors are particularly vulnerable to a long 'winter' of low oil prices. Without a diversified export base, these countries' macroeconomic performance quickly worsens and their residents experience income losses."[29]

In these cases there is a significant, traceable shift of economic activity from production to consumption, and away from production for exports.[30] Academics who study this field seem to be describing what happened in Venezuela. They explain that most businesses respond to the discovery of natural resources with an extreme form of "rent-seeking behavior."[31, 32] The chief entrepreneurial motivation of the business class shifts from "building a great company" to earning a steady income from a commission, a deal, or a payout from an extractive scheme. Economic facts force even companies with strong foundations to shift their focus. When an enterprise fights for subsidies and easy loans, rather than for a new export market, the economy becomes a "feeding frenzy" in which different interests struggle over the new resources. Suddenly distinct business, regional, and political interests end up fighting over available monies.[33]

As the Venezuelan oil democracy reached the 1970s and 1980s, few trends accelerated faster than the business sector's rent-seeking behavior, resulting in a grand battle over the oil resources available for distribution.

Apotheosis of Oil

Americans and Europeans remember the 1970s as a time of economic uncertainty, gas lines, crime, urban decay, and terrorism both at home and abroad. Venezuelans have the opposite memory of the decade. As political turmoil in the Middle East forced an oil embargo against Western countries, followed by a dramatic escalation of oil prices, Venezuela's oil royalties reached record levels. The price of a barrel of crude had tripled in five years, with benchmark prices rising from US$3.56 a barrel in 1970 to US$11.16 in 1975 in nominal dollars.[34] The country's GDP doubled in those sixty months—an earth-shattering economic and social change, even in the context of the sustained transformation of the prior thirty years.[35]

Far away from the conflicts and wars rocking the world, Venezuelans felt a brand-new pride in their economic status. The national consensus pushed for the symbols to which a small, powerful country was entitled. They included a national airline with brand-new DC10s crisscrossing the world, the best in Brutalist architecture, expensive museums chock-full of modern masters, sprawling elevated highways splicing their capital city, and local outposts of French chefs and fashion designers. The arrival of the supersonic passenger jet Concorde at Maiquetía Airport seemed to be the final proof of progress.

Right about this time, Carlos Andrés Pérez was commanding the national stage. He had been the hard-charging Minister of Interior under Betancourt, right after the 1958 coup that had overthrown General Pérez Jiménez. Carlos Andrés, as he is popularly known, had ruthlessly fought right-wing conspiracies that got as far as planting a bomb that almost killed Betancourt and scarred him for life, as well as battling Cuban-financed guerrillas that were not defeated until 1969. But by 1972 the gray warrior of democracy shed his sharkskin suits and thin ties to don off-white safari outfits in the style of Yves Saint Laurent.

His new look, speeches, and energetic style articulated a language in tune with the times. And in 1973, Pérez declared his campaign for president with a memorable slogan, *Democracia con Energía.* The campaign promised to combine Betancourt's social and political project from the 1960s, in other words a wider distribution of oil revenues, but with an emphasis on turbocharging economic growth. The landslide in the 1973 election was definitive, and President Pérez set out to become a beacon of a new energetic and confident Third World.

All over the world, oil-producing countries were changing their relationships with the companies that extracted the raw materials from their land. The Saudi Kingdom's massive new revenues allowed them to buy shares in the Anglo-American oil conglomerate that had run production in that country since after World War II. Oil-producing countries were wresting back control of their mineral treasure. The era of royalties was coming to an end. Pérez saw the writing on the wall: he would buy outright every oil company operating in Venezuela, including every asset owned by Exxon and Shell.

From 1975 onward, the Venezuelan government would own not only the oil underground, but every machine, truck, refinery, and ship used to extract it, process it, and sell it to the world. The symbolic and actual economic meaning of the straight buyout, which the government called a "government takeover" or "nationalization," was enormous. For the first time, the professional middle classes and the elites had a chance at running a real industry from end to end. For the country, the takeover was about pride, sovereignty, and profits for all.

As the price of oil stayed up and projections for future profits continued to escalate, President Pérez and his government embarked on countless development projects, each more ambitious and expensive than the last. They were all meant to turn Venezuela into a First-World country. Because the government had purchased an entire oil industry, the president and his collaborators thought it would be just as simple to will, and finance, entire economic sectors into existence.

1970s Economics

This frenzy of activity was inspired by the most famous economists of the Latin American 20th century, Celso Furtado and Raúl Prebisch. While their insightful analysis of Latin America's economic development was transformational, a simplistic version of their ideas spread like wildfire.[36]

The crux of underdevelopment for Furtado was the challenge faced by countries producing raw materials for export in isolation from their broader national economies.[37] In Venezuela an advanced oil industry lived alongside subsistence farming in the countryside and a backward manufacturing base. No matter how much money oil brought in, there seemed to be no way to get the economy as a whole to make progress.[38] The simplistic solution to this conundrum was parroted by policymakers throughout the region: substitute imports with subsidized and protected local manufacturing.

Presumably, this would pull the entire population into a modern consumer economy that was productive.

In cash-rich Venezuela, this formula of top-down, *desarrollista* development on oil-cash steroids made sense to policymakers and business elites. As the plans went ahead in every direction, ranging from agro-industrial schemes to tame the flooded plains of Apure to the building of massive steel and aluminum-making capacity, the symptoms of Dutch disease appeared everywhere. None of the projects thought up in Caracas ministry offices could generate better goods than those found in the world market, much less sustainably compete with better prices. While Venezuelan state enterprises dreamed of ever-bigger steel production lines in the Guayana region, US steel industries had seen their production peak in 1973. In a few years, the industry would pivot to mini mills. Ministry planners, disconnected from the reality of international markets, pushed ahead to build the kind of facilities that were fast becoming outdated in western Pennsylvania and the Ohio Valley. There was little emphasis on the specific market conditions where these Venezuelan heavy-industry products would compete. The competitive advantages that might or might not exist for the nascent industries were not part of the top-down frenzy. The Módulos de Apure project to transform the flooded plains into fertile Pampas was equally, if not more, farfetched, as were hundreds of proposed and fully funded ventures that ended up producing minimal results.

While a lot has been written about how governments wasted oil revenues for decades, Dutch disease was very much a part of the private sector as well. Mid-sized and large companies that, in retrospect, had a real chance of global success, were never able to do anything about those prospects.

The shoe industry born in the Catia neighborhood of Caracas is a perfect example. The know-how of Sicilian and Neapolitan families that had emigrated from the old country to continue their shoe trade in Venezuela could never become globally competitive with a strong bolivar. Their companies were very prosperous for decades because the Ministries of Education and Defense would buy millions of shoes and boots. But the future was bleak without a consumer market big enough for the factories to reach substantial scale. The overvalued bolivar never let them export successfully, and cheap Chinese manufacturing eventually hit them hard. Later, they would be crushed by globally integrated and truly competitive retailers such as Zara.[39]

The degree to which the out of context *desarrollista* policies failed the country is made evident by comparing two key Venezuelan companies and their Mexican counterparts. As early as 1979, well before NAFTA, Mexico's Grupo Modelo managed to reinvent their weak and cheap working-class beer Corona into a "cool and light" alternative for American "Yuppie" consumers. The venture's success turned Modelo into one of Latin America's most valuable companies while Venezuela's brewery Polar, awash in 1970s overvalued bolivars, did not take export markets seriously. Decade after decade Polar's businesses expanded domestically, remaining tied to the price of oil and the swings of Venezuelan politics. Another Mexican company, Cemex, exploded out of humble beginnings to become the biggest cement company in the world. While its take-off did not happen until the 1980s, everything started with a financial consolidation, a series of acquisitions, and a listing in the local stock exchange in 1976.[40] Right around that time, Cementos de Venezuela was happy to feed the building boom driven by the strong bolivar, a prelude to its eventual bankruptcy.

Rather than getting ready to expand through exports, the simplistic theory of import substitution allowed the Venezuelan private sector to use overvalued bolivar revenues to obtain dollar-denominated loans. Foreign banks at the end of the 1970s and the beginning of the 1980s were ready to lend dollars against future bolivars. On top of every other challenge, the borrowing proved catastrophic.

An extraordinary study by the economist and future Minister Miguel Rodríguez reveals that the fast-ballooning Venezuelan external debt of that time, which went from US$2 billion in 1973 to US$32 billion in 1982, neatly correlates with a jump in private assets (bank accounts, real estate, stocks) held by Venezuelans outside the country: from US$3.7 billion in 1978 to US$22.1 billion in 1982.[41] In other words, the private wealth of Venezuelan citizens held in Miami and New York apartments, Swiss bank accounts, shares in the New York stock market, and other assets grew by almost US$20 billion between 1978 and 1982 (or US$62 billion in 2019 dollars).[42]

Nothing speaks to the role of the overvalued bolivar better than those US$22 billion sitting in the United States and Europe, mainly financed by the US$32 billion of debt the entire country now owed.[43] What happened next turned out to be extremely painful.

The Recadi 1980s

The dawn of the 1980s, and the first years of Ronald Reagan's presidency, marked the end of the 1970s oil bonanza, and the incentives to secure dollar-denominated loans. By mid-1981, the American prime interest rate reached its record high of 20.61%, and by year's end the price of oil had started a slide that would last, save a few hiccups, for twenty-four years—until 2004.[44] By the end of 1983, the price of oil had dropped 40% from its 1980 peak, while the prime interest rate remained stubbornly above 10%.[45]

Venezuela's foreign debt stood at US$32 billion by July of 1983, with about US$16 billion in obligations due within eighteen months.[46] The entire sum of oil income for that year was expected to be below US$14 billion.[47] The spectacular rise in interest rates was adding billions to the debt service payments. It was a fast-moving train wreck in the making. At the same time, thousands of private Venezuelan citizens, and companies, were changing every bolivar they had into dollars at the ridiculously low rate of 4.30 bolivars per dollar. The central bank was subsidizing hundreds of millions in currency exchanges when it did not even have enough to pay its own dollar-denominated debts.

It all came to a head on February 18, 1983. The government of then-president Luis Herrera massively devalued the bolivar in relation to the dollar and created exchange controls on what came to be known as Black Friday. The bill for the *desarrollista* and its closely related *consumerista* shopping sprees of the 1970s had come due.

In a similar situation, a government in a different country would have liberalized the exchange rate and established a floating bolivar. If people wanted more dollars for their bolivars, they would have to pay the right price. But the problem was much deeper than that—at least fifty years deeper. Twentieth-century Venezuela had been born on the promise of cheap dollars, courtesy of bottomless oil exports.

This was not a question of what people felt they were entitled to; it was about feeding and clothing and taking care of the health of every Venezuelan. Because almost everything was imported in full or in part, a radical spike in the dollar would bring about a countrywide breakdown. The solution in 1983 was far easier to find, and it came with a classic bureaucratic name: Recadi.[48]

The government, specifically the Recadi program, would sell businesses the few dollars it could find at a substantial discount to the free market price. In theory, companies were supposed to use the currency to buy everything that was needed in the country, and then sell their products at a fixed price in bolivars. The discount on the price of the dollar was supposed to give businesses their profit margin and guarantee a constant supply of goods for the population at artificially low fixed prices. While it did stop the free exchange of all available bolivars into cheap dollars and helped avoid the shock of a profound devaluation, Recadi ended up perpetuating the worse aspects of Venezuelan economic activity. The government was now actually paying businesses to import all kinds of goods.

Even when raw materials were imported to be finished in-country, factories had no incentive to become more productive. What had been implicit practice now became clear policy: the economic engine of profit for all businesses lay in securing a flow of subsidized dollars. Ultimately it was more profitable to bring in finished goods and sell them to a hungry market than to assemble products from imported parts and raw materials. The country's already small production capacity declined as entire companies were transformed by armies of expediters and paper pushers who could get cheap dollars, import whatever was in demand, and sell it locally. Exports were explicitly banned for anyone participating in the program.

As oil prospects kept worsening, the price of the bolivar in the parallel free market kept plummeting. By the time Jaime Lusinchi, the next president of the Recadi era, took the reins of power, the program had become a scheme.

Businesses began importing fewer goods than they had been allotted dollars for and went straight to the black market to sell their leftover currency at seventy or eighty bolivars to the dollar. One hundred thousand dollars diverted from real goods would yield as much as half a million dollars at the height of the program. An entire population and a business class had grown up believing in the magical country: wealth was found, it was never created. For many, the most significant opportunity of their lifetimes was too big to pass up.

Soon an entire industry was set up to falsify imports and create the paperwork needed to apply for more government dollars. The Recadi program multiplied existing fortunes, created a new crop of millionaires, and further distorted every Venezuelan's idea of wealth. In Caracas an entire neighborhood of luxury apartments was briefly nicknamed *"Colinas de Recadi,"* the only ironic memory left from that tragedy. Not long after, Recadi was already considered by some academics as "… Venezuela's (and possibly Latin America's) biggest single corruption case."[49]

While few paid attention, the logic of free, or almost free, dollars slowly degraded the government's ability to deliver the traditional services the majority of the population had counted on since the 1930s and especially since the 1960s: safety, infrastructure, health care, and education. The state's energy, and its money, was focused on the orgy of imports. It added up to a massive redistribution of income, favoring those close to the flow of Recadi dollars, and profoundly affecting those far from it.

By 1988 Venezuela's population had multiplied to 18.6 million compared with 7.5 million twenty years before.[50] Most of the growth was concentrated in the cities, where huge favelas had grown. Petare, probably by then the largest continuous informal settlement in the world, occupied several hills in the eastern part of Caracas. Newcomers would arrive daily to settle farther and farther away from the city's urban core. According to the government's own very imprecise figures, extreme poverty grew 12.5% from 1985 to 1990, and then 55% from 1990 and 1995.[51]

As the informal city grew, an epidemic of cocaine and crack cocaine exploded, along with a rise in petty crime, as well as organized gang activity. The police were still equipped and organized to confront the public safety challenges of the 1960s and 1970s. The entire country went from nine to twenty-one murders per 100,000 inhabitants between 1985 and 1993.[52] The government retreated on all fronts, except the awarding of cheap dollars.

El Presidente

This was the setting for the 1988 presidential campaign and the return of Carlos Andrés Pérez to the domestic political scene as president for a second time in 1989. He had left office in 1979, vowing to return to power. In the meantime, he had traveled around the world to learn where he had failed the first time around. He needed to imprint his name in the history books and was determined to make it happen during his second term. His first attempt had been memorable. His second would bring about the end of an era.

By the mid-1980s, young economists at US universities were blaming the wreckage in which much of Latin America found itself on the vast *desarrollista* top-down spending spree of the 1970s. This was not just a theoretical issue. Mexico, Argentina, and Brazil had defaulted on their foreign debt, and Wall Street bondholders lost billions of dollars after betting that, with enough capital, Latin American countries could reach full-fledged development. If the losses were not enough, Margaret Thatcher and Ronald Reagan had fanned a movement of believers in unleashing the creative and financial power of private enterprise. The way forward, reasoned the new consensus, was to empower civil society and private enterprise to do what central governments had failed to deliver.[53] Given the economic and moral disaster of having Recadi run all economic activity in Venezuela, it was simple for Carlos Andrés Pérez to connect the dots that validated the theory.

He surrounded himself with a new generation of Venezuelan economists educated at Yale and Harvard. They were as confident that they knew how to fix the economy as anyone had ever been. They told Pérez that markets had to be deregulated, that private capital was needed, the government had to be downsized, and that an economic miracle would follow. This would be led by a stronger civil society untainted by the corruption of political parties and government officials.

The overly optimistic premise was that once free of Recadi, the business community would roll up its sleeves and get to work creating real wealth with real work. Plenty of young journalists and professionals got on board without much hesitation. The fact that private citizens and companies had diverted most of Venezuela's foreign debt from the 1970s for their personal enrichment, or that Recadi had required the complicity of everyone participating in the program, was glossed over. But before anything happened, Carlos Andrés Pérez first had to get elected.

The most expensive and sophisticated political campaign in the history of Venezuela up to that point would have as its sole objective winning by as large a margin as possible. The former president's collaborators would not try to get a political mandate for the tough changes ahead. Instead, they focused on a single message: Carlos Andrés, the president who had brought unprecedented wealth, prestige, and flash to Venezuela in the 1970s, would do it again for his people in the 1990s.

A massive advertising campaign featuring *"El Presidente"* was rolled out. Pérez campaigned tirelessly from one end of the country to the other, hitting the same notes that had worked before: he would bring back unprecedented wealth, and he would be strong enough to spread it all around. If elected, he would deliver founding fathers Bolívar and Páez,

20th-century dictator Gómez, the 1970s version of himself, and King Midas, all wrapped into one.

The message and its skillful messenger would have captured the country's imagination at any time in history, but as voters experienced a worsening economy and a deterioration of public safety, the effect was overwhelming. Carlos Andrés Pérez won the presidential election with over 50% of the vote at over 80% voter turnout.[54]

Presidents, prime ministers, and dictators from all over the world converged on Caracas for the inauguration, so many that the ceremony could not be held at the Congress and was moved to a large concert hall. The spectacle, represented on the country's most prominent stage rather than at the Capitol building, turned into a huge bash with plenty of pomp and circumstance, Cristal champagne and, according to *Time* magazine, 650,000 hors d'oeuvres.[55] All over the country, Venezuelans tuned into the glamorous party Carlos Andrés was throwing for himself. It seemed money was about to fall from the sky directly into everyone's pockets. Nothing could ever bridge the gap between campaign promises, the party of the century, and what was about to happen.

The new government was facing a credit crisis of monumental proportions. The country's mounting foreign debt would crush it, unless the International Monetary Fund came in with financing to pay interest and principal on the billions that had been borrowed over the previous ten years, and everything that had been refinanced from before. In addition, there was not enough free cash flow from oil operations to be able to sustain imports at the Recadi rates. Something would have to give, and fast.

The new government's behind-the-scenes economic plans contained exactly what the international financial community wanted to hear. Moreover, the ministers themselves, the ones who would get on planes to New York and Washington DC to fend off the catastrophic chain of events, were perfectly in tune with their counterparts. A letter of intent to start an IMF program was signed by the new government.[56] Fresh capital would flow shortly. The second order of business, required by those providing the funds but in perfect alignment with the wishes of the new administration, was to eliminate the Recadi system and its rules, overnight.

It is hard to convey how radically this threatened to change the rules of the game for every part of Venezuelan society. For years distributors and retailers had imported most goods, and domestic producers would import semi-finished parts and raw materials. Even in the years before the government had gotten into the business of providing foreign currency to importers, the Ministry of Fomento (economic promotion) would pay direct subsidies to producers in hard cash to maintain low prices of certain goods. Strict rules had always made it difficult, highly taxed, or outright prohibited to import certain goods. It had been illegal to import cars for decades, though approved car manufacturers could import all parts for assembly within the country. The system made cars awfully expensive to produce, but the subsidized dollars given to Ford or Fiat to bring in the parts made them relatively affordable.

The same story was replicated across the economy. Local producers and distributors could sell cheap low-quality milk because everything involved, from the cows' feed to the refrigerated truck that brought the product to market, was heavily subsidized. This system had never asked a business to find ways to produce better milk at lower prices, and the business community had never mounted a serious challenge to this state of affairs. The only things that mattered were relationships with government officials who dispensed cheap dollars, special tariffs, subsidized loans, distribution privileges, and set producer, wholesale, and retail milk prices. Now that there was no more money for subsidies, the production of any product in Venezuela became unbearably expensive.

The new economic team recognized the difficulties, at least on paper, but felt that without dismantling the vast system of controls it would be impossible to create a civil society and a robust private sector. And that was critical to begin replacing the economic activity primed with oil cash with a real, sustainable economy. Yes, there would be pain, they agreed, but the result would be worthwhile.

Yet no amount of theory could gloss the radical gap most people perceived between the message sent by the government, and the reality they were witnessing. *El Presidente* had promised to take care of everyone, but the government set the entire economy loose.

Interest rates were set to float in a free market and went from 13% to 40% almost overnight. The dollar was left to float against the bolivar, which immediately suffered a 170% devaluation.[57] Non-tariff barriers on almost all imported goods were lifted. Rates for electricity, phone service, and public transportation remained fixed by the government but were substantially increased.[58] Ministers and newspapers were talking about the free market, deregulation, and the end of big government, but people could only see how their lives had suddenly been turned upside down.

The most symbolic price increase was that of gas at the pump. The one thing Venezuelans felt most entitled to was gas, sold at a predictably cheap, fixed price. Yet now even that was going up in the name of a better economy, a free society, and a strong civil society. By then it was very unclear who was taking care of whom.

Bloodbath

Things got ugly twenty-four days after the bash celebrating *El Presidente's* takeover, on February 27, 1989. Twenty miles from Caracas in the small working-class city of Guarenas, laborers and service workers were lining up to wait for the owner-operated buses that would take them to their jobs in the big city. That Monday morning, the trip would not happen.

The prior Friday, the government had approved a rate increase for the bus drivers, but the drivers felt it was not enough. Prices for tires, car parts, and everything else were escalating in real time. The specter of free markets was spreading through the country, and they saw no reason not to join in by raising their own prices. Ignoring the government directive, they decided to increase their fare by 200%.[59] For laborers and service workers standing in line, a ticket at twice the regular price, barely three months after the election and three weeks after the inaugural bash, was nothing less than a personal affront. Scuffles broke out throughout the small city as people vented their frustration. They burned busses, and within minutes a full-fledged riot had started. In another time and place, people would have dispersed, and little else would have happened. But within an hour at most, upheavals had started in Petare, the impoverished suburb at the western edge of Caracas. Looting followed almost immediately. Within a few hours, the entire city was in a state of chaos.

The police were utterly unprepared. Ten years of under-investment had decimated every public safety function. No single action was or could be organized by the authorities to contain what had become citywide looting. Most police officers, as seen in the available footage and photographs, limited themselves to providing some organization to the mayhem, standing at entrances as people entered super-markets and department stores to get their share. Privately held radio and television networks covered the looting in real time, with regular interruptions for commercials that, by definition, invited consumers to acquire all kinds of products. If the initial riot had spread in the organic manner of 19th-century European revolts, by noon, privately owned television networks were sending the message that it was open season on every store in the city.

Carlos Andrés Pérez, confused by this unprecedented turmoil, and leading a three-week-old government, did not or could not respond. The next day, as looting spread beyond all control, he put himself in the hands of the army. The Minister of Defense started flying brigades into the capital. A curfew was declared, and one of the most expensive planes on the planet, an F16 interceptor, was flown over the rioting areas of Caracas to show the looters who was in charge.

Nine thousand well-armed troops moved into the areas most affected by looting, mostly the city's western neighborhoods, to enforce the curfew.[60] While there is no evidence of an order being given to shoot on sight, the streets turned into killing fields, unlike anything that had been seen in Venezuela since the Federal War of 1859. Officially, 279 people were shot and killed by the army and the National Guard over two days.[61] NGOs point to as many as three thousand dead.[62] No government before, during, or after Chávez has dared take a serious, in-depth look into the events of 1989. As a result, there is no definitive account of what actually happened.

The original black and white photographs published by *El Nacional* show the desperation and raw violence that could not be reconciled with what many believed to be an exceptional oil democracy.[63] After the bloodbath, with streets deserted, the government declared a return to "normalcy."

The Great Turn, continued

Most of the political class, the middle classes, and the wealthy acted as if nothing had happened. They blamed the entire event on inept policing and went back to their Great (economic) Turn.

Convinced that good macroeconomic figures could solve everything, the new government and the media focused almost exclusively on the big numbers. The results probably came faster than expected. By renegotiating the terms of debt payments to foreign banks, the government had lowered yearly interest payments by a third, at least in the short term.[64] The sale of the phone company to US giant Verizon and the liberalization of the stock market led to a flood of foreign investors that poured billions into the country.[65] Then

Saddam Hussein invaded Kuwait in 1990, and the First Gulf War broke out in 1991. Oil prices went through the roof. And if all that money pouring into the Venezuelan economy and its foreign reserves were not enough, the government started running larger deficits.

Predictably, the economy took off like a rocket, expanding by 6.4% in 1990 and 9.7% in 1991.[66] But the remarkable fact about these figures is how much they had to do with oil prices. The bolivar, strengthened by the inflows of dollars into the country, slowly appreciated, and imports rose. Following the old pattern of oil-fueled consumption, little of consequence was being produced internally. It was cheaper, and now that tariffs had been eliminated, easier to bring everything from abroad. The Great Turn became the Great Re-Turn to the most basic patterns that had shaped the oil country from its beginnings in the 1920s.

The role of oil in the economy was such that despite the government's resolve to jump-start a robust private sector and create an export economy, there seemed to be no way out. The government was a more significant economic force than ever, not smaller as had been planned. The strong currency led to the growth of consumer imports, rather than the creation of productive export-oriented enterprises. A new, deregulated financial sector looked much more like a casino than a tool to finance real growth.

But not everything was the same. While the basics of the oil economy remained in place, Carlos Andrés' reforms amounted to a significant redistribution of power and resources. The central government's many prerogatives had been reduced. The unraveling of the system that had been in place since the 1930s and the 1960s came fast. Ministries no longer controlled who had access to dollars and who did not. They lost the right to decide what retail prices should be or to assign subsidies, control tariffs, or decide other import controls. The free market would now make those decisions.

By getting out of the banking industry, and by liberalizing all rules regarding loans, the government ministries no longer controlled who could get financing or on what terms. With the sale of the phone company and hundreds of other enterprises, the ability to give jobs and dispense preferential treatment to governing party faithful vanished overnight. Over decades, something as mundane as awarding a fixed phone line had been among the basic tools used by governments to manage their hold on power. In addition, the government accelerated a program of decentralization that sought to create a more federal state. Heads of local and state governments, which up until then had been directly appointed by the president, would be democratically elected by voters for the first time. These new local and state governments would be able to raise their own revenues. By any measure, the true turn was a massive devolution of power from the presidency to external factors out of the central government's control. This was unprecedented in the history of the country, and ultimately unraveled Carlos Andrés Pérez's presidency.

The Financial Casino

The financial deregulation of 1989 became a huge media event. The deregulation was partly a result of the dismantling of Recadi's subsidized dollar scheme. However, it also involved a broader liberalization of banking and financial controls. All

Venezuelans were familiar with inflation and devaluation. It was another thing to see the Caracas Stock Exchange as a center of global financial action. Through some mysterious alchemy, millions of dollars were being traded there every day. Out of nowhere, yet increasingly visible in the media, young men in Italian suits, slicked-back hair, and brick-sized phones that worked like walkie-talkies, acquired a new kind of power. They were brash, flashy, and their brand-new BMWs traversed through the city as the moving banners of a new era.

Banks started to pay exorbitant interest rates to anyone who would deposit their money with them. The old rules that had strictly limited the ability of private entrepreneurs to start banks, merge insurance companies, or use brokerage firms to buy government bonds, were thrown out the window. Then, the country's first bank, "safely" in the hands of the oldest families, became the subject of a very hostile and very public takeover by entrepreneur Orlando Castro.

Unlike Argentina's or Colombia's experience with futures commodities markets throughout the 19th century, or Brazil's long history of bond-financed railroads, Venezuela's new financiers had no experience to draw on. Instead, they saw this new financial gold rush through the lens of mining, and oil. The main ideas and events informing journalists, politicians, even the young stock traders themselves, were the oil gushers of the 1920s and the dreams of gold and diamonds that had brought so many explorers and adventurers to the country over the years. Old Spanish ideas about wealth, and how it was extracted rather than created, were the only historical reference with which to interpret the strange financial revolution taking shape.

And it was destabilizing because the steady government hand that had guided economic activity since colonial times seemed to have disappeared. Instead, government ministers kept talking about "deregulation," "disintermediation," "free floating currency," and countless other codewords belonging to a new, foreign language that celebrated something no one understood. The only thing that was clear, apart from a rate of inflation over 30%, was that a few people were getting very rich, very visibly rich.[67]

Inequality

All along, a parallel reality was experienced in the ever-expanding informal settlements of the big cities. As inefficient and unsustainable as it had been, the old Recadi system had kept extreme poverty in check. Some resources had reached those at the margins, partly because the welfare state built in the 1960s and early 1970s was still agile enough to deliver some services, and because the political party organizations that reached deep into the poorest areas still functioned as vessels of patronage.

Extreme poverty had affected 7.64% of the population in 1985 while critical poverty affected an additional 20.74% in that year. By 1989, the first year of massive deregulation, the numbers jumped to 14.09% for extreme poverty and 27.25% for critical poverty, or 40% of the entire population suffering under terrible circumstances.[68] The expectation had been that government reforms would change the situation. Yet, by 1991 extreme poverty was still at 11.18%, and critical poverty at 23.46%, so that almost 35% continued to live under terrible conditions.[69]

In the early 1990s it was common for government officials to cite data on food consumption and the rise of the overall consumer market as evidence their program was succeeding. Poultry consumption rose by 41% in 1991 over the prior year, rice by 30%, and sugar by 20%.[70] Apparel consumption grew by 28% and the overall markets for consumer goods and all food products reached ten-year highs.[71] However, extreme and critical poverty had only been reduced from around 40% in 1989 to around 35% in 1991, which means the increase in consumption was not shared by all.[72] That explains much about the effects of an economic policy that generated a great deal of growth, did not substantially alleviate poverty, and accelerated a more visible inequality.

For more than a third of the country the collapse of government services, political parties, state industries, and government jobs proved devastating. On the heels of the Caracazo bloodbath, the massive changes undermined most of the president's and his ministers' political capital.

The Elites

The unraveling of Carlos Andrés Pérez's second presidency came from a long-established dynamic. Oil revenues and GDP growth were at their peak, but the distribution of resources among elites, regions, ethnicities, and industries had broken down. The different groups who had counted on their slice of oil revenues for so long were rocked by deregulation and decentralization. They wanted to stop the process in its tracks at any cost and were stubbornly united in their resolve to topple the president.

The anti-Carlos Andrés Pérez coalition replicated many of the historical battles that had been fought in Venezuela over centuries. Starting in the mid-1600s, the descendants of the original Spanish Conquistadors who had settled in Caracas had been determined to make their city the center of power over and above the original seat of government, Coro, or the rich cities of El Tocuyo in the west, and Cumaná in the east. No one was a stronger advocate of this idea than Bolívar himself, who as a bona-fide member of the Caracas slaveholding Creole elite, wrote and fought tirelessly to make his city supreme.

After independence, the few original Creoles left in the city, along with newcomers from all over Venezuela and abroad, would adopt the manners and outlook of the original Caracas elites. Together, they would slowly and surely make the original dream a reality. Throughout the 19th and 20th centuries, British, German, and Corsican families, along with a few of the original Creoles, fought for a socially conservative, hierarchical society anchored in Caracas and ruled by a strong central government. Their sense of entitlement over the land developed into a nationalism that in turn legitimized high tariffs and all manner of prerogatives and protections for their national businesses. By 1989 they controlled companies in the financial, industrial, retail, export-import, and service sectors. President Pérez's reforms threatened them with extinction. They had thrived for over a century on fixed prices, government loans, special licenses, subsidies, import duties that protected their businesses, and myriad other ways in which strong governments can help. The old mercantilist Spanish colonial ways, or at least its outlook, still mattered at the Caracas Country Club.

The traditional business community had a ready ally in the Catholic Church. The clergy was outraged by the socially liberal government policies driven by the most Jewish cabinet in the country's history. Union leaders could also see the end of a mediated, highly regulated labor environment in which their voice, vote, and veto had been a pillar of the prior power arrangement. The Left, which included parties still supporting the Soviet Union and those aligned with socialist Euro-communism, were incensed by the Reagan-Thatcher approach to free markets and deregulation. The establishment political parties, including the president's own Acción Democrática, were witnessing their entire system of patronage being dismantled before their eyes. The Chamber of Commerce represented the protectionist interests of the legacy mid-sized businesses adamantly opposed to the entry of foreign companies into the domestic market. If that was not a broad enough coalition, nationalist army officers outraged over the government's efforts at forging close political and trade ties with Colombia were ready to defend their sense of the country's honor. The army's middle ranks could not forget that President Pérez had made them kill at least hundreds, and possibly thousands, of innocent civilians to put down the rioting and looting created by his own policies.

The established political, business, and military elites felt the floor cracking under them. Carlos Andrés and his government had created an enormous power vacuum, and little in the way of a political foundation that would prop them up.

In the popular imagination, the president and the state, who were responsible for the distribution of the country's wealth, had given up their age-old responsibility. The world of every person, every social class, every region, that had expected to receive what they believed to be their fair share, was shattered. Worse still, Carlos Andrés Pérez had asked for their vote by telling them he would mediate on their behalf and between them. Instead, he worked every day to create a big hole where there had been countless ties, connections, certainties, and flows of money.

As with every political vacuum throughout history, all kinds of theories began to circulate. It was now conventional wisdom that the "free market" rhetoric was a lie invented to cover a grand theft being perpetrated by the president and his cronies. Many Venezuelans believed Pérez wanted to scale down the state's regulatory power and blur the border with Colombia to gain fabulous wealth for himself and Cecilia Matos, his former secretary and future wife.

Throughout the country's history, any disturbance in the balance of expectations and rewards between the government and everyone else had always led to violence. This ranged from the very bloody Wars of Independence, to the desperately violent Federal War of the mid-19th century.

On the night of February 4, 1992, Hugo Chávez was simply following a long-standing practice, one he knew intimately. He gained the country's attention, and its admiration, because his actions and his words filled a vacuum. When he put his life on the line and then, having lost it all, said that he would take full responsibility, it was an implicit promise that he would restore every piece to its rightful place.

He might as well have said, "I will wield all power, I will be the benevolent mediator, and I will give everyone their due. Do not worry about the price of oil. This has always been a rich country. All we need to do is stop a few from stealing from the rest of us."

The forces that wanted to stop the government's reforms bolted into action. The failed coup, Chávez's words, and then a second coup attempt in November 1992, created the perfect storm to get rid of Carlos Andrés and his government. The political, business, and labor worlds were united in their resolve. It did not take long for such a coalition to find the right institutional mechanism to force matters. A trial was started against President Pérez on charges of illegal use of funds. The Supreme Court sent him into house arrest, and the Senate stripped him of power in August 1993.

In the following election, on December 5, 1993, the conservative engineer of the opposition to Carlos Andrés Pérez, former president Rafael Caldera, won a solid victory on the back of a wide coalition of leftist and conservative forces united in their hatred of free-market and socially liberal reforms.

The new president, a strict Catholic, led a nostalgic return to the old days: he nationalized banks, re-regulated the financial sector, pardoned and freed Chávez from jail, and sought to stop, or at least slow down, the devolution of power to state and local governments. But he could not arrest the growth of informal settlements and the country's general poverty. No one could stop the decline of the welfare state's ability to address inequality, and the growing social divide in Venezuelan society.

A fundamental change in the country's demographics that had been in the works for decades was about to transform the political landscape starting in 1998. It would not be the first time in the nation's history that a demographic transformation had led to conflict and utter chaos.

The population shift from the 1770s to the 1810s led directly to the Wars of Independence. Understanding this phenomenon is critical to decoding the turn of the 21st century and the Chávez era.

III
Ethnic and Racial Wars, 1498-1821

«Okonkwo wondered what was amiss, for he knew certainly that something was amiss. He had discerned a clear overtone of tragedy in the crier's voice, and even now he could still hear it as it grew dimmer and dimmer in the distance.»
Chinua Achebe, *Things Fall Apart*

On the eve of July 6, 1814, Simón Bolívar, "The Liberator", was feeling the pain of utter and humiliating defeat. In a few hours he would escape from Caracas, riding at the head of 20,000 refugees, among them the wealthiest people in the city and most of its light-skinned population.[1] A Spanish colonial functionary describes in his memoirs people fleeing on a road called Sabana Grande "in fright, on foot, each taking what they could …"[2] They were escaping an invading Royal Spanish army that had spread panic and destruction on its path toward the capital. Thousands of Caraqueños would die in the long, disastrous retreat through mountains, tropical forests, and deserted beaches. Imagined by Tito Salas in his canvas *Emigración a Oriente*, the refugees and their leader seemed to be on a forced march to hell.[3] The 1913 painting shows the extent to which the drama of Creole ladies and gentlemen turned into hopeless refugees remained in the collective imagination for decades. At least until the oil boom erased the memories.

The month of July in 1814 had dashed all hopes in the republican efforts against royalist forces. Independence from Spain had been declared in 1811 but the first republic had collapsed by 1812. Bolivar's invasion of Venezuelan territories had routed royalist in 1813, but a year later he was again on the run.

Ironically, the two royal armies at the gates of Caracas in 1814, so menacing and overwhelming that The Liberator could not put up a final fight against them, were not made up of Spanish soldiers. They were fighting in the name of Ferdinand VII, but very few of the fighters or officers were Spanish-born.

As Bolívar and his relatives, friends, and practically every native-born light-skinned Caraqueño marched east, many local Pardos, as the mixed-race caste was called, rejoiced, and started to loot.[4] Enslaved Africans and their descendants abandoned plantations to join the King's army or flee to free African communities in the mountains and faraway plains. Just fifteen miles away in the strategic Port of La Guaira, a full-fledged slave rebellion was underway.[5] The republican forces were made up of those who wanted to break from the Crown, but that did not seem to include the mixed-race and those of African descent making up the majority.

In Caracas, the royalist archbishop Narciso Coll y Prat awaited the Crown troops he hoped would restore a semblance of order. So did the few other remaining representatives of the Spanish King, now that native-born light-skinned Creoles, in power over the preceding months in defiance of the Crown, had left the city.

Three of the leading Royalist men, including Fernando Ascanio, Count of Granja, went to the outskirts of Caracas in El Valle to confer with the invading forces. They were presumably confident their presence would convey enough authority before the King's troops.[6]

The Royalist commander was Manuel Machado, a mixed-race former foreman at the Count's plantation of Las Mercedes; the Caracas royalists had naturally assumed he would be the perfect point of contact.[7]

Yet why would a Count take the trouble of riding several miles to confer with his mixed-race former foreman? More surprising still is what happened next.

Approaching the royal troops, the Count of Granja recognized Machado and rode toward him. After all, he had come to talk to the man he had bossed all his life. No one knows what they talked about, but legend has it that Machado did not utter a single word. Instead, he took out his sword and cut his former master's head off. What is beyond doubt is that the King's commander killed the helpless Count.[8]

The few seconds during which the Count of Granja lost his head encapsule what happened in Venezuela in the year of 1814. The battles that ended the Second Republic were not a war between the King of Spain and the noble liberators of a "young and exciting new nation" in the Americas. They were not even about the Spanish-born against the native-born, or Crown and religious officials against those who wanted an independent republican government.

Instead, the Wars of Independence in the Venezuelan territories had morphed into an openly declared conflict between slave-owning landowners and an army made up of poor mixed-race soldiers, cowboys, recently emancipated slaves, Africans who had been free for years, and many riders of indigenous descent from the region of Alto Apure. The vicious battles of 1814 are a crucial episode within the Wars of Independence. Yet, their importance has been underplayed in the popular histories of Venezuela, and most of Bolívar's biographies. If not for the almost forgotten classic book by Juan Uslar, *La Rebelión Popular de 1814*, we would know little about a conflict that resonates throughout history and down to our days.

The rebellion's origins went back centuries.

Mantuano Power

The story of independence—at least from the point of view of native-born descendants of Spanish colonists— starts in the 1520s. The territories of Venezuela were of little interest to the Habsburg kings of Spain. The lack of available resources when compared to the colonies along the North–South Pacific axis between Mexico and Peru, or the soon to be thriving plantation economies of the Caribbean, made the place a forgotten corner in a vast empire. A traditional dynasty more comfortable with feudal, decentralized arrangements, the Habsburgs were content to receive their taxes as long as their subjects recognized their authority, followed the strictures of the Roman Catholic Church, and obeyed their rules of trade. The strong tradition of local sovereignty and self-governance in Castile dating back to the 1300s carried over, at least in part, to the Venezuelan territories.[9]

Throughout Spanish America, the issue of political power between native-born Creoles and Spanish-born Crown administrators was at the heart of 17th-century politics.[10] In Mexico, the struggle between the two factions was contentious. In Venezuela, on the other hand, the descendants of the original Conquistadors enjoyed even more autonomy in matters of local government.[11] The territories of Venezuela were poor and had little strategic importance to the Crown, leaving the far way colony to its own devices.

Yet, in time, the slave-owning Creole families gained wealth, although not nearly to the extent that Creoles in Santo Domingo or Cuba would soon amass. By the 1600s there were three centers of power in the Venezuelan territories: to the west, around the agricultural powerhouse of

El Tocuyo and the coastal city of Coro; to the east, around
Cumaná and Carúpano; and in the fertile central valleys
around Caracas. While the latter grew progressively wealthier
due to its more fertile lands and proximity to two major ports,
the political and cultural ties between the east, the center, and
the west were weak.[12]

This ended as the 1700s began. Europe discovered the
pleasures of hot chocolate, and a cocoa bubble got underway.
The crop grew well in the coastal tropical forests, and Venezuela's second boom market (after pearls) exploded.

The economic surge came alongside a political earthquake
in Spain. As the final Utrecht treaty put an end to the War of
Spanish Succession in 1715, the French-born and educated
Philip V was ratified as king of Spain. The new Bourbon
monarchy replaced the Habsburgs' loose administration of
the colonies with a centralizing vision of the state. Every
jurisdiction in the Americas and the Pacific would answer
to a modern bureaucracy styled on French absolutism. The
planets had aligned themselves against the Creoles' political
privileges. In addition, the cocoa boom and the suitability
of the coastal range for its production had finally made the
colony attractive to Madrid.

Soon the French-inspired Bourbon dynasty started
paying attention to the territories and set about reorga-
nizing its governance. The cabildos, from where Creoles
had ruled aspects of daily life for two centuries, took a back
seat to a series of royal institutions that were reinforced or
newly created. The Crown's tax authority and its legal arm,
the Audiencia, became increasingly involved in every aspect
of commerce and daily life. By the late 1700s, a series of

measures were put in place to fully centralize military and political power in the colony, with a Captaincy General created in Caracas in 1777. What had been three distinct regions over modern-day Venezuela were suddenly a single political entity ruled by a de facto capital. Much to the chagrin of Creoles in Cumaná and El Tocuyo, the eastern and western cities that were older than Caracas, their direct political line to Madrid was now dead.

Most humiliating of all was the Crown's 1728 award of an exclusive trading monopoly for all exports and imports to the Caracas Guipuzcoana Company, a Basque trading concern.[13] Creole landowners could no longer sell their cocoa directly to Cadiz or buy anything from abroad. Landowners revolted in 1749 to protect their right to sell cocoa to Mexico, but the Crown reacted by sending troops and the company's monopoly was reconfirmed by 1752.[14]

Everything produced from as far as away as Carúpano, Maracaibo, or San Cristobal in the east, west, and southwest, would now be handled by the Basque company from Caracas, the new power center.

In the territories, the effects were evident. Following a duality characterizing the Spanish colonial enterprise, the Guipuzcoana's monopoly's extractive nature did not prevent its bringing stability and prosperity to the cocoa economy. Yet the wealthier the Creoles became, the more resentment they felt at not governing their cities and regions as they had, or at least they thought they had, for centuries. For the Caracas Creoles, who supported making their town the capital of the entire country, the sense of entitlement and ownership was even more profound.

Things came to a head in 1808, more than thirty years after the United States had declared its independence from the British Crown, and right in the middle of Napoleon's systematic toppling of old European monarchies. A new wave of nationalism was sweeping the world, and in Caracas the local Creoles were paying as close attention as ever to every new fashionable idea.

While Spain had been an uneasy ally of Napoleon, the Corsican decided to lure the Spanish King Ferdinand VII and his father into a trap on French soil. Once kidnapped, the king abdicated, paving the way for a formal invasion of Spain by French troops. The war of Spanish Independence broke out on May 2nd and 3rd, 1808, in the streets of Madrid. The violence, so vividly painted by Goya, quickly spread throughout the Iberian Peninsula.

For the Creoles of Caracas, this was the opportunity of a century, literally. If the now-independent former British colonies in the north were prospering, why couldn't they do the same at the head of their very own country?

Quickly enough, La Junta de Caracas, an ad hoc committee created by the Cabildo council that had run the city before the Bourbon reorganization, declared independence. The First Republic of Venezuela was born in April 1810. But a majority of different castes, classes, and races were against the move. Some because they were pro-Spanish Royalists, but most because they felt no allegiance to the Caracas elites. The city of Coro, the territory's first seat of power, and the provinces of Guayana and Maracaibo were officially against the Venezuelan Republic from the outset. The war started then.

Domingo Monteverde, a Spanish army officer, arrived from Puerto Rico with 230 soldiers. According to a 19th-century chronicler, the Spanish had also brought "a priest named Torellas, a surgeon, ten thousand bullets, a cannon, and ten quintals of biscuit."[15] Starting with such meager resources and defying all expectations, Monteverde cobbled together an army of thousands to fight a Republic representing the dreams of Caracas Creoles.

If the political and financial leadership behind independence was firmly in Creole hands, the army was another matter. Francisco de Miranda was named commander of the independence forces. He had been born in Venezuela but had spent most of his adult life in military service abroad, first with the Spanish army in Spain and then in the King's service as far away as Florida and New Orleans. His most famous exploits were with the French republican armies during the revolutionary years. His feats in the early battles against Prussian armies earned him a place in the Arc de Triomphe in Paris, where his name is still etched along with those of another 660 heroes of the revolution.[16]

Opposition to or support of the French revolution marked a dividing line between the slave-owning Creoles who sought to preserve the colonial social order within an independent republic, and those who saw the occasion as a moment of social revolution. Though Miranda was the most experienced military man in sleepy Caracas, many among the Creole elites were uncomfortable with his experience in France, and his alliance with radical local factions.[17] His command would be fiercely opposed even as the war intensified.[18]

The extent of the fraught politics within the army is made clear by the appointment of young and inexperienced Simón Bolívar to command the strategic garrison of Puerto Cabello. Having no military experience, the heir to the biggest Creole slaveholding fortune lost the garrison to Crown forces soon after taking its command.

Beyond the Puerto Cabello debacle, the republican armies were fragmented within and facing a growing enemy. Despite the lofty dreams of independence, it was soon clear the First Republic was not to be.[19]

Besieged by a growing Crown army in the west, a significant slave rebellion to the east, and imminent and real uprisings by those enslaved up and down the coast, Miranda surrendered his troops to Monteverde, and fled.[20] Bolívar captured the fleeing Miranda, delivered him to Monteverde, and secured himself a passport out of the country.

The betrayal of the low-born Miranda by the high Creole Bolívar is that brief war's most chronicled and least interesting event. What should matter is that Venezuela's First Republic was lost in 1812 while Spain itself was in the grip of a savage civil war, and two years before the Spanish King returned to the throne.

The question traditional histories and films ignore is that of how Monteverde, a Spanish officer landing in a faraway colony with 230 soldiers and with his King imprisoned, managed to reclaim power. Spain was at war against French invaders on Iberian soil, and nothing could be further from anyone's mind than events in far-off Venezuela. Yet Monteverde ended up sending Miranda to prison and Bolívar into exile. Plenty of ready explanations have been advanced throughout the years. Some blame the deadly earthquake of 1812, others Miranda's ineptitude, or Bolívar's naiveté, or the 'immaturity' of the independence forces. The implicit theme in these narratives is that either an external factor, or a personal failing on the part of military leaders, led to the debacle. What few want to mention is the deep social conflict that had been running through the colony for centuries.

The fracture between Creoles from Caracas and those who had steadily lost their trading and political privileges in towns and regions throughout the territories was real. The deep conflict between Creoles and mixed-race Pardos throughout the 1700s has been thoroughly documented. The untenable situation in which those enslaved found themselves and the existence of dozens of rebellious communities made up of those who had escaped the plantations made for a precarious social order. Tens of thousands of potential soldiers of indigenous descent living at the margins of the colonial order could not give the Crown, and later the First Republic, any hope of an easy peace. But for unsung historian Federico Brito Figueroa and his work exploring an alternative version of events, we would understand little of the long history that preceded and explains the events of 1810.[21]

For the historian, the first 150 years after the Spanish arrived in 1498 involved a slow-burning, and sometimes explosive, series of violent conflicts between the conquerors and the native populations inhabiting the territories. These battles overlapped, and were followed by, almost two centuries of intermittent slave revolts and permanent warfare against thousands of escaped slaves in Cimarron communities.

Between 1510 and 1810, argues Brito Figueroa, "there was not a single region not affected by some rebellion or armed insurgency by slaves, free Blacks, free Indians or those under the encomienda system, peons, or 'free population of color.'" In addition, "there had been extensive areas of the Venezuelan territory which were at all times under the control of former slaves" who had escaped plantations.[22] As if that was not enough, the three centuries of colonial rule were marked by several Quixotic rebellions against the Crown by Spanish soldiers, including that of the infamous Lope de Aguirre.

As the Caracas Creoles were getting ready to launch their flaming republic in 1810, they seemed oblivious to this violent history and its consequences. There was no blank canvas for republican and monarchical armies to battle over different ideals of government because, more than anything, the Venezuelan territories were a social time bomb. Yet, the Creole's focus, and sole grievance until 1814, was their conflict with the Spanish Crown, fueled by a centuries-old sense of entitlement over the territories of Venezuela.

Indigenous Wars

When the Spanish explorers reached what is now Venezuela in 1498, they did not find a single, centralized indigenous nation they could control by killing their leaders. Or a large settlement like Tenochtitlan—current-day Mexico City—which they could occupy. Instead, several nations and native tribes speaking very different languages, controlled different parts of a varied geography. Exploiting the divisions, conquering, enslaving, and imposing feudal relationships of servitude on each of these groups, or at least controlling the territories they once held, would take at least 100 years of wars, skirmishes, savage killings, and finally, waves of missionary Capuchin and Franciscan friars.

In 1520 the settlement of Cumaná, one of the first Spanish cities and a future key colonial outpost, was destroyed by an Indian raid. The settlement was built again in 1521 and renamed Nuevo Toledo, only to be sacked and destroyed by the native inhabitants. It was built yet again under the name Nueva Cordoba and destroyed yet again.[23] Diego Fernandez de Cordoba, in 1569, could not find any trace of its inhabitants, any buildings, or even a street grid (*"ni traza de pueblo"*).[24] He established yet another settlement, which eventually disappeared as well.

The story repeats itself in every Spanish settlement in the east, where most of the early colonization took place. The chronicles tell of a permanent state of violence in which Spanish colonists were routinely hunted down and killed on the road between the main coastal towns of Píritu, Barcelona, and Cumaná, and even within sight of the towns. As late as 1693, indigenous raids allied with, or supported by the French, destroyed many towns that never came back to life. Among them were settlements founded in Pozuelos y Trinidad, Santa María de Manapire, and Nueva Tarragona, first settled in Uchire and later in Batey.[25]

The earliest Spanish towns in the western part of the country, Coro and El Tocuyo, close to where several indigenous nations had practiced agriculture, enjoyed more stability. Yet all attempts by early German and Spanish settlers to explore beyond the confines of the towns involved them in continuous warfare throughout the 1500s.

The Welser Banking family was granted a license by Charles V in 1528 to settle and conquer the western part of Venezuela. Their representatives arrived in Coro, after which they renamed the entire eastern region Klein-Venedig. Obsessively looking for El Dorado, and sometimes for the Pacific Ocean, the colony's three successive leaders, Ambrosius Ehinger, Georg von Speyer, and Phillip von Hutton, died at the hands of native warriors, fevers, or Spanish soldiers exasperated by never-ending battles.[26] The general sense of desperation felt by Europeans because of their lack of territorial control is recorded again and again in the early histories of Venezuela.

The bloodiest part of the conquest took place in the more fertile central valleys and the territory around Caracas. The original inhabitants, divided into different nations that eventually unified themselves against the Spanish, fought a tenacious twenty-year war. The allure of conquest is explained by the idyllic, fertile, and temperate valley of Caracas, protected from the Caribbean by the Avila mountains.

Despite the valley's potential wealth, the Spanish had stayed away for almost sixty years after their initial arrival in the territories. This ended in 1560 when Francisco Fajardo, son of a Spanish lieutenant and an Indian woman, founded the future town of Caraballeda on the coast north of today's Caracas. As happened so many times before, the original settlement was raided and abandoned by 1562. But as the Crown's fortunes and those of the Creoles from El Tocuyo improved, a substantial expedition was mounted. Diego de Losada founded Caracas proper in 1567 after defeating the Mariche nation, but that was just the beginning of a long and bloody war in the central valleys.[27]

In the conflict's most famous encounter, the Battle of Maracapana in 1568, the leader of the Teques was able to forge a coalition of many nations occupying the central region.[28] While there is scant historical evidence, Chief Guaicaipuro is thought to have gathered between 10,000 and 20,000 warriors for the battle.[29] The Spaniards marshaled as many warriors as possible from competing nations, probably from the western part of the country. (As a point of comparison, the patriot army in the Battle of Carabobo, the most important in the country's official military history, amounted to between 6,500 and 8,000 soldiers, including all the British troops. The Royalist Spanish troops did not exceed 5,000 men.)[30]

Guaicaipuro lost the battle and was later betrayed and killed, but the terrain played to the Amerindians' advantage as the conflict continued for years. Different nations harassed the Spanish without any final resolution until an epidemic wiped out as many as two-thirds of the native population by 1580.[31]

Many warriors headed south toward The Plains to flee Spanish control. They continued fighting colonial armies, and later Creole armies, for successive generations into the 19th century. Others were captured and placed into slavery or servitude to their new Spanish masters. Those who had fought alongside the Crown assimilated to the colonial system as free artisans. By 1800 the indigenous population is thought to have comprised 76,000 people in various forms of servitude: 26,000 assimilated to the colony and "free," and 60,000 "not conquered or evangelized," accounting for a total of 18.4% of the territories' population.[32]

Slave Rebellions

One of the first recorded slave rebellions, led by Negro Miguelote, dates as far back as 1553.[33] It took place in the Buria gold mines near El Tocuyo, in the western foothills. After breaking free and killing their captors, those enslaved escaped to the nearby mountains to establish a free community of Cimarrons. Either because the Spanish colonial authorities were weak, the local Creoles too poor to band together and enforce slavery, or the territories were too vast and menacing for effective military action, or likely a combination of the three, Negro Miguelote became King Miguelote. Not much more has been historically established about these events, but the Cimarron community became a Venezuelan legend and a reference for similar *"rochelas"* and *"cumbes"* down the centuries.[34] King Miguelote was eventually killed in an assault on the city of Barquisimeto. His legend inspired hope in his fellow slaves, terror among slaveholders, and was a model of survival and organization down the years.[35]

As the slave trade expanded with the cacao boom in the early 18th century, so did the pace and intensity of rebellion. By 1730 Andrés López del Rosario, better known as Zambo Andresote and originally a slave in the city of Valencia, led armed bands that seemed to control large swaths of the Yaracuy Valley as far as the sea town of Tucacas.[36] The fighting went on for decades; Andresote gained the support of Dutch smugglers intent on protecting a beachhead for their contraband trade.[37] The connections between free Blacks in towns like Morón and Alpargatón and Andresote's armed bands allowed him to defeat at least one large Spanish army, and to routinely block roads from Puerto Cabello to San Felipe.[38]

By 1749 the central government had become aware that a large-scale rebellion was planned in the central valleys. Official documents reported that 40,000 slaves, allied with indigenous peoples, came close to rebelling simultaneously in the territories' richest region (granted, official documents likely exaggerated these numbers).[39] After a gruesome session of torture and interrogation, it was "established" that the revolt was set for the Night of San Juan, and the plan was to kill every white in sight.[40] The historical record is full of episodes like these.[41]

The permanent state of war documented throughout the 18th century has been underestimated, if not erased, by the pastoral, nostalgic view of colonial times in fashion during the 20th century. The management and perpetuation of the slavery system required bloody and brutal violence, even when those enslaved were compliant and the countryside was peaceful. The day-to-day of slavery in Venezuela has been partially documented: confinement in caged environments, complete lack of private space, heavy and painful bodily restraint for minor violations, and whippings and isolation cages for any challenge to the rules.[42]

Yet to a large extent, contemporary perceptions of slavery in Venezuela have been shaped by the stories of those considered "house staff" (Negra Hipólita, Bolívar's nanny), those eventually freed by their owners (Pedro Camejo, aka El Negro Primero), or those in positions of power on behalf of their owners (El Esclavo Manuelote, José Antonio Páez's mentor). The reality was quite different. Keeping one in eight people in chains year-round, for life, and across generations, could only be accomplished through systematic terror.

Dozens of movies and books romanticize the sugar, indigo, and cocoa plantations in the central valleys and coastal ranges. Instead of the beautiful haciendas represented by nationalist films, these plantations resembled modern prison complexes housing hundreds of inmates each. Documents from the Chuao cocoa plantation spell out the specific height of steel and adobe fences built to enclose the slave quarters, as well as procedures to secure the inmate population under lock and key to prevent them from having "any contact or communication with outsiders."[43]

A large number of escaped slaves living in Cimarron communities appeared to have ready allies among the many Indians forced into servitude to the Crown or those outside of the colonial system. This makes sense in the context of the long wars of territorial conquest that preceded, and in many places, overlapped the massive arrival of African slaves.

The story of Venezuela's violent birth would take hundreds of pages. Yet even these few paragraphs make it clear that the Creole claim of independence, and their ambitions for the First Republic, were untenable given their minority status, and a 300-year history of carnage.

After the monumental disaster of the First Republic, these conflicts came to frame Simón Bolívar's writings.

Bolívar's Obsession

The future Liberator—humbled, but already planning his next move—left the territories in a hurry after the defeat of 1812. Once in Cartagena, modern-day Colombia, he wrote a Manifesto to analyze what had gone wrong with the First Republic and to rally forces for another attempt. The "idealist" scion of one of the region's largest fortunes writes about his defeat with clear-eyed realism. He had gone into the revolution bright-eyed and sure-footed about the power of his social class, but failure ushered in a new tone.

The Cartagena Manifesto is a search for answers about centuries of regional conflict, savage wars, killings, rebellions, and endless battles. For Bolívar, the perennial conflict of interests and ensuing violence is the only way to explain why his idealized Venezuela had not come to be. For him, the First Republic's debacle was not rooted in the delusion of a few slave-owners about the ideal country they wanted to lead. Far from it—for him the "Venezuelan nation" was a "natural" fact, but one that would only be realized with considerable force. Only a robust, top-down state could gather enough power and authority to control the differences within.[44]

In his telling, the First Venezuelan Republic of 1810 had relied on an informal all-volunteer force, but victory would require a different kind of army. American colonists had defeated the British Crown without paid "mercenaries," he writes, but these would be required for Venezuela's independence. Only a ruthless and well-paid army of any national origin, enabling a central government against all opposition, would create his dream nation. This is what he set out to do.

After convincing the Republican congress of Nueva Granada—modern-day Colombia—to grant him military command of a small army, Bolívar set out to defeat a series of Spanish strongholds in the eastern territories. In a few months he had reached the border with modern-day Venezuela and, without hesitation, crossed the Andes Mountains to attack the Royalists from the west.

The army descended from the steep mountains on the Venezuelan side and entered the city of Trujillo. There Bolívar prepared his final march to Caracas by issuing the remarkable "War to the Death" decree.[45]

This military order compelled every one of his soldiers to kill those born in Spain who were not actively helping the independence cause. The lives of those born in the Americas, even if they were fighting for the Crown, would be guaranteed. The War to the Death decree became the rallying cry of Bolívar's army and ultimately of the Second Republic as a whole.

Today such an order arguably fits the legal definition of genocide.[46] Even in 1813 it was an extraordinary measure. Nothing like it had been employed in the War of American Independence, fought thirty-eight years before, or in the Napoleonic wars ravaging Europe at that time. An order issued by the head of an army to implement the systematic, wholesale killing of a civilian population on account of its national origin whenever they were not explicitly cooperating, was something contemporaries of Bolívar would read about in the histories of Roman and Greek conquest. Such a specific definition of national origin, in a public order of extermination coming from the highest level of government, makes the decree unique. A few years later the American wars against Indian Nations, the policy of forced Indian removal, and the public-private armies that killed tens of thousands of indigenous descent would lie at the founding of the American West. But there was never anything close to Bolívar's written decree issued by the president or a flag officer.

For Venezuelan historians from the left and the right, Bolívar had merely turned a conflict that was a reality on the ground into written orders. But no matter what the situation was on the battlefields, it is impossible to sugar-coat the nature of the order: the targeted killing of combatants and non-combatants according to their national origin.

Yet Bolívar comes across as a person of his Age. His voluminous correspondence suggests a romantic, gritty, tireless, authoritarian man, but one who was keenly aware of the mores and rules of the Enlightenment world to which he felt he belonged. He had been to France during the revolution and had likely read everything his contemporaries had written on the sanctity of every human life. Why then would he go as far as to issue such an extraordinary instrument of terror? Those enslaved and the descendants of those who attained their freedom, and the poor of mixed-race did not feel they were part of the Americas, or Spanish, or even remotely Venezuelan. They had been born on the land, but their blood did not mix with the soil. Those of indigenous descent had no stake in Bolívar's ideal country. None of them shared the sense of belonging and ownership so keenly felt by the Caracas Creoles. In fact, the Creole beliefs about their ownership of the land had been at war for 300 years with the beliefs of those they had enslaved, or their former slaves who were now free, and with the original inhabitants and their descendants.

Most impoverished Spanish and Canarians who had arrived throughout the late 1700s and early 1800s apparently could not feel anything for their new land. Ultimately they were the ones specifically targeted for extermination in the military order.

As if that was not enough, the light-skinned slaveholding and trading classes in Maracaibo, El Tocuyo, Coro, and Cumaná had little interest in or use for a central government run by Bolívar and his class. Until 1777, or less than forty years before, those colonial cities had operated independently of Caracas. It had been a relationship of equals. They had voted as much when the First Republic was unequivocally declared a loose "confederation." For many, that was already too much central government. Everywhere Caracas Creoles turned they could only, at best, expect to face enemies uninterested in their fanciful idea of nation. Historian John Lombardi notes "the state invented for the First Republic was an institutional structure without foundation in Venezuela's past or its reality."[47]

The death decree sought to provide that solid foundation, regardless of how much violence it entailed, that had been missing. Few seemed to care who was Venezuelan and who was not, but Bolívar was determined to draw the distinction at any cost. Those born in the New World would be Venezuelans and be spared regardless of their actions or beliefs. Those born in Spain and the Canary Islands would have to earn their allegiance to their new land or be killed. If the ensuing bloodbath did not tie people's identity to the soil, it seemed nothing ever would.

The announced wave of terror, and the fact that Monteverde's forces had to defend themselves on the eastern flank as well, led to an easy path for the Republican army.

Bolívar arrived in Caracas as a hero in August of 1813. There he was proclaimed "Liberator" by his people, the local Creole assembly, a title he would embrace until the end of his days.

The Second Republic

Once in Caracas, Bolívar started the Second Republic of 1813 by trying to revive an economy shattered by years of war and the devastating earthquake with British-styled free trade. He also set out to organize his vision of a centralized, authoritarian government.

Several traders and concerns took advantage of the new situation. They set up shop in Caracas after centuries of absolute control by the Spanish Crown. The landowners' cocoa would now be sold on the global market, and goods would be freely imported for the first time.

At first, Bolívar turned to the two obvious challenges on his western and eastern flanks. Monteverde remained a real threat. After independence armies had taken Caracas, the Spaniard had retreated to the Puerto Cabello garrison on the western coast. He was soon recruiting a new army, just as he had done two years before to defeat the First Republic.

To the country's east, Bolívar faced a different issue. An independence army, led by Santiago Mariño, had defeated the Spanish Royalist troops. Mariño's army started with just forty-five men from the island of Trinidad but had quickly grown to several thousand men. By 1813 they controlled the critical towns of Barcelona and Cumaná. Mariño kept in communication with Bolívar but ultimately had no interest in subordinating his actions to orders coming from him. Although he occupied the trophy town of Caracas, Bolívar's position was weaker than Mariño's. To the west, Monteverde's growing menace continued to require Republican troops and resources. Coro and Maracaibo, on that side of the country, remained openly defiant to any independence project.

Between October and December of 1813 Bolívar's luck started to turn, but only if the conflict is understood as a purely military engagement between armies. Monteverde was wounded in the battle of Las Trincheras and retreated to his garrison in Puerto Cabello. Determined to destroy the Royalist army and validate his claim over all independence armies, Bolívar took command of the Republican troops in the west.

Royalist troops from Coro, Maracaibo, and The Plains, outnumbering the independence forces by several thousand, met Bolívar and his soldiers in Araure, on the western plains. This would be the Second Republic's final stand. Against all the odds, Bolívar's forces prevailed. The Liberator returned to Caracas confident the Royalist cause was done for. Yet he was further from realizing his idea of a cohesive country than he would ever be.

Waiting for Bolívar in his hometown were more than 1,000 Spanish prisoners in the garrison of San Carlos as well as those wounded and confined in the Hospital of La Guaira. Bolívar ordered that they be executed and burned, without exception, and in strict compliance with his death decree. Most were butchered with knives and lances by order of General Juan Bautista Arismendi.

The executions marked a turning point. Creating a nation would not be a matter of just accumulating power, paying for an army, or enforcing an identity with a sword. The citizens of this new nation needed to feel bound to something, and in the territories of Venezuela in 1814, what bound and divided a majority of the population was their status as slaves, mixed-race free subjects, and those of Spanish descent. What mattered to people was their place within the caste and slavery systems.

To any reader familiar with the traditional historiography of Venezuela's independence, this essay's emphasis on ethnic and racial conflicts might seem like an exaggeration of events—a new idea unduly influenced by recent intellectual fashions. Yet Juan Uslar's assessment of Bolívar's situation after establishing the Second Republic in Caracas, written in the early 1950s and partly based on Vicente Lecuna's 1947 book on the wars, could not be clearer:

"The peace appeared to be secured in the republic's center. Everything appeared to be still. But that was not the reality. In the countryside the situation was different. The King's rule was seen with fondness, since the islanders (T.N. Canarian) had not committed the excesses that had taken place in the cities; the monarchy was seen as a protector of the popular interests against the overlords' tyranny [...] While in Barlovento slaves were taking up arms against the whites, armed bands with lances and pikes, led by gray leaders without relevance, started to appear in Los Llanos. They were going to patriot towns killing their inhabitants and proclaiming the King as they satisfied their hunger for social justice by beheading whites and distributing the stolen wealth."[48]

As Bolívar pushed his death quest to the limit, a people's revolution led by one José Tomás Boves was gaining strength and would soon envelop the entire country. The first truly popular leader in the territories would lead a national battle against the caste system, and to a lesser extent, against slavery. Above all he waged a war to the death against Bolívar, his social class, and the nation they wanted to build.

Boves would single-handedly topple the Second Republic and send Bolívar into exile yet again. At least in name he would do it on behalf of the Bourbon King Ferdinand VII. But to understand the nature of Boves' successful uprising, along with the histories of indigenous suppression and slave uprisings, it is critical to review the story of the caste system.

(Out)Castes

The caste system in Spanish America was the most important, and likely the least understood, organizing principle of colonial society. Contemporary historians, particularly at American universities, have debated for decades how the caste system worked, to what extent its rules were enforced, and how relevant it was to everyday society across Spanish colonies.[49]

No one disputes the extent to which the Venezuelan society of the late 1700s, more than that of any other Spanish American colony, was gripped by a furious battle between Creoles and those of mixed-race over the future of their society. The legacy of violence from battles between Indians and Spanish, and the enforcement of African enslavement, had shaped the Wars of Independence. But underneath the conflicts there was a revolt against the caste system.

The lives of distinct social groups marked by religious and ethnic descent had been tightly regulated for hundreds of years in the Muslim and Christian strongholds of Spain.[50] Muslims born of Arab and Syrian ancestry in the Emirate of Granada had different privileges than Mozarabs (Muslims of Spanish ancestry),[51] those of Jewish ancestry, or the Slavic or Berber warriors in the employ of Sultan Boabdil. Those rights, regulations, and privileges would change for different social groups in Christian-controlled cities like Avila or Valladolid but were just as rigidly enforced, if not more so. Everywhere in the Iberian Peninsula there were rules determining where different ethnic and religious groups could live, who they could marry, and what kind of work they could do.

The Spanish exploration and subsequent invasion of today's Dominican Republic and Cuba came only a few years after the conquest and occupation of the Emirate of Granada. The fall of the Emirate in 1492 had been followed by the reorganization of the social hierarchies, with Muslims dispossessed of their lands and castles, some enslaved, those Mozarabs that opposed the Spanish punished, and those that had collaborated, and professed Catholicism rewarded. Many of the men arriving in the Caribbean had been the same Extremeño and Castilian soldiers fighting in Granada.

Historians of Spanish America tend to see the caste system in its uniquely European and Catholic sense. In the classic *Race Mixture in the History of Latin America*, Magnus Mörner argues that castes were "created by transferring to the New World the hierarchic, estate-based, corporative society of late medieval Castile and imposing that society upon a multiracial, colonial situation."[52] But he forgets how multi-ethnic Spain had been since the Muslim invasion of 711. Something else he fails to mention is the extent to which the Mexicas and the Incas in Peru had perfected their own rigid caste systems.

Tenochtitlan and Cusco were organized on even more fixed social lines than Granada or Avila. Hierarchies of lineage, genealogy, ethnicity, and work ruled much of the lives of every inhabitant.[53, 54] The canal that used to separate today's Zocalo in Mexico City from the market in Tlatelolco, for example, signaled a completely different set of rights and regulations for the ethnically specific inhabitants of each area. In the Mexica city there were slaves and traders from different nations, a priestly class, a warrior class, an aristocracy, and carefully designated guilds for different types of labor. It was in Mexico City and Cusco, cities built on civilizations based on caste-like groupings, that the Colonial Spanish American imaginary was created, and exported to lesser colonies such as Venezuela.

Equally relevant to this discussion is the speed of change in the ethnic composition of colonies like Venezuela from the 1550s through the early 1800s. In 1503 Queen Isabella I issued a royal proclamation encouraging the Spanish and those of indigenous descent to intermarry. By 1514 intermarriage was fully codified in a Royal Edict.[55] Promoting ethnic diversity was an intuitive choice for a Spanish monarch of the time. It would dilute the power of the former rulers and legitimize the new ones. Previous rulers in different parts of the Iberian Peninsula had taken similar actions for the same reasons over the previous 1,000 years.

Later in the 1500s, kidnapped Africans would be transported in substantial numbers to work as slaves in the Spanish

Caribbean, where plantation economies were beginning to thrive. The conquerors' early ideology of slavery was based on the ancient practice in North Africa—a place that the south of Spain was still culturally tied to. It was not racialist in the way the word is understood today: anyone captured in the Mediterranean Sea by pirates would be routinely sold into slavery well into the 1700s. Miguel de Cervantes, before writing *Don Quixote*, had been captured on the high seas and sold in a Tunisian market as a slave. Five years later he was able to purchase his freedom and write his famous novel.

That is partly why in Spanish America, as opposed to the British colonies and later the southern United States, it was easier and more culturally accepted for the enslaved of African descent to buy or be granted freedom. Once free, they would establish themselves as free artisans near their former plantations or in the cities.

Ethnic diversity in cities was not only a long legacy of both the Iberian Peninsula and the great pre-Hispanic empires. It was a fact created by the bringing together of people of different races and backgrounds in one place. The new colonial social order even made it possible for people from formerly enemy indigenous nations, and their descendants, to now live in peace near each other.

By the mid-1600s, the Spanish and their descendants born in the Americas, Indians and their descendants, enslaved and free Africans and their descendants, were procreating across ethnic lines in the Venezuelan territories. Spanish men had the power vis-à-vis those enslaved, indentured, and free, but in a new society that did not look like any other in history.

By the 1700s the growing diversity, and the growing non-white free population, created a backlash from colonial administrators and the Creole castes. The newly centralizing Crown authorities wanted more social organization and stability. The answer was to strengthen the world of castes. The system was a wide and uncoordinated set of laws, regulations, and customs that continued the Spanish and Muslim, and the Mexica and Inca, traditions of social organization along lines of ancestry, work, and religion.

By the 1700s the formal and informal societal organization of castes for free, non-enslaved people had Crown officials born and raised in Spain at the top of a pyramid. The light-skinned descendants of the original Spanish conquerors, now wealthy slaveowners, were below the Spanish and above everyone else. Then there were sizable numbers of Spanish colonists who had arrived recently from the mainland, as well as those coming from the Canary Islands, not quite "Spanish" but certainly close to them. The poor Spanish and Canarians were, in practice, if not by law, below the landowning class. The system recognized two kinds of Amerindians: those assimilated to colonial life and those outside of it. There were free Africans and their descendants. And then what would become the most important part of the population: those of mixed-race. While in Venezuela they are mostly seen as a single group, Pardos, some of the literature and official documents from that time speak of further categories: Mulattos (for those of European and African descent), Zambos (from those of Indian and African descent), Mestizos (for those of indigenous and European descent), and Cuarterones (those mostly of European descent who were at least a quarter African).

Because people had been mixing for 200 years these classifications grew ever more complex. As 18th-century Europeans became obsessed with classifying everything from plants and animals to types of societies and ways of thinking, Spanish American castes became a particular subject of fascination. In Mexico City, the hemisphere's most culturally advanced outpost, intricate paintings classifying every caste became all the rage. These caste paintings do not have a basis in law or regulation, but rather in the encyclopedic desire to represent and organize society's presumed diversity of ancestry.

In a poor colony like Venezuela, people of mixed-race were understood as Pardo, and within that broad category those of Mulatto ancestry would be singled out. But the actual laws regulating the life of Venezuelans were specifically aimed at controlling Pardos and their marriages, taxation, access to the seminary and the university, promotions within the army, and access to professional guilds.

The laws sought to bar those of mixed ancestry, specifically called "soiled" and "dirty," from marriage with Europeans and their descendants; the laws excluded them from government, higher education, the officer corps, key professions, and from obtaining different kinds of commercial licenses.[56] They also sought to insure those of mixed-race were taxed at the higher rates not applicable to those of European descent.

The laws, regulations, and customs functioned as a broad ethnic classification designed to block the political, economic, and educational advancement of a specific group of people.

The marriage regulations, in the context of colonial life, had a direct implication in the inheritance of property by the offspring of mixed-race inhabitants.

But soon after the Crown imposed these regulations, it was clear they would not work in the long term. Resentment and resistance to the caste regulations would grow as the territory's changing society resulted in a new balance of power. The demographic shift that would determine the course of the Wars of Independence, and the future of the country, is unmistakable.

A Demographic Tsunami

The most compelling evidence of social transformation in the colony are the census numbers compiled by Brito Figueroa from the Aragua Valley of the 1700s. It is in the heart of the slave plantation economy that the demographic change becomes most obvious.

By 1786 the population of the Valley numbered about 10,000 whites; 12,000 free mixed-race and free Blacks; 3,000 Indians in servitude; and 3,000 enslaved of African descent.[57]

By 1804, just twenty-eight years later, the population of free non-whites would reach just over 30,000, while the Spanish and those of Spanish descent barely registered any change.[58] A demographic explosion was happening alongside the new cocoa wealth.

It is helpful to look at comparable numbers from the American South to fully understand the shape of the emerging Venezuelan society. In the 1810 US census, for example, there were 105,218 slaves; 252,433 whites; and just 1,801 free non-whites in the state of Georgia. The numbers look similar in the wealthiest slave states: Virginia and South Carolina, where the percentage of free non-whites does not exceed 3%.[59] In the Central Valleys of Venezuela, the heart of the country's plantation society, free non-whites made up 64% of the population.[60]

Anglo-Americans were obsessed with clear and simple lines to explain the world. They had established that a single drop of non-white blood immediately made an individual Black. To be designated as "Black" in those southern states, with rare exceptions, meant being subject to capture and enslavement. In this sense, the institution of slavery in America was inseparable from how people understood racial identity: both theirs and others.

In the Venezuela of the 1790s things were infinitely more complex. The open power struggle between those of mixed-race, Creoles, and officers of the Crown, was increasingly tilting the balance against those of light skin. The century's prosperity was empowering a new class of Pardos who had enough money and education to openly challenge the strictures against them.

Toward the end of the 18th century, the Bourbon Crown reversed course by allowing a more flexible interpretation of caste restrictions. The change might have been unavoidable given the new demographic reality, or it might have been intended to counter the power of native-born Creoles. While the specific intention behind the shift has not been historically established, the 1795 *Gracias al Sacar* statute allowed individuals to petition the King for a reclassification of their caste from mixed-race to Creole.[61] The right appearance, money, education, and accent could now legally change someone's legal and social status. Only the King could issue such a dispensation, and fees were set at 500 Reales for Pardos, and 800 Reales for Quinterons (offspring of Cuarteron and white, where a Cuarteron would be the offspring of Terceron and Spanish, and Terceron the offspring of Mulatto and white). Six years later fees would be raised to 700 and 1,100 Reales respectively.[62] The attempt to differentiate between Pardo and Cuarteron in the statute attests to how dynamic the social situation was. In Venezuela and in New Granada—the colony next door—the new ambiguity was making ethnicity more fluid by the day. For some, this new regulation signaled the impending collapse of a society of castes.[63]

But the reaction to the regulations and to the idea that ethnicity could be defined by an individual, even a King, was swift and violent. Creoles' share of the colony's population was dwindling. Now their birthright privileges and entitlements could be acquired by someone from a different caste by paying a fee to a revenue-hungry Crown.

The Cabildo, the municipal authority that represented the Creoles' interests before the Crown, expressed its feelings directly to the King in a letter from November 1796. The proposed reclassification law, the Cabildo went on, is "horrifying to the neighbors and those naturally born in the Americas because only they know due to long years of intercourse, the immense distance that separates whites from Pardos; the advantage and superiority of the former, and the low nature and subordination of the latter ..."[64]

The document makes clear that colonial Creoles, or Mantuanos, were the first ones to bring ethnicity to the center of Venezuelan politics, where it has remained for over two hundred years. Where moneyed Pardos simply wanted to enjoy Creole rights and privileges, colonial Creoles used their substantial political capital to maintain the separate and unequal status quo. Should the new statutes stand, the letter continues,

> "the public government will come to be influenced by men of infamous and crooked lineage, lacking in education, easily moved to the worst excesses, and from whose fierceness, owing to their own principles and manners, we can only expect scandalous and subversive movements against the order established by the wise Laws that have ruled us until now..."[65]

The Creole political offensive was not only against the principles and general regulations loosening the caste system; a vigorous legal strategy to contest specific individual claims was also set in motion.

By 1806 the right to an education became a battleground, and the institutional weight of Caracas's university was thrown against the right of admission even to those individuals the King had already granted reclassification as Creoles. Appealing to the Crown, university officials claimed,

> "If the career in letters should open the doors to honors and employment to them, if enlightenment and knowledge should unfold the pernicious seed of their ideas of equality and supremacy, if the will to copy books and found libraries, a course of action that follows the literary profession, all these things will

put in their hands some of the monstrous produc-
tions subversive to the maxims of our government,
and destructive of every social order, and enemies of
all domination ... if these books that so flatter their
self-love, that exalt with such daring the rights of man
and that feed the pride of the vulgar people, make
them reflect on their past slavery, on their current
dejection ... with such seductive maxims they would
communicate to their brothers their contagion with
that much greater ease ..."[66]

Although we primarily know about these conflicts from
the legal record, it is not hard to imagine the social tension
that must have permeated the streets of every city in the
territories. The naturalist Alexander Von Humboldt sensed
it upon arriving in Caracas, remarking that Creoles, or
Mantuanos "... would want to give up rights rather than share
them with others; and would even prefer foreign domination
than authority exercised by those born in the Americans of
a lower caste ..."[67]

A social earthquake was shifting demographic power
in the colony, and plenty of people were unhappy about it.
Across the territories, the scope of demographic change
was shattering.

By 1800 the free Pardo population already amounted to
407,000, or 45% of the entire country, while free Blacks and
Mulattos made up 4%. There were 24,000 former slaves in
open rebellion, or 2.4% of the population. Free and indentured Indians numbered over 100,000, or almost 12% of the
population. There were almost 90,000 slaves, or about 10% of

the total. Yet only 12,000 people had been born in Spain or the Canary Islands, and there was a total of 172,727 Creoles and poor whites born in the territories.[68]

By the time the Wars of Independence broke out, the light-skinned population amounted to just over 20% of the entire colony. Eight out of every ten people living in the territories of Venezuela were either enslaved or in a subordinated caste.[69]

The popular uprising of 1814 had been brewing for a long time.

Boves From Asturias

By 1814, a bear of a man hailing from the rugged mountains of Asturias came into sharp focus within Venezuelan history. José Tomás Boves had studied at the Royal Marine Academy at Gijón. He probably traveled to the Caribbean at first before venturing into the Venezuelan territories. Like many Spaniards of his generation, educated but with no prospects on the mainland, he sought his fortune in the colonies.[70]

Boves' options in Venezuela were clear, if not particularly hopeful. The now wealthy descendants of the first Spanish conquerors, and those Basques associated with the Guipuzcoana Company, monopolized all paths to upward mobility. For young Boves, a skilled merchant mariner with a meager job at the port, the only choice was to join the contraband trade, to this day one of Venezuela's enduring activities. Soon, he was caught and imprisoned.[71]

Luckily for him, a family friend was able to intercede on his behalf and he was granted an early release. Penniless, he decided, or was forced, to go where every other outcast in the colony found themselves: the southern plains.[72]

The Llanos was the Venezuelan frontier. Long a home to those escaping slavery, renegades, and tens of thousands of wild horses and cattle, it was as far away as a young Asturian seafarer could go. He ended up in the town of Calabozo, in today's Guárico state. In a few years, the expanse would be enclosed to create ranches as big as European duchies, but in the early 1800s, Los Llanos meant openness, freedom, and poverty.

Eventually, Boves appears to have come into his own as he found the rugged Llanero culture a perfect match for his independent streak. The poverty and simplicity of life on the frontier must have been familiar to a descendant of Celtic tribes that had settled in the mountains of Asturias.

Boves opened Calabozo's general store and developed a sideline in horse-trading.[73] Like hundreds of Canarians and mainland Spaniards who owned and ran general stores throughout the territories, he was key to its social fabric. The general store owner was both the connecting vessel between the town and those traveling through it, and a focus of resentment. Apparently wealthy in the eyes of locals, and always the last link in the long chain that delivered the products of daily life, he was held accountable for price increases, shortages, and the unpredictable quality of anything made in a preindustrial economy. No matter what the general store owner did, he was bound to lose.

Boves lost everything soon after the Wars of Independence started. Once the local landowners took control of the town from Spanish officials during the First Republic, the

Asturian was accused of favoring the Royalists.[74] His store was looted and burned and he was thrown in prison.[75]

It seems he was imprisoned not out of jealousy but simply because he repeated what he had been told: the First Republic was disintegrating, and it would be a matter of time before Calabozo's Republicans fell too. He languished in jail for several months. When the Royalist commander Antoñanzas took Calabozo from the Republicans, he freed Boves from prison and gained a soldier for the Crown.

By 1813 Bolívar had entered Venezuela from the west while Mariño was easily winning over the eastern part of the country. At that time, Boves was already fighting with the Crown's troops in the unsuccessful siege of Mariño's stronghold in Maturin. By September, the Royalist armies were disintegrating. Boves was allowed to return to Los Llanos and raise an army of horse riders. Without any significant Crown presence in the territories, he was on his own.

While Bolívar tried building the Second Republic in Caracas, an army of native-born men of all races led by Boves quietly gathered strength. Its backbone were the mixed-race Llaneros, who had made a living rounding up wild cattle and horses on the plains. But a significant number of freed slaves who had escaped their plantations amidst the chaos of war were joining this novel army. Men of indigenous descent were also eager for a fight.

At that point, a small contingent of Republican soldiers was sent from Caracas to reinforce Calabozo. When Boves would not march on the town, Republican troops left Calabozo and went out looking for him in open country. The

Republican battalion made camp overnight by the Catalina river, but woke up to a surprise dawn attack. They were swiftly defeated, and most of the Republican cavalry went over to the Boves camp. Most of the infantry were executed. Then, Boves marched on his hometown of Calabozo. What happened next changed the course of the war Bolívar had started with his death decree.

Every single light-skinned man, woman, and child, Republican or Royalist, was killed. The town was looted, the booty distributed among the rank and file, and all property seized from whites was distributed among the mixed-race rank and file troops. Boves made a point of issuing new property titles.

The Republican commanding officer, Diego Garcia, fled to the nearby town of Villa de Cura with Boves in close pursuit. Once he caught up with him, every single light-skinned person in that town was killed as well. Garcia's head was placed on a pike and displayed on the main square. Boves controlled the lower Llanos, but his fame would spread like wildfire all over the territories. A full-fledged race war against all whites, led by a big, blued-eyed Spanish man, had started.[76]

Events over the following months accelerated beyond the Creoles' comprehension. Few writers have stopped to think about the nature and scope of what happened during this period. The most prescient of Venezuelan historians, Juan Uslar, provides the main clues.

Boves led tens of thousands of mixed-race warriors set loose by the collapse of the colonial system against a pro-slavery, Creole-led Independence Army that enforced the hierarchies of castes and fought to keep them intact for the entire country.

By July 1814 he entered Valencia after a long and difficult siege. His troops flew both the skull and crossbones banner, and the King's colors.

Valencia, in the central valleys, was the first major town Boves had conquered and one well outside The Plains. The local Creoles, regardless of allegiance, were convinced the unruly Spaniard would behave after capturing such a prize. He did, at first. Boves attended mass and swore on the altar that there would be no reprisals. He organized a grand ball to celebrate with the local elites. Yet Cajigal, the leading regular officer of the Spanish army that had participated in the takeover of the city, would not be in attendance. He had ordered his troops to pick up and set up camp outside the city earlier that day, providing no explanations.

At the party, everything proceeded brilliantly. Boves was not dancing but seemed to be participating in the celebrations. At some point, the military leader asked that a piece of music, *"el Pariquito,"* be played. It turned out to be the signal to his troops to start rounding up and killing every light-skinned man in sight. The massacre lasted all night, both inside the house and on a riverbank nearby.[77] The country remembered the river running red with blood for decades.

The conflict was fundamentally about race and ethnicity. This fact is openly discussed by the Spanish officials at least nominally allied with Boves. In a letter to the King, José Ambrosio Llamozas summarizes his view: "from the very beginning of the campaign Commanding General Boves made clear what he proposed, and from which he never deviated: it was based on the destruction of all whites while preserving, flattering and indulging the other castes (...) distributing the homes and other goods of the dead and exiled among Pardos, and giving them property titles."[78]

Moreover, Boves' army had been transformed. As described by the Spanish archbishop of Caracas, the leader "enforced a factual equality among the white officers that stayed in his army and the ferocious multitude of Blacks and free zambos and slaves he took out of The Plains."[79]

A Military Revolution

Despite Boves' personal brand of sadistic cruelty, his success at the head of his army explains the course of a race war he started. His story is the story of the unique frontier region of Los Llanos, or plains.

Throughout its history, most of Venezuela's economic activity had concentrated on the coast spanning 800 miles from eastern Cumaná to western Maracaibo. The vast plains to the south were culturally disconnected from the slave plantations and very rigid racial and social mores of the coastal regions. The main economic activity was cattle herding, and significantly the catching of wild cattle and horses to be sold to local ranchers and horse-traders, such as Boves.

Before the massive enclosures of the 19th century, the Llaneros of the early 1800s could still be considered independent horsemen leading semi-nomadic lives. The harshness and poverty of the landscape made these superb riders everything European armies were not: agile, fast, and able to improvise on their own. Pablo Morillo, the Spanish general who much later in the war would have to fight them, offers an unforgettable description of the landscape:

"On several occasions, I have informed his excellency of the inclemency of this weather and of these plains for European troops, the rigors of which make themselves felt in the health of the soldier ... The passage of rivers and spouts, entire days through swamps and quagmires, with water up to the waist, along with meager and miserable food for the soldier in the scorching sandbanks of the Plain, has resulted in many sick, as well as many wounded by 'rays,' and bitten by fish called 'caribes' ..."

Of the men that thrived in this hostile wilderness Morillo noted:

"... the baggage does not disturb them, because they're naked, and they could care less about subsistence because meat provides them with a healthy and robust existence; they make swift and happy movements that cannot be stopped no matter how much our soldiers force themselves in their marches. The plainsmen throw themselves from a horse on the riverbank with saddle on their head, and their lance in their mouths. They can pass two or three thousand horses in a quarter of an hour as if they were going through a wide bridge, without fear of drowning or of losing their weapon or their clothing. In this way, they tire out our columns that chase them in the most painful marches imaginable. We lose in a few days a great number of soldiers that get sick in the quagmire, and when they consider those losses, and our tired and useless horses that have no place to repair, they come to attack us or wait for combat ..."[80]

The Llanero riding skills, along with their use of the long lance, would be the decisive military factor of the entire Wars of Independence. Lightning-fast and ruthlessly violent, the Llanero cavalry could form wide, enveloping lines in the manner of Alexander the Great. They also executed the explosive flank charges in vogue during the Napoleonic wars. Their signature maneuver was to feign a chaotic retreat that lured the enemy into chasing them, and then turn around to destroy their pursuers. Lethal against fixed infantry formations and fast enough to evade the 18th-century single-charge musket firing-lines, the Llaneros would underwrite power in Venezuela until the end of the century. Or until Andean traders in 1899 got hold of repeating rifles that would devolve power to the foot soldier on the battlefield, tipping the country's regional balance of power away from Los Llanos.

The political consequences of having an army of empowered horsemen were radical.[81] Llanero warfare was based on free, autonomous men who needed nothing from anyone. They had their horse or could easily rope a dozen more. Their lance would work for life. Their all-beef diet did not depend on agriculture or army logistics. Like similar armed societies throughout history, each Llanero had a lot to say about who he would fight and, most importantly, under whom. The leader would come from within, live like the rank and file, and fight from the front. Once chosen, the leader would be followed to the death, so long as his men stayed loyal to him.

As if this was not sufficiently subversive, Llaneros were as racially diverse as anyone in the Americas. The frontier territory had been the natural retreat of all indigenous groups from the very beginning of the conquest. The original inhabitants of the central valleys who had not died of European-borne illnesses, or had fought for the Crown, had fled south toward the Llanos. To the south and beyond the Orinoco River, indigenous populations have survived outside of any Western influence until today. The Llanos have always been the middle territory between the Amazon jungle and the coastal cities. Throughout the 1700s, the place was also a natural refuge for escaped slaves. The Cimarron communities would hunt for cattle and horses and eventually integrate into Llanero life. The region's egalitarian culture became a rod against the established social arrangements of the colony, slavery and the caste system.

A common belief is that Llanero fighters would go wherever their leader took them, and to explain their violence by the harshness of the landscape. Add a psychological profile of Boves and one might conclude that he led his men down his rabbit hole of madness. (Something similar was said of Zamora during the Federal War, half a century later, and of Chávez in the early 2000s.) Yet even a brief look at the social structure of the Llanos and its deep-seated values of independence, individualism, and racial diversity provides an alternative explanation. Their struggle against Creole society was rooted in a history of cruel violence.

The original Declaration of Independence from Spain was ideologically driven by the slave-owning classes. Those at the top of the caste system in the central valleys wanted to kick out the Spanish and lead a new slaveholding, caste-bound country.

As late as 1814 Bolívar's armies were busy hunting escaped slaves to return them to the plantations, and putting down slave rebellions.[82] And the Creole leadership in the armies of the First and Second Republics had maintained the same hierarchies that existed in their cities: native-born, slave-owning, light-skinned officers at the top, and everyone else below them. It is not difficult to see why Llaneros fought against Creoles with such fury.

The Race War

By the end of 1814 Boves had raised three separate Llanero armies of more than 5,000 men each. His third army, raised in the frontier town of Guayabal, better known for its population of escaped slaves, might have reached 10,000 men between May and June.[83]

While Boves oversaw daily arrivals of men of all races, he carefully trained them in the light cavalry maneuvers that Llanero General Páez would later make famous. Boves had won his first battles with the open, single-line cavalry lines that would envelop and suffocate the enemy's flanks. In his one major defeat at Mosquiteros in October of 1813, this same formation had broken when the enemy refused to come out in the open. The same thing happened when he proved unable to dislodge Bermudez from San Mateo. At Guayabal, he trained for concentrated flank attacks based on surprise, the tactic that had allowed him to crush Bolívar and the Second Republic's army at La Puerta. In that battle, his cavalry had waited in the lowlands of a canyon while the battle progressed, eventually breaking out in concentrated force to crush their opponents.

As the Race War of 1814 continued, Boves' army continued amassing victories and territories. After the Valencia bloodbath in which every Creole man was executed in cold blood, Boves marched toward Caracas. The big city was already safely under the control of his men, Manuel Machado and Chepino González. As we have seen already, Machado himself had sliced off his former master's head before leading the Royal Army into Caracas.

By then, Bolívar was well on his way to Barcelona at the head of a rapidly dwindling column of light-skinned refugees. The Liberator was hoping that Mariño's troops, in the east, would fend off the Boves tsunami. Back in Caracas, the Asturian took possession of the territories' most crucial town.

The sight of Boves lording over a Caracas almost entirely made up of Pardos, free Blacks, and those slaves who had escaped the plantations would have seemed, to the proud Mantuanos of the 1700s, like an impossible tale concocted by the Devil himself. And yet, most light-skinned residents, except for a few Crown and church officials, had joined the refugee march, managed to board a ship bound for exile, or had been killed.

In the meantime, Boves ordered Machado to go after Bolívar and harass the rearguard of the refugee march. If the challenge of jungles and arid expanses was not enough, Machado's raids proved deathly for the refugees. There are no reliable numbers on who finally reached Barcelona, but many died along the way.

Once in the eastern city, it must have become apparent to Bolívar that there would be no haven for him in the Venezuelan territories. The military situation in the east was precarious at best as Mariño focused on defending the stronghold of Maturin. He had defeated Royalist armies in that city before, even fighting a younger Boves there during the First Republic, and he was getting ready to do it again.

In time, Boves left Caracas to chase Bolívar. If he prevailed, most of the territories would fall under his direct control. A victory would also destroy the Creole cause once and for all. Bolívar did not have the slightest chance of defending Barcelona and chose to flee further east. The few thousand surviving refugees placed their last hope in the town of Cumaná, the very place which had been burned to the ground by Indians, and rebuilt by Spanish, over and over again throughout the 16th century.

Boves easily marched into a Barcelona vacated of Republicans, though many local Creoles had chosen to stay. Having heard that Boves had refrained from violence toward the few white Spaniards and royalist Creoles who had stayed in Caracas, the elites of Barcelona flew the King's banner and stayed put. Their fate was sealed as Boves once again promised peace and organized a victory party for the locals. The bloodbath that night was apparently as gruesome as Valencia's, and the killing started with the same piece of music that had been the cue for the first slaughter. But the Asturian would not rest until Bolívar had been vanquished and quickly left in pursuit.

The remaining refugees and a few soldiers were all that was left of Bolívar's Second Republic. Entrenched in Maturin, Mariño would not come to his help. At the end of his rope, Bolívar got on a ship with a few of his men, the little Republican treasure left, and fled to see a better day.

Boves set out to join his own troops near Maturin, where everything would be finally settled. The battle of Urica in December 1814 would mark the end of an incredible year.

In this hard-fought action, Republican leader José Félix Ribas initially put Boves on the defensive with a strong cavalry charge that broke the Asturian's lines. The Llaneros managed to counterattack to a deathly draw.[84] But the Republicans did not have much left afterward and were defeated. Among the countless corpses on the ground lay José Tomás Boves himself.

Bolívar's Reinvention

Even though he was dead, Boves still won the War of 1814. And Bolívar, on his way to exile, could only wonder about the forces that had defeated, killed, and exiled his kin.

The Liberator had a unique ability to learn and grow from every setback. He had contributed to the loss of the First Republic of 1810 with his loose and possibly inexcusable command of the Puerto Cabello fort. By comparison, the Second Republic saw a strong, tireless, and centralizing Bolívar who never lost sight of the action and led from the front. Yet he was roundly defeated again.

By early 1815 he was bound for Haiti and Jamaica, from where he organized a third, and ultimately victorious, attempt to forge his ideal country. His first destination in exile says much about his reflections on defeat. Another kind of leader would have gone to the United States or Europe to hobnob with the journalists and political luminaries of the time. Instead, he chose to go to a devastated country born out of a slave rebellion.

Just a few months before arriving at Port-au-Prince, Bolívar had led a Second Republic that was hunting down slaves on the run and putting down uprisings at slave plantations. His officers had rigidly enforced the caste system at every level of the Independence Army. This racial and ethnic agenda had caused the Republic's defeat.

Boves, on the other hand, had prevailed over the Republican Army with considerably fewer resources and a radical message of racial vengeance and revindication. His army's terrorist actions and his reputation for sadism undoubtedly helped his military objectives: opponents feared his men. But those armies would not have fought as tenaciously as they did if they had not believed in a cause that made sense to them. Boves fought at the head of a novel multi-racial army that had banished castes from its ranks. He had articulated a multi-racial vision that rallied his fighters.

During this Caribbean journey, Bolívar could only be reflecting upon defeat and the role the social imaginary of his colonial childhood must have had in it. The lessons of Boves' popularity among the people and the nature of his victories must have been obvious.

In Haiti he spent time with Alexandre Pétion, the first president of a country founded on a slave rebellion. He promised the Haitian leader that he would abolish slavery. From there he went to Jamaica to continue his fundraising efforts.

By 1816 Bolívar was back in the Venezuelan territories. While he would not keep his promise to Pétion, Bolívar's actions and words in those years would have been unrecognizable during his previous campaigns of the Second Republic. He dispensed with Creole formalities and widely held prejudices on the military front by giving General Páez and his multi-ethnic army the leading role in the independence effort.

By 1819 Bolívar delivered the justly famous Angostura speech to the second Venezuelan Congress.[85] What he said then laid out a plan based on Boves' insight into colonial society. For years, the Angostura text has been read as an example of a centralizing Bolívar advocating for a strong state that accommodates patrician institutions like a hereditary House of Lords. The most radical aspect of the speech is seldom mentioned.

Going well beyond what he had written in the Cartagena Manifesto, Bolívar seeks to explain the fragmentation and hatred within the colonial territories. Many decades before Vallenilla Lanz and Uslar Pietri had articulated the fracture at the country's heart, he already speaks of a society on the verge of falling apart: "The diversity of origin requires an infinitely firm grip, an infinitely delicate tact to manage this heterogenous society whose complicated artifice can be dislocated, divided, and dissolved with the slightest altercation."[86]

The key phrase is "diversity of origin," which acknowledged at the very beginning of the 1800s that Venezuela was, at its core, a multi-ethnic and multi-racial society. The explanation goes into considerable detail,

"We must be aware that our people are not Europeans, or North Americans: they're a composite of Africa and the Americas rather than a product of Europe; even Spain itself is no longer European due to its African blood, its institutions and its character. It is impossible to properly decide to which human family we belong. The largest part of the indigenous population has been annihilated, the European has mixed with those of the Americas and those of Africa, and they have mixed with Indians and with Europeans ..."[87]

No one had ever described the facts and uncertainties of ethnic and racial differences in this way. Boves' de facto solution had been to promote the extermination of all whites. Creole society's program sought to reenact the colonial caste system. Many ignored the issue and pretended it was not relevant. As the years went by and a battery of constitutions dismantled the caste system's nominal rules, and later, slavery, most of the country's intellectual establishment chose to ignore the subject.

The speech's enduring passage defines the conundrum faced by countries in the Caribbean basin: "our parents, different in origin and blood, are foreigners, and all have visibly different skin: the dissimilarity brings a challenge of the highest order."[88] In the context of his time, and that of many decades after him, Bolívar proposes a radical solution: "The blood of our fellow citizens is different. Let's mix it in order to unify it ..."[89]

The speech promotes a mixed-race country with a historical dimension and a spiritual path. Boves' men had lived their day-to-day in a new kind of army: multi-ethnic, horizontal, and devoid of rankings based on skin color or national origin. This had been a revolutionary social experiment. Bolívar wanted a society based on that model and included his ethnic group in the mix.

While the concept of nation proposed at Angostura had nothing to do with the Creole ideals of the older Cartagena Manifesto, Bolívar continued to advocate for a powerful ruler and a centralizing seat of power.

The speech summarizes the late Bolívar's prescription for the country: fuse all nations and races and ethnicities into a new brown Venezuelan identity and superimpose a powerful central state to combat factionalism and special interests.

Although this was never clearly stated, one hundred years later Rómulo Betancourt founded his political project upon those ideas. Acción Democrática would create a vast and centralized welfare state unimaginable to Bolívar in its scope, reach, and sheer power. And the party and its leaders would work tirelessly to create one nation around the idea of Juan Bimba, a racially mixed John Doe that stood for the average (and ideal) Venezuelan.

The End of Spanish Rule

Beyond his grand social program, Bolívar needed to turn words into reality. His legend was still in the making, and to many, he was just another white Creole slaveholder from Caracas. While he envisioned his army's multi-ethnic future, his forces then were more of a loose ensemble than a force with a clear sense of identity.

On the practical side of things he needed both money and at least some troops on his side. He worked hard to secure foreign financing and to open trade in his stronghold on the Orinoco River. And he set up an agent in London to recruit British mercenaries. These hardened and disciplined troops would assure his safety and give him critical military leverage in the battles ahead. A number of troops in the final, definitive Battle of Carabobo were British and Irish.

But Bolívar knew that real military power was in the hands of the deathly Llanero riders that Boves had rallied. All the words and money in the world would not be enough to win the war. He needed a Llanero leader and thousands of horsemen to overcome the Spanish forces. As it happens, a former ranch hand by the name of José Antonio Páez was that leader.

Bolívar worked to seduce Páez with a barrage of flattering letters, and later, in person. The Llanero leader was already on the Republican side, but Bolívar needed his absolute allegiance and complicity to complete his ambitious project.

José Antonio Páez would prove to be an infinitely savvier version of Boves and would ultimately outmaneuver and outlive Bolívar and the rest of his contemporaries. But in the beginning, The Liberator had enough British money and troops to keep Páez in line while they fought successfully for the same objective. Without that leverage, he might not have kept Páez and his essential Llanero cavalry in check.

Finally, Bolívar had to deal with the rival pro-independence *caudillos* from the east whose refusal to bow to a Caracas Creole had cost him dearly at the end of the Second Republic. To accomplish this, Bolívar had one of their key military leaders, Manuel Piar, shot for treason.

Emboldened by his new mixed-race vision, British treasure, British troops, and with Páez fighting the war, Bolívar was able to consolidate power in a way that had never been possible before. The real battles over independence from Spain started in 1816 as Bolívar and Páez set out to face the largest Spanish army ever sent to the Americas.

General Morillo and his 20,000 hardened troops had landed in Venezuela in 1815. By then, Napoleon had been thoroughly beaten in Spain by British forces and Spanish guerrillas. King Ferdinand VII was back in control, and the Spanish bureaucracy, the trading aristocracy, and the army were now unified behind a reassertion of the Crown. For the first time since the first rumblings of independence in 1808, Spain focused on squashing the rebellion. Realizing that a full-fledged ethnic and racial war had been fought in the name of the Spanish King and painfully aware that Madrid had no control over Venezuela, the Crown decided to start there. Pablo Morillo arrived in the eastern city of Carúpano. Without Boves, the Royalist Llanero cavalry and the soul of the racial uprising had disintegrated. For the remainder of the war, the Royalist side would be genuinely Spanish.

And for the first time, Bolívar had an army that was Llanero at its core. This time, there would be a war between mixed-race Venezuelans, with British help, against European Spanish troops. As had happened in the War of 1814, whoever had the Llanero warriors' loyalty would win the final war of independence.

Morillo's force was slowly worn down in a stretched-out battle that merits its own book, and finally left the country. Led by Bolívar, Páez and the British legions eventually defeated the Spanish army at the Battle of Carabobo. In time The Liberator decided to continue his wars beyond Venezuela.

After Angostura, his mind wandered to the idea of a much bigger country encompassing the territories that stretched from Venezuela's east coast to what is today Peru's border with Chile. It would be called Gran Colombia. Once again, he was forced into the kinds of battles over identity and local control that had initially overwhelmed him in Venezuela. Where the Spanish Crown had patiently built fiercely independent fiefdoms in Peru, Ecuador, and Colombia over 300 years, Bolívar tried to impose a single authority. He tried to sell his Angostura multi-ethnic ethos in places where thousand-year-old cultures like those of the Aymaras, Q'ero, Quechua, and Chibchas had been firmly established.

He would quickly find out that the demographic balance in those territories had nothing to do with Venezuela's unique situation. It was one thing to create an identity for a majority of mixed-race Pardos and free Africans and their descendants, who did not live in the land of their ancestors. But it was quite another thing to persuade indigenous Andean nations, who had lived their way of life for thousands of years, that they were now "Great Colombians" instead.

Bolívar had won many battles with multi-ethnic armies in the Andean countries by harnessing a deep hatred of Spanish rule. But that would not translate to a positive, multi-national and multi-ethnic identity in a post-Spanish world. A vast majority of the populations of current-day Peru, Ecuador, and Bolivia all spoke different languages, and few spoke Spanish at all.

No sooner had Bolívar died in 1830 than Páez formally separated from the Gran Colombian federation Bolívar had built between Venezuela, present-day Colombia, Peru, Ecuador, and Bolivia. The wily Llanero orchestrated the creation of a newly independent country, the Republic of Venezuela, but had waited until Bolívar was gone.

Most Spanish, Canarians, and the native-born inhabitants of light skin had been exterminated and exiled during the long wars. There would not be another demographically significant light-skinned population in Venezuela until the 1950s and 1960s.

IV
Dismantling the System, 2004-2019

«*There are times made to decimate flocks,
confuse languages, and disperse the tribes.*»
Alejo Carpentier, *Explosion in a Cathedral*

The year 2004 brought the beginning of a wild run-up in the price of oil and a sense of victory for Hugo Chávez's project. The historical forces that had shaped modern Venezuela, oil revenues, and social identity, were about to explode.

The tragedy had been foretold. By 1936 Arturo Uslar Pietri wrote that fossil fuels would turn the country "into a giant oil parasite, swimming in a temporary and corrupting abundance and driven towards an inevitable and imminent catastrophe."[1] By 1819 Simon Bolívar observed that "our parents, different in origin and blood, are foreigners, and all have visibly different skin: a dissimilarity that brings a challenge of the highest order."[2]

The extravagant oil bonanzas had been part and parcel of the 20th century. Uslar Pietri merely described the inevitable if oil continued to overwhelm society or, as in 2004, started a price run that would break all historical records. Bolívar stated a fact evident in his time and unlikely to go away. For hundreds of years, national, ethnic, and racial groups had fought each other with extreme violence. The long and bloody Spanish conquest, the wars over the settlement of Caracas, the many slave rebellions then and afterward, the vicious Wars of Independence, and the chaotic Federal War would weigh like a nightmare on the minds of every succeeding generation.[3]

As told by Juan Uslar in his brilliant 1968 account *Historia Política de Venezuela*, four generations of rulers deployed distinct models of power and authority to wrestle with the country's twin challenges of ethnic conflict, and scarcity or sudden windfall of resources, from the 1820s and until his days.[4] By now we can speak of Chavez's generation, a fifth one, putting its stamp on Venezuela's story. The first generation fought against the Spanish Crown and then inherited a ruined country. José Antonio Páez and his successors, two independent-era generals, ended the formal caste system and eventually outlawed slavery. They advocated British free trade to generate a coffee economy over a destroyed countryside. The experiment initially infused much-needed resources but never enough to establish a proper state organization over the territories. Páez's unique political gifts achieved a tenuous post-war peace that held for twenty years. Still, the countryside's misery, the constant violence, endemic malaria, and the predatory rule of Paez's immediate successors, the Monagas brothers, led directly to the Federal War of 1859. The mid-19th century civil war started where Boves had left off in 1814: a mixed-race and free Black population, and those of African descent who had been recently liberated, were united by deep grievances and the fact that they had nothing to lose.

The violence, the proliferation of battles in a countryside that had nurtured gangs and private armies for decades, the feudal conditions for the few who could find work, and sharpened rhetoric of ethnic hatred, gave the Federal War a bloody and destructive character. The conflict ended in 1863. Its aftermath brought the second generation of military men to power and a long period during which General Guzmán Blanco dominated the country's politics. In his diligent mind, Venezuela needed a strong centralized state at any cost. He crafted a new paradigm of government inspired by French-styled statecraft and leveraged

by a new global bond market. He represented a generation
of leaders who were convinced that British free trade would
never let the country prosper. Guzmán's efforts gave the proto-
state a legal and administrative architecture while the wealth,
knowledge, and power gap between Caracas and the
countryside deepened. The general became spectacularly rich
by comparison to any prior rulers. Meanwhile, the poverty,
illness, and decay in the countryside, where more than 90% of
the population still lived, continued unabated. Guzman and
his generation of Federal War generals ruled until 1899. That
year, a third generation of chieftains since independence from
Spain brought in yet another approach to power and authority.

The first two rulers were cattle ranchers from the
commercially prosperous Andes region, Cipriano Castro
and Juan Vicente Gómez. They had modern artillery and
repeating rifles that made their troops immune to Llanero
cavalry charges. Their territory had not known malaria
due to the altitude of its towns. A healthy young army and
modern guns ushered in fifty years of rule from the conservative highlands of Táchira, starting with Castro in 1899
and ending in 1959 with Marcos Pérez Jiménez. Unlike
their predecessors and successors, these men never talked of
poverty, misery, or the rights of the oppressed. Their solution
to the challenges of the age-old social divide was inspired
by the colonial order and driven by new nationalist rhetoric.
Juan Vicente Gómez ruled for twenty-seven years and
imposed an iron-handed peace throughout the country after
winning every military battle he fought. High cacao and coffee
prices during World War I financed the beginnings of a state
organization that could reach the entire country for the first

time since colonial times. The sudden and spectacular oil boom of the 1920s allowed Gómez to grow a ruthless governmental machine, despite the continued poverty, illness, and misery of the mixed-race inhabitants in the vast countryside. Between 1821 and 1958, each generation that conquered and retained power had different approaches to dealing with the social scars running through the country. Whether they enhanced the ethnic and racial divide to sustain their rule or ruthlessly repressed it, every generation's political project eventually ended. Sooner or later, the tensions would resurface, bury an era, and usher in a new one. Rómulo Betancourt and his early socialist allies brought about a fourth era in this political history. They were mostly of mixed ancestry and firmly believed they could escape the historical trap announced by Bolivar. Betancourt and his fellow adecos would get their turn, their own era, by removing the last of the highland generals from power in 1958. They founded a republic that would last forty years. Betancourt's father was Spanish-born, and his mother was of African-Venezuelan descent. Raúl Leoni, his closest ally and successor as president in 1964, had a Venezuelan-born mother, while his father had emigrated from Corsica as an adult. Throughout the party's history, four out of five elected Acción Democrática presidents had foreign and native-born parents. Unlike their immediate predecessors and many contemporaries, these presidents believed they could build a peaceful society out of disparate origins—and oil profits. Betancourt forged an unprecedented liberal democracy with a grand bargain *(El Pacto de Punto Fijo)* designed to mediate all conflicts and distribute the oil treasure.

The culture of inclusiveness and negotiation engineered into the Pacto prevailed for decades. A welfare state vanquished malaria and illiteracy while raising the standard of living of all Venezuelans to unprecedented levels. But by the 1990s, too many years of low oil prices, an exhausted welfare state, decentralization, and the privatization of public services had mortally wounded the levers of Betancourt's consensus. Bolívar's words about Venezuela's social dynamics fit the last years of the 20th century like a glove: the complicated artifice stitching together a heterogeneous society had been dislocated and dissolved. The old social conflict that would not go away had returned like a ghost and was now front and center in the political arena. That was Chavez's political moment. The rule of two generations best describes the 19th century's political history, that of the Independence Wars generals and then those that came of age during the Federal War. The 20th century was marked first by the Tachira highland generals and then the adecos' republic. The early 2000s saw the Chavista turn. The different eras of Venezuelan political history provide a broader historical context to the Chavista revolution. Just as prior generations of rulers had imposed new paradigms of power and authority, Chavez sought to destroy what came before him. The difference is the violence with which the largest state structure the country had ever known was ransacked and the speed with which the established civil society disintegrated. In the end, everything Chavez's predecessors—the mid-century adecos—feared could happen given the history of Venezuela, and much worse, came to pass by 2019. The depth of the tragedy has been such that many questions still elude academics, journalists, and politicians. Why would

Chávez plunder a state oil company under his control and destroy the ability to extract the most extensive fuel oil reserves on the planet? Why dismantle the national welfare and health networks staffed and led by his subordinates? Why weaken security functions already under his control? Why force the exile of hundreds of thousands of people with college degrees and years of valuable experience? Those unaware of the country's history cannot understand why Chávez would destroy a state and a country he already ruled.

The same question arises about José Tomás Boves and his soldiers, whose remarkable takeover of Venezuela is chronicled earlier in this book. As they galloped unopposed out of the Llanos during the racial war of 1814, they destroyed a countryside they already controlled. The writers who have taken the time to study Boves' movement see a motivation: those at the bottom of the caste system, and those formerly enslaved, were involved in a vicious war against armies primarily led by Creoles who wanted to reinstate the social arrangements of colonial society. By 1813 Bolivar's troops were hunting down those who had escaped slavery, while republican armies typically enforced the caste system. In the heat of a brutal war against an enemy fighting under the banner of a death decree, Boves' men burned down everything associated with the Creole and Spanish colonial universe, come what may. No lesser literary achievement than Uslar Pietri's *Lanzas Coloradas* is a treatise on this original grievance and the destructive impulses it nourished. As events recounted later in this chapter make clear, Chávez and his political and intellectual supporters had something in common with the furious armies of 1814.

Spiral

The early Chávez government, from 1999 to early 2004, had little margin of action as oil prices remained stuck in a two-decade trend. Despite the central promise of the presidential campaign, there was no hidden treasure to redistribute. Chávez and his collaborators filled the vacuum created by the lack of resources with an ever more radical discourse. A new constitution, new laws, and a torrent of words and images sought to deepen the ethnic divide while speaking of a new kind of justice. Chavismo became an echo chamber for newly current Jean Jacques Rousseau's ideas about the virtues of unmediated government and the wisdom of rule based on a "state of nature." According to the new constitution and the president's speeches, originary rights, people's democracy, and popular sovereignty were the keys to justice.

Borrowing Rousseau's ideas for similar political ends was as old as the French revolution.[5] At the height of Robespierre's revolutionary rule, he unleashed a terror campaign against the elected convention and most of his opponents in the name of the "general will."[6] For Robespierre, "kings, aristocrats, tyrants, whoever they be, are slaves rebelling against the sovereign of the earth, which is the human race, and against the legislator of the universe, which is nature."[7] The idea that the originary will of the sovereign people could be conjured to squash all dissent was something Venezuelans would hear about countless times after 1999.

Rousseau's revival within global leftist circles catalyzed the original Chavista impulse. Against the transactional nature of representative democracy, now stood the purity of popular sovereignty emanating from the rights of originary peoples and enslaved Africans that had toiled the land. Instead of equal justice for all, the wisdom of ancestral truths. Against the parties of 20th-century democracy, a single "general will." And to be cast as the embodiment of the originary nation, Chávez himself. But initially, the impetus did not go beyond rhetoric.

On the other side of the divide, and seeing their standard of living still dropping, the middle classes coalesced around a rhetoric of ethnic anti-Chavismo. It was common to hear lighter-skinned professionals and small business owners disparaged the lack of "education," "manners," and "violent nature" of their opponents. The still-private media fed audiences a constant barrage of vitriol, often crossing into racialist hatred. The word "monkey" became a standard private and even public epithet to describe those in power.[8, 9] Chávez welcomed the polarization and responded by demonizing his opponents.

In the minds of Chavistas, between the years 2000 and 2003 their ethno-nationalist movement had defeated an all-out attack by a threatened light-skinned oligarchy. Their success vanquishing the enemy had convinced them they were part of a historical, even transcendental movement led by a once-in-a-lifetime leader.

The momentum to destroy the old society fed on itself: the old wounds of history, enhanced by vicious political polarization, returned under the guise of a new mythology of originary restitution. A messianic call to action took over Chavista politics.

And then oil surged as 2004 was ending. The amounts of money involved remain unbelievable, not just in the context of the previous twenty-four-year drought. The decade of high oil prices would bring between seven to nine times the value of the Marshall Plan, which had rebuilt France and Germany's economies after World War II's destruction.[10]

The young Chavista cadres, and Chávez himself, were convinced they could deliver, or more precisely purchase, a utopian society after destroying the current one. The old state, its institutions, culture, and rules would be torched in the name of an oil-financed ethno-nationalist redemption.

In Chavez's own words: "We are Guaicapuro's children, right here. Who among us feels they are Guaicapuro? We are all Guaicapuro. And his war cry against the Spanish Empire, 'ana karina rote.' That's where we come from …"[11]

According to the Chavista mythology of origin, Guaicaipuro, the indigenous leader who fought against the Spanish conquest of the Caracas valley, led his warriors with the Caribe war cry "ana karina rote."[12] The phrase means "only the Caribe are people." Here was the idea defining ethnic frenzies throughout history, whether barely whispered or violently acted upon: demonized social groups are less than human.

An entire group of outsiders, immigrants, their children and grandchildren, and those educated abroad or inspired by European and American institutions would be ostracized and then pushed into exile.

The country's social fabric was broken while forces on both sides pushed for more radical confrontation. Never-seen-before oil revenues unleashed the "inevitable and imminent catastrophe" described by Uslar Pietri. Such an amount of free money would break apart any healthy society, never mind one gripped by ethnic hatred.

The firestorm lit in 2004 would burn brightly for a long time. The oil bonanza acted as a gale speeding its spread and carrying embers in every direction. And after ten years, a savage humanitarian crisis exploded. Bolívar and Uslar had eerily predicted it, and nothing Betancourt and his adecos had ever created would help stop it.

Dismantling in Six Acts

Chávez's revolution after 2004 can be examined through six distinct efforts:

1. A massive government exchange control system intervened in every corner of the private sector, effectively ruining it.
2. The new leadership at the oil company, other state enterprises, and the expropriated concerns started managing those businesses in the service of identity politics.
3. Dozens of quasi-state organizations, mostly known as Misiones, subverted and replaced most executive functions of government.
4. Many of the government's safety functions were weakened in favor of non-state actors who functioned as proxies for Chavismo.
5. Tens of thousands of local committees became an alternative legislative branch channeling originary power.
6. Hundreds of generals and colonels were forcibly retired to remake the army in the image of the ethno-nationalist revolution.

The following sections chronicle each of these massive transformations of the status quo, starting with the exchange control system.

Currency control schemes had been part and parcel of the oil democracy. But the Chavista experiment at controlling currency flows would take the concept to a new level. There had never been so much money at stake as in the once-in-a-generation oil bonanza of 2004-2014. And this happened as the legal and ethical edifice of the liberal state was dismantled.

Destroying the Private Sector

If the oil state controlled the entire energy sector in Venezuela, it followed that politics would always be more important than economics. For Chávez, the power equation was based on which ethnic group controlled the oil company, every other facet of government, and the army, and not necessarily in the broader issues of business. This explains why one of the government's most visible efforts selectively handed out hundreds of billions of dollars in subsidies to individuals and companies under the banner of 21st-Century Socialism.

Despite the agenda's grand name, the objective was not to destroy a business elite and a professional upper middle class it enriched beyond their wildest imagination. The idea was simply to make them obedient (if fabulously wealthy) clients in a system where they had little to no power. Yet the subsidized dollars, bogus bonds, and crass credit card schemes corroded the private sector from the inside out while destroying any semblance of the civil society that had existed before. This collapse of the Venezuelan private sector, key in the country's self-destruction, was more a byproduct than an objective of Chávez's ethno-nationalist plan.

Reviewing the sequence of events helps understand this confusing aspect of the Chavista legacy. The economic trendlines of the 20th century had continued in the 2000s. The Venezuelan economy exported almost nothing other than oil, and whatever it produced internally, it did so with raw materials, machinery, and technology that was brought in from abroad. Every product or service required foreign currency to operate, or to exist at all.

As had been done many times before, the Chávez government distributed dollars at subsidized rates to the private sector, which was supposed to import whatever was necessary to keep the country fed, clothed, housed, entertained, educated, and policed.

Taking a page from those previous experiences, the government's controls set an artificially low price for the dollar in relation to the bolivar, but it would not sell these openly. Every business had to apply to the government to get these "cheap" dollars. When the oil bonanza filled the treasury's coffers beyond anything that had ever been seen, the exchange control policy degenerated into a scheme best described by a 2018 US Federal indictment of a Venezuelan businessman:

"Venezuela has a foreign-currency exchange system under which the government will exchange local currency (Bolivars) at a fixed rate for US Dollars. The fixed exchange rate has been well below the true economic rate by a substantial factor for several years.

For example, in 2014, the Venezuelan government fixed exchange rate was approximately six Bolivars to one US Dollar. By contrast, the true economic exchange rate was approximately sixty Bolivars to one US Dollar. The difference between the fixed rate and the true economic rate creates opportunity for fraud and abuse. For example, in 2014, an individual could exchange ten million US Dollars for 600 million Bolivars at the true economic rate. Then, if that individual had access to the government fixed rate, he could convert that same 600 million Bolivars into 100 million US Dollars. Essentially, in two transactions, that person could buy 100 million US Dollars for ten million US Dollars."[13]

The black market was a parallel, illegal exchange for dollars that came up with an informal daily "rate" reflecting the true economic value of the currency. An extensive network of underground retail money changers, both large and small, set up shop using foreign bank accounts to settle the ballooning volume of transactions. In theory, every government dollar issued was supposed to return to the country in the form of goods and services—anything from raw materials to finished products and all manner of services required to keep Venezuela running. Most of the subsidized dollars ended up in the black market.

Things got out of control as companies focused on finding every possible way to get cheap government dollars. It started with fake invoices and degenerated into fantastic schemes involving ghost companies, empty crates, and all sorts of imaginary transactions. The vast majority of the private sector refocused most of its energy, legacies, capital, infrastructure, and know-how on maximizing their advantage in the toxic triangle between themselves, the exchange control authority, and the illegal exchange shops. The government would not crack down on the scheme, busy as it was on its ethnic project. Most in the middle and upper classes took the government's indifference as a green light to make as much money as possible, in part because it was clear Chavista officials and supporters were implicated in every facet of the new cottage industry.

The operative capacity of most companies eroded while the paper-pushing, financial, and political skills required to navigate the arcane world of Chavista exchange controls became razor-sharp across industries. That's how 21st-Century Socialism ended up destroying the ability of most companies to manage anything other than exchange controls.

The travel sector is a perfect example of how the exchange policy affected not only the economy, but an entire generation. The exchange control law prescribed that any citizen could get several thousand dollars at deep discounts, to cover "travel expenses," if they could prove an impending trip. Bogus travel companies immediately sprouted up. At first, Venezuelans would fly to a nearby island to allow the tour operator to run their credit card for the entire permitted annual amount. Cardholders would then be paid a set amount of bolivars for their trouble, while the operator would keep the dollars. Because airlines were receiving their subsidized dollars to fly anyone from Venezuela, tickets were unbelievably inexpensive, the difference being made up by the Venezuelan treasury with payments in the US.

Eventually, thousands of college-educated professionals focused on the retail opportunity of their lifetimes. They found a way to perfect the scheme so that people did not need to leave Venezuela to cash in their yearly dollar quotas. Local operators would now just need the citizen's credit card to buy them an airline ticket that was never used but was required for the dollar quota to be activated, and proceed with the monetary operation. Airlines were ecstatic with the prospect of more sales.

The travel subsidies became a dark, tragic comedy. Entire "exiled" Venezuelan families living in Miami and Panama would begin their Far East trips at the Caracas airport to cash in their birthright first-class tickets to Hong Kong or Tokyo for a few hundred dollars each. This was the sort of coup de grace that would be giddily reported at dinner parties in Miami, right after the obligatory recounting of the latest "horror story" about Chávez.

Beyond Travel

Away from the very visible retail currency schemes, billions were being moved in all sorts of dollar-bolivar and bolivar-dollar bond schemes. The operations ranged from those that were legal, directly sanctioned by the Central Bank, even if clearly immoral, to those that constituted a straight theft from state coffers. The latter came from new government-controlled financial institutions that had the power to originate all sorts of convertible dollar debt, guaranteed by the state.

To most in the government and the private sector side, this was a once-in-a-lifetime opportunity to hit the jackpot. For several well-known bankers, whose families and friends were stridently anti-Chávez, Venezuela had always been "corrupt," and this was no different. For the younger, and more cynical, set in the mold of Jakubowicz's fictional character Juan Planchard, the stakes were uncomplicated:

> "That is how anyone who wanted money and knew how to do it got rich. Zero risk. Everything straight to your pocket, all perfectly legal and Bolivarian. It is sort of like robbing the country, except that robbery by popular consent stops being robbery and becomes a collective philosophy …"[14]

By any world standards, the scope of the extractive arrangements between traditional Venezuelan elites and the new government officials that now had power is astounding. Today it is common to speak of the "bolibourgeois" as a separate group of newly-rich people who found untold wealth through their connection to the Bolivarian government. But all along, the schemes involved members of the traditional elites.

A group of friends from some of the country's most prominent families, all in their twenties and thirties, managed to obtain more than one billion dollars' worth of contracts to revamp the electric grid. Some think the massive blackouts of 2018 and 2019 are evidence very little was ever done for the money. The same group was later implicated in an alleged multi-billion-dollar scheme to launder oil company bribes through a Swiss bank partly controlled by them. Yet their accomplished ancestors show up at every period of Venezuelan history starting with independence, the life of enlightened Caracas throughout the 19th century, and the liberal glories of the 20th century. Alongside the infamous *"bolichicos,"* as they came to be known for their connection to the Bolivarian revolution, there were hundreds of American-educated lawyers and financiers enabling bond transactions, exchange-rate schemes, bogus contracts, and myriad other operations to milk the system until the very end of the oil bonanza.

The lasting effect of the extractive activities, and the fixation on exchange rate schemes, fundamentally degraded the private sector's capabilities. Professionals with specific technical, management, building, and logistics know-how who were unwilling or unable to join the exchange control madness, left the country. The exchange control authority gave companies more dollars if they could prove a larger volume of "legitimate" imports. Local production of anything was shunned.

Contracts for building, maintenance, and control of the government infrastructure were taken away from firms with built-in capacity. They were given to a crop of paper companies with deep ties to the import schemes.

The substantial wealth transfer was a sideshow, one which conveniently put the elites aside, and disarmed them politically. The money ended up transforming the real estate market in Miami and later Madrid, and years later, billions still sit in bank accounts around the world. But most of the oil money that ended up in private hands was spent as quickly as it arrived. Little of it has been visibly invested in anything other than further speculative ventures.

The money nullified an entire social class economically and politically. With a few notable exceptions, like the Polar company holding, the private sector's willingness to focus on sham transactions crippled it. Companies across Venezuela forgot their knowledge of business and ignored the skill capital of their employees. The private sector that had been born in the 20th century died at the altar of quick, shady profits on the foreign exchange market. This broke the broader civil society's ability to influence anything. By the end, most of that legacy and its energy ended up dissipated throughout the world or destroyed.

Destroying Government Enterprises

If the government's foreign exchange policies eroded the private sector, the fate of state enterprises was even more tragic. As early as the 1970s the liberal state had followed a European model of development by owning and operating major enterprises in energy, raw materials, utilities, transportation, and finance. As the global swings for and against the virtues of free markets had influenced Latin America over several decades, the Venezuelan government had controlled or shed dozens of companies.

As in many European countries, these state enterprises were run more or less independently of government but with a general view toward profit-making. The most important of all was PDVSA, the holding controlling all oil production, processing, and transportation in the country. The company had enjoyed a reputation of independence from government influence during the thirty years before Chávez became president. Its isolation from the rough and tumble of politics would quickly end.

A key demand of Chavismo's bottom-up participatory revolution was that any enterprise in the hands of the state be thoroughly politicized. Everything, after all, was political. More to the point, it was imperative that every single company in the hands of the government be staffed by "real" Venezuelans.

This started in the oil sector as part of the effort to break up the strike of 2003. Most middle managers and company leaders who had studied abroad, had roots or an outlook from North America or Europe, were summarily dismissed. Then the Tascón List, bearing the name of every single citizen demanding a recall referendum against the president, enabled a massive purge of light-skinned employees across all government-related enterprises.

Adding to the list of companies already owned by the state in 1998, dozens of infrastructure, food, raw materials, and agricultural enterprises nationalized by the Chávez government became embroiled in a farfetched experiment.

Nationalizing and running government-owned enterprises had been perfected by socialist governments for one hundred years. From the examples in France and Germany, to the more recent profitable state ventures in China and Vietnam, there were many successful formulas to choose from. In Venezuela, participatory identity politics drove an entirely different agenda.

This story has been chronicled in the book *Comandante*, a first-person account by the *Guardian*'s Caracas correspondent Rory Carroll. Published in 2013, the book provides a unique view of events unfolding between 2004 and 2012, the years before Chávez died.[15]

In one chapter Carroll describes a visit to Ciudad Guayana, the place where every Venezuelan government since the late 1960s had invested in the promise of a non-oil economy based on hydroelectric power, ore, bauxite, gold, and diamond mining. Ciudad Guayana would become tragically violent by the 2010s, and already bore the hallmarks of squalor and massive de-industrialization. At the city's aluminum plants, in the hands of new worker-managers, everything had collapsed well before Chávez's death.

"Political managers from Caracas with no background in industry. Ideological schools set up in factories. Investment abandoned, maintenance skimped, machinery cannibalized. A catalog of grievances detailing blunders, looting, and broken promises. Venalum, they said, had at a time stopped exporting to the United States to vainly seek 'ideologically friendlier' markets in Africa and South America. After months of stockpiling, aluminum managers returned to US buyers, but then the market had crashed, losing the company millions. To curry favors with Miraflores [the presidential palace in Caracas A.N.], another company imported trucks from Belarus, Chávez's European ally, but the cabins were too high for the region's twisting paths, terrifying drivers. The trucks were abandoned. Managers at another factory halted production and sold the company's entire stock before disappearing with the cash. On and on went the denunciations, one anecdote bleaker than the last. Worst of all, said the union men, was that for the previous years bosses had refused to renew collective agreements, meaning workers lost their rights and half their wages to inflation."[16]

Carroll's descriptions show the new priorities in the running of these enterprises. The formal world of management seems to have been trumped by the personal feelings and experiences of the new leaders. Most importantly, by the intuitive sense of their ethnic legacy. In this view a government company's assets did not represent an opportunity for the country's future profit. Rather, it was booty stolen from the blood and sweat of centuries. It was treasure. And the fair and right thing to do with treasure was to distribute it.

On a grand scale this was the fate of PDVSA, the state oil company. Because the value of treasure was perceived to be intrinsic to itself, and had no relationship to exploration, extraction, refining, and its sale in global markets, the new Chavista leadership's priority was its distribution among the people. After 20,000 highly skilled managers and middle managers were fired in the PDVSA purges of 2003, more than 100,000 bona-fide Chavista party members were hired to work at the company.[17] One of the best-run energy companies in the world had become a patronage machine tasked with running myriad welfare programs. The government would distribute the treasure while crude production capabilities degraded, refining capacity dwindled, and entire operational capabilities were destroyed. Actual production sank to about a million barrels a day in 2019, down from the 3.5 million that had been produced the year before Chávez assumed power.[18] It was the lowest level in almost seventy-five years.[19] The trendlines for production into the 2020s looked bleak.

The oil story is well known and has been thoroughly reported, which is why Carroll's book is so critical in illuminating a broader nationwide trend. In passages devoted to an agricultural cooperative on confiscated land, the story repeats itself. The religious fervor of a revolution that has done away with rational thought and modern notions of wealth is everywhere:

> "I spent three days there. Conditions were primitive. Most of the men wore rags and went barefoot despite mosquitoes and snakes. They slept in hammocks in a roughly hewn wooden bungalow. There was no toilet, shower, electricity, so they answered nature's call in the fields, washed from a barrel of soapy water, and cooked over an open fire. Rice and beans for lunch, rice and beans for supper. There was no tractor or mechanized agricultural equipment, so clearing brush, chopping wood, harvesting crops, and milking cows were done by hand. It could have been the 19th century. Then at night, the same workers would gather around the fire to dream of revolution: 'This is part of something bigger. We're building up the country, we're fixing it.'"[20]

The ideas, the philosophy, and the outcomes would repeat themselves in many instances beyond government-owned industries and farms.

The Venezuelan welfare state built in the 20th century is perhaps the prime example. Its reach had been vast, all-encompassing, and critical to the lives of millions. In health, safety, education, infrastructure, and many other sectors, Venezuelans had depended on the work of ministries and their large operations.

Dismantling the Government

The fate of the country's public health system is a perfect case study of how Misiones destroyed the executive branch of government. The Misión Barrio Adentro started as a small pilot project in 2003 to bring Cuban doctors and health workers to the most impoverished communities in Caracas.[21] Informal settlements that had seldom seen health aid reach them would be showered with the sort of bottom-up attention that seemed impossible before. Cuban health workers working for their government and paid for with Venezuelan oil went where no Venezuelan doctor dared go to service these desperately poor communities. The missionary doctors and nurses lived in the impoverished, violent communities while attending to their health.

Sending health workers to the places they were most needed made perfect sense. And because of the unique characteristics of Cuba's totalitarian society, there would be no shortage of missionaries. Where the prior Republic had failed, here was a turn-key solution that promised spectacular results.

Quickly, an emergency measure to bring a few hundred Cuban health workers to desperate favelas in early 2003 was turned into a grandiose idea by 2004: make Misión Barrio Adentro the centerpiece of the government's health program. Eventually, 15,000 to 20,000 Cuban health workers would be working all over Venezuela.[22]

Understanding the structure and role of Barrio Adentro can be confusing, even when reading the government's own explanation. A 2006 document submitted to the World Health Organization and co-signed by nineteen Venezuelan and Cuban government experts, and three academics from Venezuela, Canada, and Germany, offers some ideas.[23] According to the document, Barrio Adentro was charged by a presidential decree with "coordinating and implementing" all primary health care functions across the government. The organization would take "precedence" over the Ministry of Health and would not be subordinated to any "health plan or program" from preexisting health authorities. Funding was to come from "extraordinary appropriations," meaning those outside of the regular budgetary process. The "design" of all health programs would be performed in conjunction with "neighborhood health committees."[24]

The fuzzy legal structure of the Misión would be elaborated upon by one of the WHO document's co-authors in a later academic paper. Dr. Carles Muntaner explained that Barrio Adentro was "administered by the 'Oro Negro' [Black Gold, A.N] Civil Association, [and] was responsible for the implementation and coordination of the Primary Health Care Program, with participation by the ministries of Health, Labor, Energy, Defense, the president of PDVSA and Frente

Francisco de Miranda [an organization of social rights activists, A.N.], and the mayors of two Caracas municipalities, Sucre and Libertador."[25]

The organization's day-to-day operation seems to have been just as confusing. As reported in the original WHO document, Cuban health workers conducted extensive health surveys, but there is no mention of coordination with the legacy Ministry of Health's epidemiological division. Instead, the data went back to the Barrio Adentro headquarters, the Social Security Administration, and municipal health authorities.[26]

When the system was initially conceived, patient referrals to the network of existing public hospitals were not planned. Instead, patients were referred to hospitals deemed supportive, like the Military Hospital. Within a year, a directory of "friendly" doctors identified across the system would be used to refer all the organization's patients.[27]

The WHO document's authors make it seem as if the Ministry of Health and its decades-old network of rural and urban primary care clinics, and its large public hospitals, did not exist. They would play no role in the revolution. By design they would be left to wither away unfunded, and without a clear role in national health efforts. However, by 2006, the year the document was published, the Ministry of Health had been part of two consecutive Chávez administrations and led by his political appointees for seven long years.

Only a brand-new, independent, and all-powerful organization would be able to bypass what in other parts of the world has been called the "deep state." In the 2004 words of Alí Rodríguez Araque, a key Chávez ally and at various times head of the Energy, Finance, and Foreign Relations ministries:

"the Missions are nothing other than a seed in a new way to conceive of institutions; before a great obstacle such as that of the bureaucratic state, inefficient and ineffective, we begin to see, next to it, parallel structures."[28]

While the original organizational planning did not concern itself with the Ministry of Health, there was plenty of thought given to grassroots health committees, themselves affiliated with neighborhood councils. By decree, Barrio Adentro had to work alongside these organizations to create its health programs.

By 2006 Barrio Adentro had hired, and trained, 150,000 "health promoters" charged with disseminating critical public health information door to door. The World Health Organization reported that in just the first three months of that year, 41,639 community health assemblies (with the participation of 1,423,815 people) were held all over Venezuela.[29] Dr. Muntaner and his colleagues leave no doubt who was to be in control: "The design and realization of all activities is controlled by decisions made by the community, while residents of the neighborhood participate in administration and delivery of primary health."[30]

This was vintage Jean-Jacques Rousseau: people knew their health problems better than the experts. The sick knew better than their doctors. The never-ending popular assemblies encouraged people to discuss and participate in every facet of their own health on a permanent basis, regardless of their work hours, chores, difficulties commuting, or other familial obligations.

By 2007 the Misión Barrio Adentro, still for all practical purposes acting independently of the Health

Ministry and within an ambiguous legal and budgetary framework, had spawned three sequels. Barrio Adentro II, charged with building or taking over government care centers for advanced diagnoses, rehabilitation, and something called Advanced Technology Centers. Barrio Adentro III, and then another iteration, Barrio Adentro IV, which plunged the organization into highly specialized facilities like a newly opened infant cardiology hospital.[31] The government propaganda machine went into overdrive with slick short documentaries showcasing state-of-the-art new hospitals and smiling children, alongside relentless television commercials heralding a new dawn in health care.[32]

The revolution was in a rush to transform every facet of society. Barrio Adentro had little in the way of a legal or compliance framework or an internal auditing system. Amid "social transformation" there was no time to plan, ponder, or coordinate. Instead, billions of dollars would be spent buying whatever was necessary to fix Venezuela's health care, now, immediately.

Health care services were being delivered by two separate organizations that did not talk to each other. The Cuban medical mission managed thousands of "popular" and hundreds of midsize clinics.[33] There is no evidence of coordination with epidemiological vigilance networks, vaccination control databases, or, presumably, contact with doctors and public health officials who had intimate knowledge of the history of these issues in the country.

By mid-2010 Dr. María Sader, the air force doctor who led Barrio Adentro, was named Minister of Health. Eleven years after becoming president, Chávez turned full circle with an official takeover of the legacy health institution by his revolutionary start-up.[34]

Yet there is no evidence of a sustained effort to properly merge both organizations. No efforts appear to have been made to rescue the legacy health infrastructure. The government's objective seemed to be to multiply the number of primary care facilities across the country. The sheer number of units and of their mirror popular health committees, not the functional integration of the entire health care system, became the measure of success.

But the inevitable consequence of dismantling the health care sector would soon be evident. By 2014 oil prices faltered before eventually caving in, severely affecting the financing of health missions.[35] By 2016 most of the Cuban medical health workers in Venezuela had left.[36] The momentum of political assemblies and unsustainable participation of transient health workers stopped. Misión Barrio Adentro collapsed, while the century-old foundations of the legacy health care system had already been destroyed.

Measles, TB, malaria, and other preventable diseases reappeared without any organized way to confront them. In the words of an academic paper published by the CDC's *Emerging Infectious Diseases* journal:

"The circulation of measles in Venezuela was preceded by the progressive interruption of the national immunization program since the year 2010, along with the dismantling of the primary healthcare infrastructure."[37]

By the third quarter of 2018 Venezuela had 5,525 measles cases, or 68% of all reported in the Americas, as well as 85% of all measles-related deaths.[38] According to Human Rights Watch, quoting the Pan American Health Organization, there had been only a single case of measles in Venezuela between 2008 and 2015.[39]

Malaria cases surged 359% to 136,402 cases between 2010 and 2015, and then rose 71% between 2016 and 2017 to reach 411,586.[40] At the main tuberculosis clinic in Caracas, which had shown 5% positive rates for TB in all adults tested between 2013 and 2015, the figure jumped by 9% by the fourth quarter of 2017. By January of 2018, it had reached 14%.[41] According to Human Rights Watch there were 13,000 cases of tuberculosis in 2017, the highest recorded in forty years.[42]

After nine years with zero reported cases of diphtheria, from mid-2006 to mid-2008 2,000 cases were reported nationwide.[43] The government's own numbers show that maternal mortality rose 65% while infant mortality increased by 30% between 2015 and 2016.[44]

Citing the Pan American Health Organization, Human Rights Watch indicates that 87% of the more than 79,000 people living with HIV who were registered to receive anti-retroviral treatment from the Venezuelan government were not getting anything by 2018.[45]

Dengue cases, as measured by recurring epidemics, rose more than fivefold between 2010 and 2016. Six increasingly large epidemics were recorded between 2007 and 2016, compared with four in the previous sixteen years. A Chikungunya outbreak saw an estimated two million suspected cases, more than twelve times the official count.[46]

Between 2017 and the second half of 2018, hospitals all over the country reported having no supplies of any kind, in addition to being unable to cope with frequent power shortages, and a monumental malnutrition problem that compounded every single health issue.[47]

The collapse of the health care system by 2017, beyond these numbers, was confirmed by experts and impartial organizations throughout the world. "The situation in Venezuela is dire," according to John Spiegel, director of the Johns Hopkins Center of Humanitarian Health. For him, "to see this incredible decline in the health infrastructure in such a short period of time is quite astonishing."[48]

Chávez, Chavismo, and its intellectual supporters in Venezuela and abroad, had argued since 2004 that the old liberal state could not produce people who cared for the well-being of the majority. The "representative" governments from the 20th century had not been able to deliver for all. But if there is an area where the liberal state was able to create long-lasting institutions with veritable results, it was health care.

The first nationwide, publicly funded efforts to eradicate malaria started during Rómulo Betancourt's first government in 1945.[49] The program had begun under the old generals in the mid-1930s. Dutch, British, and American oil companies had been active in the eradication of the disease in their areas of influence.[50] But Betancourt's social priorities and taxes on oil companies provided a new impetus. The efforts led by Dr. Arnoldo Gabaldón started with a massive campaign to eradicate mosquitoes in malaria zones. Within three to five years malaria had disappeared from the areas where the infecting mosquito predominated, although the WHO would not certify the disease had been eradicated from the country.[51]

Betancourt and his party would be thrown out by a coup in 1948, only to return to power by February of 1959. One of his first acts the second-time around was to name Dr. Arnoldo Gabaldón as Health Minister. The renewed emphasis and funding would officially free the country of malaria by 1961.[52] Gabaldón's work did not stop as efforts to build a robust central health authority continued for a decade. Critically, his lifework had been dedicated to getting the academic and practical experience necessary to build such an organization.

Gabaldón had started work as an assistant at the Ministry of Health in 1928, when generals still ruled the country. This gave him an early acquaintance with the ins and outs of the health bureaucracy across the country. He then studied at the German Institute of Naval and Tropical Diseases and the Italian Experimental Station for the Antimalarial Battle, before returning to Venezuela in 1932. He received a health science doctorate from Johns Hopkins University in 1935 through the Rockefeller Foundation and interned at Rockefeller University in New York City.[53]

Upon returning to Venezuela, he joined the Ministry once again. At that time, fighting malaria was the country's number one priority. By 1945 no pathogen, including the influenza virus that caused the 1918 pandemic, caused more deaths than malaria in Venezuela. The population had declined between 1891 and 1920 because of the disease.[54] The historical devastation caused by malaria no doubt contributed to the zeal with which a generation of reformers fought a tireless battle against it.

First in his front-line role eradicating malaria, and then as the builder of a first-class health ministry and epidemiology network, Gabaldón delivered the most enduring results in the history of Venezuelan health care. Over three decades he dedicated himself to reforming, modernizing, and growing an existing, prior organization. The deep differences between Betancourt's perspective and that of the military governments he had overturned had no real impact on Gabaldón's work. His formula of achieving scale through incremental reforms, long-term training of middle cadres, deploying compliance systems, and creating strong legal frameworks, continued until the 1970s. Gabaldón was able to defeat every health challenge he met, to international acclaim. The epidemiology systems he created prevented the return of any serious epidemic for more than forty years, until everything he had built was dismantled.

Gabaldón's legacy was overturned in the name of the people's originary wisdom and the virtues of intuitive decision-making in health matters. Yet, no one suffered more than those in whose name the health sector was destroyed. By 2017, over a decade into the Chavista dismantling of the liberal state, more than 400,000 Venezuelans had been infected by malaria. This increase amounted to 84% of the rise in malaria cases between 2010 and 2017 around the world.[55]

The Violence

The health care implosion was not unique. When the humanitarian crisis broke out, safety and safe passage across the country, macroeconomic and monetary stability, food import and distribution, the oil infrastructure, and the power grid, also crumbled under the weight of a comprehensive political transformation inspired by a romantic ideology of people's sovereignty.

How Venezuela became one of the world's most dangerous places is ultimately related to the same strands that made health care collapse. But the way this calamity unfolded was different.

In the traditional revolutionary playbook, governments and rulers must centralize all law enforcement functions. At first, and at least in appearance, the Chávez government followed that path. Initially the government advocated the creation of a federal police to unify several criminal justice organizations. From day one, Chavismo was against the idea of decentralization of municipal power and explicitly opposed to the idea that mayors would have police forces. Chávez supported police reforms that sought to organize and streamline the more chaotic administration of justice from the previous century. These reforms sought to improve statutes and clarify lines of authority, and, at least to some academics, seemed somewhat promising.[56]

But those efforts turned out to be either a false start, or a smokescreen. Or plans changed. The 2002 coup d'état against Chávez, and the massive oil workers' strike a few months later, revealed the extent to which his opponents could influence the state and reach its vital functions. While Chavismo seemed to win every battle, it had been constantly forced to fight on the defensive and on its opponents' turf.

Chávez understood his opposition in the upper middle classes, within the middle ranks of government, in the most conservative parts of the army, at the banks, stock exchange houses, and the US embassy, had plenty of money and the ability to influence events. Hawkish President George W. Bush had just won reelection in the United States.

Back in the early 1960s Fidel Castro had faced determined opposition to his rule, but he had been able to isolate his enemies. He and Che Guevara concentrated all power, built an army and a security apparatus from scratch, sent thousands of enemies to the firing squads, and frightened the rest to flee into exile. At the height of the Cold War, an island so close to the United States offered tantalizing possibilities to a rich and powerful ally like the Soviet Union. In retrospect, Fidel Castro had taken advantage of a unique situation to get a complete grip on Cuba.

The realities of Venezuela were different. Chávez faced a security situation he could never really control. The National Guard remained a threat. Their potential involvement in profitable businesses at ports, border controls, logging sites, gold mines, national parks, and jails gave them financial autonomy. The Caracas Metropolitan Police had opened fire against his supporters during the 2002 coup. American embassy officials and military liaisons at bases throughout the country had on-going relationships with middle-ranking officers in the navy, air force, and even the army. While he had worked hard at neutralizing their power, Chávez had no way of knowing the extent of their real influence. In the end, there were too many factors beyond his control.

On the other hand, other factors played to Chavez's potential advantage. Long-standing leftist gangs in Caracas's downtown neighborhoods had proven loyal to him during the coup. In addition, the original grassroots organizations of his ruling party, Círculos Bolivarianos, had surrounded the presidential palace with tens of thousands of people while he had been detained. People on the informal side of the city seemed ready to die for him.

He could not neutralize many of the forces arrayed against him, but he could light a firestorm of violence. If Venezuelan history had any lessons for Chávez, it was that chieftains from The Plains had successfully defied substantial odds, repeatedly, by sowing chaos and death throughout the land. Their opponents had never understood what hit them.

Within weeks of the 2002 coup, Chávez and his supporters set out to multiply the number of Círculos Bolivarianos in every favela, housing project, and working-class district. A reported 8,000 Círculos became 70,000 in just a few months.[57] The Círculos were small groups of no more than a dozen people loosely tied to the ruling party organization.[58] On paper they were a nationwide network of political supporters, but ultimately it was far more complex than that.

Starting in the 1970s, left-wing activists had created paramilitary neighborhood organizations in the western side of the city.[59] At different times they had successfully battled government forces to claim a degree of autonomy in their neighborhoods. During the 1992 Caracas riots, military units were held for days by armed local gangs in the *23 de Enero* housing project, and in the end retreated. The rise of drug sales, extortion, kidnapping, and other criminal activities through the 1990s and 2000s became mainstays of financing for some of these groups.[60] When the Círculos Bolivarianos were started within Chávez's party, the blurry line between politics and crime that had defined armed political organizing within the Caracas favelas could not be suddenly erased.

The written orders or the specific mechanics of arming the Círculos Bolivarianos with military weapons after the coup remain unknown. Yet a consensus exists that such a decision was made and carried out.[61, 62] In some cases, existing armed groups became part of the Círculos organization, and in others brand-new armed cells were activated throughout major cities in the country. In Chávez's words, "our revolution is peaceful but armed."[63]

The Círculos and their successors, the colectivos, became an ad hoc network of gangs armed with military grade weaponry, operating well outside the liberal state, and mushrooming all over the country alongside the army and the police. Newly empowered, and much better armed, many of the groups moved aggressively into local drug markets, and began sustained campaigns of kidnapping, armed theft, and extortion.[64]

The bargain for Chávez and Chavismo was that this was not a pyramidal organization with a strong command at the top. For years before 2002, Chávez had grappled with the Círculos' defiant autonomy from their decades-long activism. But if Chavismo wanted to unleash a violent storm while staying out of the reach of its enemies, tens of thousands of Círculos would have to be created overnight. Only an organic and semi-independent organization in which no direct military orders could be given or would be received could grow that fast.[65] Hugo Chávez would have to flow with his new semi-independent allies, as caudillos like Boves and Páez had always known how to do in The Plains.

Arming tens of thousands of loosely tied Círculos had an immediate impact on crime throughout the country's major cities. Chávez had unleashed a wave of violence the likes of which Venezuela had not seen in over a century. The middle classes and the political opposition were completely overwhelmed by the storm.

The second critical factor in Chavez's calculations was the potential threat the National Guard presented. A cross between the Spanish Guardia Civil and the French Gendarmerie, the Guard is the armed forces branch tasked with running the country's jails and national parks, safeguarding federal highways and ports of entry, stopping contraband, and leading the fight against narcotics. In that sense, the National Guard was embedded throughout the life of the country and could easily tap into dozens of illegal profit-making opportunities. From Chávez's point of view, the puzzle was not small. He had to ask himself whether to attack frontally and tame a potentially autonomous threat or find an indirect way to weaken its might.

Skipping the chance to rein in the institution, Chavez decided to unleash it. Free to exploit its potential and sowing chaos throughout the land, the Guard would keep its gaze away from the center of power.

It soon splintered into fiefdoms, turning most domestic security functions into discrete, for-profit ventures. As a result, the state lost complete control of its jails and saw an explosion of contraband. Protected crime organizations and drug cartels became more powerful. Some suspect it was the first governmental institution to be thoroughly penetrated by Colombian drug cartels.[66] Gasoline contraband between Colombia and Venezuela would grow as a significant business.[67] Miners accelerated massive illegal mining on government lands.[68]

For Chávez and his Minister of Defense, neutralizing a significant force in the short term while further destabilizing the old order was worth any long-term consequences. This stance would turn out to be catastrophic for the country, and a critical factor in the breakdown of society that led to the humanitarian crisis.

The third critical piece of the new safety and security landscape involved the correctional system. The changes would not take place immediately after the coup, but a few years later with the creation of the Ministry of Prisons in 2011. Chávez would not only take the administration of jails away from its traditional home at the Ministry of Justice, but would also name a close political ally, Iris Varela, as minister.

By that point, most penitentiaries seemed to be run by violent gangs that heavily influenced the day-to-day running of their institutions. The National Guard appeared to control the outside perimeter of all jails and therefore supervised what and who came in or out of each building. But inside, one or several *prans* seemed to rule. The word *pran*, a new noun for a prison gang leader, became synonymous across the country with the head of any gang, inside or outside the penal system.[69]

The newly sworn-in Minister of Prisons, who would effectively run all jails for the following nine years (save for a six-month hiatus in 2017), had a clear agenda she wasted no time implementing. One of her first public activities was to pose for photos with feared gang leaders El Conejo and

Wilmito, at their jail cells in Margarita Island and Ciudad Bolivar, respectively.[70, 71, 72]

It seems absurd for the head of prisons to be photographed with an inmate, much less hugging the convicted head of a drug cartel like El Conejo, while sitting on a cot in his cell. And yet the photo's underlying message is clear: both the minister and the inmate are wearing red shirts, the color of the Chavista party. Not only is the Chavista top correctional officer playing the guest, but one of the country's most dangerous inmates plays host in his humble cell. By posing for and distributing the picture, Minister Varela formalized a new balance of power in Venezuela's jails. El Conejo telegraphed his public support for Chavismo. The *pran* did not just rule the San Antonio prison, he was also head of the Tren del Pacífico drug cartel. His power extended well outside the prison walls.[73]

The extent of El Conejo's power within the prison is evident in footage of his 2016 funeral on YouTube.[74] Recorded inside of the San Antonio jail, the video shows his gang firing an impressive and varied array of high-caliber guns into the air. An expensive gun salute by inmates, inside a jail, to their fallen leader.

Minister Varela had another picture taken with Wilmito, the then-feared *pran* of Vista Hermosa prison. There are at least two photos of him and the Minister of Prisons warmly hugging each other.[75, 76] A former boxer, Wilmito was a colorful character about whom much was written. When respected journalist Alfredo Meza visited Wilmito to interview him, the *pran* had an AR-15 assault rifle propped against the wall in his jail cell, as well as a 9mm pistol.[77]

In other interviews, he claimed his different jail businesses generated US$3 million per year.[78] His real value to Varela and the revolution was his considerable media exposure. A friendly photo with the feared Wilmito sealed a new alliance both inside and outside of prison walls. The *prans* in charge of every prison would no longer deal with the National Guard, but directly with Varela, Chávez's close political confidant. In turn, the Chavista grassroots movement that Minister Varela represented to a larger extent than most other government officials, acknowledged the *prans* as their own.

The alliance gained considerable significance as the jail population ballooned, tripling between 2000 and 2017, and organized crime exploded around the country.[79] While the state's security organizations retreated from their public safety functions, this did not mean they disappeared. Now in complicity with gangs, criminal elements, cartels, and on their own, they used every means at their disposal (including depriving enemies of their liberty) to profit and to cement their power. That is why, while crime soared unchecked, the jail population increased as well.

The connection between jails and poor neighborhoods became closer than ever. Drugs, weapons, soldiers, and information started to flow seamlessly between prisons and the outside world. Culturally, it is difficult to tell if life in prisons started to resemble life outside, or the other way around.

Just as the power of the state vanished from the running of penitentiaries, now left in the hands of government-friendly *prans*, the police literally disappeared from most neighborhoods. More important, perhaps, is how the police as an omnipresent factor of power disappeared from the minds of many Venezuelans. The stories of the time were certainly reflecting this new reality.

A series of YouTube short films by former barber turned filmmaker Jackson Gutierrez followed the lives of *petit prans* in Caracas's favelas.[80] Part soap opera, part reality television, the scripted shorts follow those fighting over control of stairways and narrow passages up and down the hilly informal settlements overlooking the formal city. The protagonists are far from the hardened gangsters of *City of God*, the genre's classic. Instead, they were cast to represent the beautified realism of soap operas: the ideal of an average Venezuelan.

The plot is the same in every video: women and men loosely tied to gangs battle each other for control of the stairways and passages of their own neighborhoods. They battle as if in feudal times, armed to the teeth and with no awareness of a central state, municipal police, or a national army. During hours of scripted video, the only obstacle to gaining control is another gang, another lord, a different *pran*. The state is gone from these YouTube stories and every woman and man is out for themselves. The informal urban grid where most urban dwellers live is depicted as another prison left to its own devices by a retreating National Guard.

Much like the picaresque narratives it borrows from, Venezuelan cinema has often told its classic action movies from the point of view of the bad guy. Protagonists need to overcome the police and their actions, be they bumbling or sadistic, in order for plots to advance. From the neorealist *Soy un Delincuente* to the psychological thriller *Secuestro Express*, the state's security forces matter a great deal in every story. It would have been unthinkable for Trece, Budú, and Niga, the kidnappers in Jakubowicz's *Secuestro*, not to worry about the police. But in the new Chavista paradigm, conflict was driven by warring independent forces in a world without a sign of government.

Fiction became reality. The real *prans* also posted their homemade videos on YouTube and Facebook. Gangs of all kinds displayed their weapons and their power at funerals, and in the middle of the day in their neighborhoods, with a total sense of impunity.[81] Looking at these images it is clear the police were no longer a factor.

These narratives of a disappearing state only make sense by thinking of a new kind of power. Chavismo was in control, but thanks to the decentralized network of proxies partly built by Minister Varela. In a broader sense, the network included armed *colectivos* within the socialist party, units of the National Guard, the new federal police, the investigative and the political police, each attending to their fiefdoms, none interested in a collective peace. The sense of chaos in the streets, partly fed by constant battles between all these actors, allowed Chavismo to thrive even as the country plunged into a nightmare of violence.

Crime numbers from the United Nations tracked the dismantling of the Venezuelan justice system and its centralized security functions. By 2005, a year after the beginning of the oil boom, murders per 100,000 reached forty-five nationwide, a substantial jump from the thirteen murders per 100,000 reported in 1998, the year of Chávez's first election. By 2012 they had reached fifty-three, the third highest in the world, and the point at which the government simply stopped counting or refused to share reliable data.[82]

Either the dismantling of the criminal justice system crippled the government's ability to compile the data, or the numbers were unpublishable, or both. No matter the answer, it seems logical to assume the actual figure grew substantially.

Local NGO Observatorio Venezolano de la Violencia, made up of researchers from seven private and public universities, continued to make projections of the growing violence based on the scant and often questionable data they could find. By their estimates, they reported ninety murders per 100,000 inhabitants in 2015, or a staggering 27,875 deaths. Around the world, only the conflicts in Syria and Afghanistan recorded more deaths per capita that year. Dr Dorothy Kronick, a professor at the University of Pennsylvania, disputed the NGO's methodology by raising the possibility that deaths were being double-counted due to overlapping journalistic reports and government raw data.[83] Yet, her own estimates of sixty-nine deaths per 100,000 people fall back on raw data from the Health Ministry and the national police, institutions undergoing massive upheavals during those years.[84]

More than anything, the confusion about the actual number of homicides points to a breakdown in the traditional categories of criminal statistics. It is even possible that violent deaths in a year when the lines usually separating the actions of governmental, criminal, and paramilitary actors were blurred turned out be much higher than has been reported. At any rate, Dr. Kronick's conservative estimate would make the year 2015 the country's most dangerous on record.

As the humanitarian crisis continued, the Observatorio de la Violencia 2017 number remained at eighty-nine deaths per 100,000. In 2018, when millions of refugees had already fled the country, the number settled at eighty-one.[85] Although overall murders were slightly down, by that measure Venezuela remained one of the world's top five most dangerous places.

If violence by gangs and individuals in the face of the state's retreat stopped its steep climb after 2017, the security situation took another ominous turn. By 2018 the model for state control through decentralized violence was significantly upgraded with the founding of a new commando unit named FAES.

Starting after the April 2002 coup, the secret police, and the nascent national police, were built out to enforce state security. This was narrowly understood as the preservation of power by Chávez and Chavismo.[86]

In the years before the humanitarian crisis, the government had such popular support, and the opposition was so weak, that these newly built security organizations did not have a lot of work. They were deployed to spy on military officers, opposition leaders, diplomats, and specific individuals posing a threat to Chavismo. But as state services crumbled, the economy nose-dived, and violence in the streets exploded, the threat of urban revolt against the government became real. No one expected an opposition-led uprising, but rather an organic explosion of rage by the hungry and the destitute.

The old armed Círculos Bolivarianos or its successor organizations, long since deployed to put down dissent during opposition marches and nationwide strikes, were not enough to face a citywide revolt.

The solution, announced by President Maduro in July 2017, was to form a wide-ranging commando-style unit within the National Police.[87,88] By 2018 the Special Actions Forces, or FAES by their Spanish initials, were operational, with headquarters next to a local morgue and a skull as its seal.

The new organization fit neatly into the Chavista world of proxies, albeit one with better financing, intelligence, and reach. Its objective was not to eliminate or oppose other gangs, regulate other violent actors, or guarantee the right of safe passage throughout the country. Its principal mission became to squelch any signs of general unrest or explicit anti-government activity. The extent of the unit's disregard for civil peace became clear by 2019, when photos of FAES commandos on duty wearing Halloween skull masks became widespread.[89] The balaclavas of 2018 had apparently not instilled sufficient fear among the country's citizens.

The United Nations affirmed that FAES was directly involved in the killing of 5,287 people in 2018. All told, the UN reported 9,000 killings by government forces "for resistance to authority" over eighteen months between 2018 and 2019.[90] The 2019 report on violent deaths by the NGO Observatorio speaks for itself: 6,588 confirmed homicides, 4,632 murders in unknown circumstances, and 5,286 deaths while resisting authority.

Addressing the ominous government category of "killed while resisting authority" the UN's Human Rights Commission was explicit: "there are reasonable grounds to believe that many of these killings [in Venezuela] constitute extrajudicial executions committed by the security forces."

Heavily armed, masked, and roving through the country's cities in pickup trucks, the new commandos were the final victory of the project to dismantle the old central state that so many progressive thinkers around the world had imagined was at the root of Venezuela's problems.

But there was still a missing piece in the grand puzzle of the new Venezuelan state power. Chávez and Chavismo needed a legal and legitimizing origin for their authority within the new society they were forging. They found it by shifting power from the "illegitimate and corrupt" representative congress to a new form of council-based popular power. It would be the ultimate Rousseauian accomplishment.

Originary Direct Democracy

As the global economic and political challenges had become more complex during the early 2000s, many around the world pined for the romantic simplicity of council-based government. Instead of a politics driven by an abstract and ever-complex state, councils were supposed to devolve all power to the people. They would bury representative legislative government. This solution had come in many flavors throughout the history of socialism, including Trotskyite and Gramscian alternatives. The American variants always had a more utopian edge, and sometimes a touch of Jefferson.

For Chávez, the idea of councils meant the realization of his identity quest. They would organize "his Venezuelans" in every neighborhood around a strong political mission. In principle and as explained in hundreds of speeches, state power no longer flowed through mediators. It was exercised directly by the people from the bottom of society.

The creation of council-based government was first announced by Chávez in 2004 and became a more articulated reality as part of the 21st-Century Socialism promised in 2005.[91] The process would be self-managed by those organizing themselves in their neighborhoods. Between 200 and 400 families within a given area could be automatically recognized as a council.[92] By 2006 the entire project was endowed with the legitimacy of a congressional law.[93] Direct funding from the executive branch began in 2007.[94]

It was no accident that Michael Albert, long-time American guru of councils, would decamp to Caracas sometime after Chávez announced his new initiative. In a 2008 interview, Albert was asked if the councils could become the only source of power in Venezuela. His answer is telling:

> "I certainly think that is possible, and that that is the goal, not just conceivable, at least in many people's minds, including in the relevant political ministries. I sat in offices and heard them explain their hopes for these councils becoming the seat of governing power throughout the country, describing the 50,000 councils that were needed with about 30,000 currently formed— and describing the gains in confidence and methods also needed within the councils, and explaining that yes, these would be above mayors and governors and even the president. So, yes, having them be the primary locus of government power is the aim."[95]

Evidently no one was thinking about how councils would fit along with the Misión organizations, created at the same time, or with the older paramilitary Círculos Bolivarianos, or the proxy armed gangs then emerging throughout the country. Albert was interviewed in 2008, when the impact of Misiones was already visible. The role of the Círculos in the revolution was also widely publicized by then. Every official Albert spoke to certainly knew of the many on-going initiatives, even as they pledged to place the power of Popular Councils above that of the president.

As Councils grew in number and importance, their objectives and jurisdiction clashed directly with that of Misiones. The latter grew exponentially between 2006 and 2010, and not just in the health area.[96] There were Misiones for literacy, for housing, and to address myriad other needs. As we have seen, Misión Barrio Adentro depended on constant political assemblies in every neighborhood. By their own count, over a million health assemblies had taken place during three months in 2008 alone.[97] Other Misiones also required considerable amounts of local involvement. Their very nature devolved all power and decision-making to the people, essentially turning individuals' private lives into never-ending assemblies.

As the political infighting shifted priorities and focus within the executive branch, new kinds of popular committees, communes, and other types of grassroots organizations were also created and recognized. By 2010 Congress passed a commune law.[98] It endowed the communes with the same kind of self-governing status of a geographical area as had been given to the Councils in 2006, mysteriously overlapping them.

After 2009, the spread of self-governing organizations, which by then also included agricultural cooperatives and worker councils whose prerogatives sometimes conflicted with the neighborhood organizations, became unmanageable.

The rhetoric of people's councils, committees, and organizations at the grassroots had convinced Chavismo they had empowered the people. Yet the spectacular growth of this kind of people-power was also driven by money. Every organization, and consequently every network of organizations, was to be funded by the oil state. A wild entrepreneurial streak drove political operators, ministers, governors, local officials, and those in the Chavista party to create and support their own networks. Council government became an excuse for the building of political platforms, each vying for their slice of power, influence, and money. Some of the financing came directly from the oil company, some from ministries, or even state governments. Whenever the president visited any of these organizations and heard the complaints of its members, he would order immediate funding from unspecified sources.

While half a dozen laws were passed between 2009 and 2012 relating to popular power, the most noteworthy effort during these years was the creation of a Ministry for Councils.[99] The cabinet-level organization was later renamed Ministry of Communes.

The ministry was supposed to coordinate the unruly edifice of people-power. Fifty thousand and probably more councils, communes, co-ops, popular defense organizations, and myriad other forms of popular power would now be organized by the executive branch. Implicitly, the Ministry of Councils became legislator and tribunal as conflicting jurisdictions, sources of funding, and legal roles needed to be sorted out.

But no single individual or group within Chavismo had enough political capital to put an end to the chaos. The very nature of a process in which executive and legislative power were being dismantled, and the fact that anyone could organize a council, delivered a stalemate.

At the highest levels of government, different factions fought for control of what had become armies of followers. The Ministry of Councils was never able to wrest control of significant sources of funding from the oil company PDVSA. The Cuban legation and a new cadre of leaders that now controlled Misión Barrio Adentro would not let go of their powerbase. Cooperatives and communes that were associated with agriculture and food production centers were related to other sources of funding and political control. Powerful state governors in agricultural states, and officials in different ministries, also had their interests to protect.

The conflicts were not a trivial political fight. Councils had been given real power and their conflicts with other parts of the new state machinery were real. In the frenzy of people-power, and the fierce jockeying between different factions for bigger budgets, the ultimate outcome was the continued degradation of the executive branch.

The 2006 law already lists among the councils' tasks the management of housing and infrastructure projects in each of their neighborhoods.[100] That the federal government had a 100-year plus legacy of public civil works seemed irrelevant.[101] Even if Chavismo considered that history politically poisoned, the mountainous terrain in Caracas and a recurring summer monsoon throughout the country made the building of roads and drainage technically challenging.

In earthquake-prone Caracas and other parts of Venezuela, it did not make sense to build, fix, or upgrade housing haphazardly.

As with much of the Chávez people's revolution, feasibility was never a factor. And reforming ministries the Chávez administration had controlled for years to make them responsive and agile in their delivery of services was never on the table.

The contradictions between council government and the real challenges of managing infrastructure works were just part of the problem. The very existence of councils further complicated the work of already "politized" health, literacy, housing, and myriad other Misiones. The work of rebuilding, improving, building access, and providing health care to neighborhoods in poverty, and extreme poverty, was refocused into endless assemblies. Every neighbor was given a voice and a vote while much of the organizational energy of each organization overlapped. The traditional government organizations that at least knew how to build resilient, sustainable, and effective solutions were specifically excluded from the process. Well before Chávez's death, the underlying conflicts between all the actors involved in the direct democracy experiment had contributed to the growing political chaos.

By 2014 oil prices faltered, and eventually caved in. The oil company that had financed a great deal of the council revolution confronted dwindling revenues and ballooning debt payments. The government felt the revenue squeeze at all levels. Councils, communes, committees, and all Misiones suffered massive defunding. After a decade of people's assemblies and very little building, the entire project crumbled.

As the humanitarian crisis hit the country, the wreckage of the council movement had left a footprint of organization in every single low-income neighborhood. Running against time and a tsunami of hunger, the ruling political party, PSUV, moved in to take over what was effectively a zombie political structure. Something called Local Committees for Supply and Production, or CLAP after their Spanish initials, were established over what had been myriad organizations. Certified party members following hierarchical orders were installed as the leadership of these committees.[102]

The council infrastructure became the government's chief food distribution network. Each group would receive weekly food boxes to be distributed in the neighborhood. As the Misiones and other government paid jobs and monetary handouts disappeared, as all other services vanished and no one had anything to eat, CLAP committees and their eponymous boxes became the only means to acquire food available to most Venezuelans.

Private distribution mechanisms and know-how had been decimated by the exchange-rate schemes, and the exile of tens of thousands of middle managers. Most Venezuelan logistics experts of that generation had found work in Miami, Tampa, and other commercial hubs around the world. Their absence proved tragic. Two years into the CLAP experiment, the average Venezuelan lost twenty-four pounds over twelve months.[103] Yet enough food trickled down, the only available to millions, for the new status quo to continue.

The Chavista state's answer to the vast welfare networks of the 20th century had put the country in a time machine. Venezuela would again look like it had in the years of the hungry 19th century. The similarities between the 1800s and the new world created by Chavismo would not stop there.

The Army of 2019

Back in the year 1819 the country was ravaged by almost a decade of savage warfare. The final battle against the Spanish Crown, in the field of Carabobo, would not come for two years. Yet the dynamic of power that would define the newly independent country was clear. With all agricultural resources ransacked, the place overrun by banditry and the structures of a once mighty colonial administration gone, feudal forces would battle for power for the better part of a century.

The largest, most organized, disciplined, and mobile of the early forces answered to General Páez. They called themselves the Republican Army, flew its flags, and were nominally commanded by Bolívar. All the same, they were Páez's men.

Over the next few years they would chase the remaining Spanish and pro-Spanish armies out, see a contingent of British mercenaries depart, and consolidate their preeminence over the territories. Yet no single armed force had enough resources, and enough of a state machinery, to control the country.

As in France and Spain in the 15th century, General Páez could look forward to an endless battle for control of the roads, cities, ports, and the meager resources at hand. Ruling, for the first European national monarchs, and for Páez in Venezuela, would be about negotiating, cajoling, threatening, and most of all coexisting with other forces they could not vanquish.

Already at its birth the Venezuelan army was limited in the scope of its power and was itself fragmented by different interests that made up its ranks. But as the biggest force on the land it was able to either destroy those that opposed it or impose terms of coexistence. That is how Venezuela was governed until the First World War. At that point the European conflict drove the prices of cocoa and coffee upwards. Dictator Juan Vicente Gómez used the money to start a modern army, which in the oil decades would be followed by a mighty state. But for the 100 years before the Andean cattle rancher rose to power in Caracas, the Venezuelan army did not have a monopoly over violence in the land.

The Venezuelan armed forces of 2019 found themselves in the familiar place of their origins. Chávez and Chavismo had turned the country into a fragmented landscape littered by the remnants of a dismantled liberal state, armed bands and *prans*, freelance miners, drug traffickers, poor and malaria-ridden peasants, informal settlements on the verge of survival, the remaining fragments of people's councils, co-ops and communes, and FAES commandos. As in 1819, the armed forces were the biggest game in the country of 2019, but not the only one.

Army soldiers had physical control of the remains of oil production, transportation, and shipment. They had enough power to informally tax, sometimes control, a growing gold rush. They sustained Chavismo's hold of the government treasury, borders, banks, and enough structures of power to rule. And to prop up President Maduro, himself besieged by powerful chieftains within his inner council, and by the specific interests of the Cuban legation.

In the new landscape and at least until 2019, the armed forces retreated from operating jails, doing policing, or aggressively maintaining the peace or the right of passage. Because all security and safety matters were transacted in a fluid field of power, the armed forces' authority was based on the careful management of its limited resources.

How the original army was unified and deployed by Bolívar and Páez back in 1816 and through the 1830s is discussed in the third chapter of this book and in its epilogue. The critical elements of their original success, and of the army's role in the following years, were always clear to Hugo Chávez. Perhaps he understood better than most the ethnic dynamics at the core of the organization at a time of scarce resources. As if that was not enough, the growing number of US indictments for drug trafficking against various officers helped cement that sense of unity.

The modern army of the 1910s had been created by Juan Vincente Gómez and his fellow conservative Creole officers from the Andean highlands. For the most part, they were descendants of Spanish settlers and generally lighter-skinned. Yet the army's ethnic composition started changing early on.

The armed forces' spiritual leader through the 1940s had been Carlos Delgado Chalbaud. He came from a wealthy military family, grew up in Paris, and studied military engineering at Versailles. He led the 1945 military coup and was assassinated in a plot by fellow officers in 1950. His murder foretold the social transformation of the Venezuelan military.

By the 1960s and 1970s the military academies were no longer attractive paths to power or wealth for the sons of the privileged. The real opportunities lay in business or politics. Instead, the academies became magnets for those of humble origins looking to rise in the world. As the years passed, the military was transformed. Chávez's early ally, General Garcia Carneiro, voiced this view when he said, "We're not part of a caste as in other countries where the commanders of the armed forces are upper class with impressive last names. On the contrary, typically the armed forces here are linked to the people."[104] The fact that Delgado Chalbaud's ancestors, the Velutini family, had been among the most influential at the turn of the 20th century, could be easily dismissed by General Garcia Carneiro. His army had been a people's army for too many decades.

From Chávez's point of view, there was no ethnic imperative to dismantle the army and create a new one, as had happened after the Cuban and Nicaraguan revolutions. The Creole influence had eroded over the years, and the immigrants and their descendants had never had any interest in joining the armed forces. By the early 2000s there were many older generals and colonels who owed their allegiance to the liberal state and opposed Chávez's leftward turn. But the institution itself was not an issue for the ethnocentric revolution. Rather, it was its natural arena.

As soon as he was elected, Chávez catered to an eager audience of receptive listeners within the armed forces middle ranks. He talked of a fusion between the "the people and its army," and of the leading role officers would have in the country's upcoming transformation.[105] In countless formal and informal talks across the country's barracks, forts, and training fields, he offered his vision of a nationalist ethno-state to redress long-standing grievances against the corrupt elites. To the young officers from poor families throughout the country for whom the army had been a ticket of upward mobility, Chávez's speeches made sense. By 2002 the massacre of 1992 was but a decade old, and Chávez would never let anyone forget the event. In his crisp telling, a neo-liberal government ordered the army to kill its own people in the streets of Caracas. All in the name of free markets.

Alongside his campaign of seduction and persuasion, Chávez orchestrated organizational changes to reshape the army's operations. He fast-tracked the careers of allies and retired his enemies, remaking the command structure. He did not hesitate to jail former allies he felt had betrayed him, some still in military prison as of this writing. He modified the curriculum at the military academy to reflect his ethno-nationalist project. He changed the songs, slogans, and military symbols of the rank-and-file army, inserting a much more political bent in everyday operations. After 2004, soldiers were ordered to salute with a new war cry: "Fatherland, Socialism, or Death!" In 2005 he severed all relations with the US Department of Defense, effectively ending decades of cooperation and training. American officers and technicians embedded at Venezuelan bases would leave the country.

The political opposition lost any connection to the armed forces. If generals and politicians from the 20th century knew each other, Chávez's military had its own language and culture. The armed forces middle ranks were a world apart from an opposition that looked to American and European public policy schools for inspiration. In contrast, captains and lieutenant colonels looked to the social and cultural traditions of The Plains, and the stories of heroism of Zamora and the Federal War. The cultural distance became a real separation, as most opposition politicians did not personally know active-duty officers. Worse still, they made no effort to connect with them.

Politically this was the Chávez masterstroke. Without a sympathetic ear in the armed forces to uphold the constitution, respect elections, ensure a peaceful transfer of power, protect the integrity of Congress, or prevent political leaders from being arbitrarily jailed, the opposition was effectively nullified. The real political battle between the early 2000s and the early 2010s had not been over elections or in referenda. Chávez had fought it in the barracks, without opposition.

The lesson from the 19th century had been that Venezuelan politics of that time started with the rank and file, to be followed immediately by the army's middle ranks. The foundation of power for Páez, the Monagas brothers, Guzmán Blanco, Joaquin Crespo, Cipriano Castro, and Juan Vicente Gómez, from 1819 all the way to 1927, had always been based on the informal armies that took them to power. Later, as Gomez created a modern army, the old loyalties were simply transferred to the more complex institution. Chávez knew his history. Subsequent events proved his understanding gave him the upper hand over political opponents that had no clue about the real forces they were confronting.

By 2014 the systematic destruction of the liberal state was followed by a humanitarian crisis. Ten years of power-devolution, ethnic identity politics, and a ferocious campaign against institutions and the rule of law had destroyed the country most had known. The most important and least-understood part of that debacle is how in the new landscape, the only structures left standing were the armed forces.

Yet Chávez, and later Maduro, were too sophisticated to give any one group too much power. The armed forces would stand above the wreckage, but they would be splintered within so as not to pose a threat of their own.

Historically, the source of army and military discontent came from middle-ranking officers who did not see a possibility of advancement. Regardless of ethnicity or politics, those with operational control of the troops had risen against the top brass every time they felt their power, ideas, or their economic interests were threatened. Captain Delgado Chalbaud had done as much by rising against General Medina Angarita in 1945. The Carupanazo rebellion of May 1962 against Betancourt was led by army captains. A month later the Porteñazo rebellion was led by navy captains. By 1992 Lieutenant Colonel Chávez had risen against President Pérez and his defense minister, General Ochoa Antich.

Chavismo neutralized this ever-present threat by fast-tracking the promotions of hundreds of middle-ranking officers. In the year 2000 the army had 150 generals and admirals. By 2017 there would be 2,000 generals and flag officers in the Venezuelan armed forces, or twice the general officers of the US's million-strong armed forces.[106]

The proliferation of officers was dealt with by turning the former strategic commands into zonal commands. This scattered the army geographically. The border area Andes command, for example, used to have six generals overseeing about 13,000 troops. The critical command was in the front line of drugs and human trafficking, regular contraband of goods, and within the area of influence of Colombian guerrillas. By 2019 twenty generals oversaw the same area.[107]

Authority had also been diluted at the top. The defense minister could not mobilize troops without the authorization of the Strategic Operations Command, an agency created by Chávez to centralize all deployments. The officer in charge of the Operations Command also reported directly to the president.[108]

As chronicled in this book's epilogue, Páez's most famous battle after independence was fought against some of his own troops. Victory in the violent melee near Payara reaffirmed Páez's leadership for a decade, but his own telling of events shows the extent to which that army was rife with rivalries within.

The 2,000 general officers which by 2019 commanded 150,000 troops must have made up a force as fragmented as that of 1830. But just as an *esprit de corps* ultimately manifested itself in the military caste of the 1830s, many shared incentives and pressures unified the 21st-century officer corps. A growing number of US indictments for drug trafficking against several officers helped build that unity. In addition to the many layers of economic incentives, and terrible consequences of betrayal, the fear of being imprisoned for life at an American maximum-security prison kept the forces together. Together enough to maintain a precarious status quo.

Chávez is Dead

For many, Chávez was a madman who hypnotized a country, squandered an oil fortune, and was succeeded after his death in 2013 by a gang of thugs that retained power through sheer force. Those who supported Chávez's ethno-nationalist project until the mid-2010s pushed the myth of a radical break, before and after Chávez's death, to justify themselves. And most within the twenty-year-old opposition pushed a narrative in which Chávez's shamanistic appeal, and the ruthlessness of a mafia-style government that came after, justified the failed outcomes their own misreading of events helped create. In the before and after Chávez version of the story, the money from the decade-long oil boom was mainly stolen by a few Chávez collaborators who acquired even more power after his death. For the millions of refugees and exiles, the explanation served just as well.

But that is not what happened. Hugo Chávez brought to fruition an ethnic identity project rooted in the country's history. The furies of an old social divide along with an unprecedented oil boom fueled the wanton destruction of the 20th-century society and its state. A vast welfare system was systematically dismantled, the government stepped back from enforcing security, and an orgy of consumption engulfed every social class. The new money fanned ethno-national flames that destroyed a society and nearly collapsed the state. It also fueled a wave of violence not seen since the 19th-century Federal War. When oil prices dropped, and Chávez died, the same trends continued.

The post-Chávez leadership likely convinced themselves the humanitarian crisis had to do with the collapse of crude prices. It was an excuse no one should believe. Even without considering the prior ten-year rampage dismantling the state and its oil company, their answer to the human suffering throughout the country was to ignore it. As society came to a standstill in late 2013, the lessons of Weimar Germany and John Maynard Keynes's prescriptions to avert economic collapse were dismissed. A treasury secretary proclaimed that the concept of inflation was a bourgeois myth.[109] The new president insisted Chávez had appeared to him in the form of a little bird.[110] Instead of finding a way to prop up oil production with modern management and technology, the leadership doubled down on the ethno-nationalist political and cultural agenda. While the country drowned, the vice president said in mid-2018, "There is no humanitarian crisis in Venezuela."[111]

'Delay, deny, and continue to hold' became their mantra. With millions of committed and potential opponents fleeing the country, the longer they controlled the reins of government, the less likely that a threat to their power would materialize. The growing exodus made time Chavismo's most valuable commodity. Chávez's successors, with much less money and under increasing pressure, merely floated over the decimated society that Chávez's identity project had bequeathed them. There is not a before and after Chávez's death, but rather a single line at least two decades long.

Back in the early 1800s, the Wars of Independence unleashed the centuries-old fury of the enslaved and those marginalized by the caste system. This was met by the violent retribution of Creoles who felt entitled to inherit the country's reins of power and intended to keep colonial society mostly intact. The savagery of a slave society, the caste system's contradictions, and the violence spawned by extreme poverty fueled ten years of wars that killed a third of the country's population.[112]

Two hundred years later, the ethnic fury unleashed by Chavismo destroyed the society built during the 20th century. Those who suffered the most were not the ones leaving through international airports. The real victims were those in whose name Chavismo dismantled the liberal state. The ones who were supposed to have redeemed their originary rights in a direct democracy. The same millions who walked away to countries throughout Latin America, and those who stayed to suffer deep poverty and death.

As in the country that emerged from Boves' and Bolívar's bloody battles in 1819, poverty and destruction were everywhere evident by 2019. A hungry, illiterate, and disease-ridden 19th century awaited those Venezuelans who had not died or left the country during the Wars of Independence.

The outcome of the 2020s and 2030s is still be written

Epilogue: Politics Without a State, 1834-1837

«*When you are writing laws you are testing words to find their utmost power. Like spells, they have to make things happen in the real world, and like spells, they only work if people believe in them.*»
Thomas Cromwell, imagined by Hillary Mantel in *Wolf Hall*

When a colonial order vanishes, an oil bonanza changes a country's society, or an entire social and economic arrangement is dismantled, the past still helps shape the new landscapes to come. Politics have always been tied to people who lived in times we barely recognize but whose ideas and arrangements still affect us, just as we will influence events taking place long after we are gone. Today the future of Venezuela is wide open. Many possibilities exist between the death of an old order and the uncertain birth of a new one. History does not repeat itself and nothing can predict the future. But as we search for tomorrow's fortunes, we only have facts known until our present times, our inherited legacies, and our memories of the past.

That is why the story of General José Antonio Páez is more relevant than ever. Alone among the well-known heroes of his time, he survived the desolation of the Wars of Independence to shape the beginnings of an independent nation.

He had always been different. His brilliant contemporaries Andrés Bello, Simón Bolívar, and Antonio José de Sucre spent their adolescence polishing their French while surrounded by enslaved workers. Páez spent his as a semi-literate peon in the far away southwestern Llanos. The ranch's foreman, a slave of African descent named Manuel, taught him everything about cattle-raising. By Páez's telling, his youthful duties included washing the foreman's feet at night.[1] He would learn to eat with a knife and fork much later in life while attentively watching the table manners of British mercenaries and adventurers Bolívar had brought to the country to fight the Spanish.[2]

By any measure, Venezuela's first self-made character lived an incredible life. His story started in an impoverished backwater. He raised and led an army to defeat the Spanish Crown's largest force ever sent to the Americas. He single-handedly orchestrated the founding of the independent Venezuela Republic and became its first president. He started dismantling three hundred years of Spanish mercantilism by introducing a liberal legal framework allowing some free trade. After dominating the turbulent politics of his country for twenty years, he remade himself again in New York City. While Paris and Madrid shined brightly in the minds of privileged Venezuelans, it was in the rough and tumble of Manhattan that Páez became an influencer of his times. His personality and his autobiography made him famous worldwide.

Páez's funeral procession in New York, delayed by his political enemies for fifteen years after his death, was led by Civil War hero William Tecumseh Sherman. Cuban poet José Martí chronicled the event. The parade took the General's remains from the grounds at the Armory to the piers, where a US Navy warship awaited to take him back to his country.

As the 2020s and 2030s decide the future of Venezuela, the challenges faced by Páez in the early 1830s are illuminating. It was then that the Llanero General straddled a path between the moralistic wrath of Caracas elites nostalgic for colonial times and the amoral self-interest of new actors who sought to profit from chaos. While navigating this tightrope, he shaped fragmented territories into the beginnings of a nation.

In the process, he invented a kind of politics that remains critical to Venezuela's power equation.

Caracas, 1834

The European and American middle classes had discovered the pleasure of coffee as the newly born Venezuelan Republic was electing its second president in 1834. Although a long war had ravaged the infant country, coffee's new value had given an economic jolt to the territories.

An old elite Caraqueño dream came back. While a significant number of the Spanish-born and their descendants had either been killed by Boves' armies or Bolívar's War to the Death or had fled during the independence conflict, a new "society" had reconstituted itself in the old capital city. This handful of old Creoles and merchants who had survived, along with a few recently settled traders and coffee planters, started to think about the kind of country they felt entitled to have, believing that they should be the ones leading the nascent republic.

As they deliberated on who the next president should be, a new culprit for the country's ills was implicitly identified: "corrupt" mixed-race generals who had all the power in the aftermath of the independence wars. The solution to this problem was to elect urbane, polyglot, well-educated light-skinned men to public office. This is how in Venezuela's second election, where only men of property could vote on an Electoral College, a venerable and well-traveled medical doctor was elected president.

As the stiffly attired Dr. José Vargas assumed power, a glimmer of the old Mantuano dream came back: to have a properly run, orderly country, anchored in beautiful Caracas. This happened exactly twenty years after a popular rebellion of mixed-race peons, former slaves, and many of indigenous descent had destroyed the Venezuelan Second Republic and sacked the capital city. In a few months, a posse of bandits had defeated the Republican Army and shown how far Bolívar still needed to travel to understand his country's social dynamics. The Liberator's youthful naiveté ultimately sent him on a march west at the head of 20,000 light-skinned refugees and an eventual exile in the Caribbean.[3] The popular rebellion of 1814 demolished the Creole's claim to power, yet the dream would not die.

By electing Dr. Vargas in 1834, the men of property were implicitly showing General Páez, the outgoing president, the door out of Venezuelan politics: "Thank you for your service, we'll take it from here." Showing them every courtesy in turn, the Llanero general graciously accepted the defeat of his preferred candidate, wished the distinguished doctor well, and retired to his ranch 100 miles away.

Dr. Vargas and his supporters believed the country needed well-written statutes and powerful symbols. While focusing on a big plan to fix the country, they ignored the precarious power dynamics throughout ravaged territories where the demobilized independence troops had reconstituted themselves into armed bands and private armies. As the months went by, the president did not attempt to forge political alliances or connect with any of the forces roaming the countryside. To sit down with bandits and outcasts was not only beneath him, it was against the notions of civilization and propriety he thought the country desperately needed.

Instead, he was content to preside over an imaginary nation while his real authority never extended beyond a few blocks in Caracas. Meanwhile, local and regional caudillos, bandits, thugs, former generals and mercenaries, soldiers, and assorted characters from the twenty-year war could not believe the size of the power vacuum arising in front of them. In a matter of months, the rumblings of war became deafening.

Santiago Mariño, who had earlier wrestled with Bolívar for control of the country's east and had later joined a challenge to the early Venezuelan Republic in a bid to create an independent country in his own region, led a group of generals and rose in arms to proclaim the "Revolution of Reforms." Not long after that another independence war general, Pedro Carujo, burst into Vargas' bedroom to tell him the game was over.

The exchange that supposedly followed between them, whether real or made up, foreshadowed the soap-opera view of politics often invoked by the Caracas elites to argue on behalf of their principles.

"Dr. Vargas, the world belongs to the brave."

"No, the world belongs to the just. Just men, not brave ones, have always lived and will forever live happily on this earth knowing they act in good conscience."[4]

In this portrayal of the story the good doctor became a hero for the ages by uttering noble sounding lines. But the fact remains that he never cared to understand or engage the power dynamics of the scarred country he thought he led.

After his short stint governing an imaginary Venezuela, he was sent into exile on a Caribbean island. The generals were once again in control of the state's symbols. The conflict to see which strongman would rise above the others had started.

What followed has become a reference-point in a new kind of politics by Llanero General José Antonio Páez. Starting days after the coup d'état, Páez's travels, battles, and letters show him wrestling with and seducing enemies and allies alike in his quest to gain a measure of control over territories without an actual state. For a million-plus Venezuelans trapped by the violence of local chieftains and the ravages of malaria, a measure of peace was the necessary beginning of any redemption. Páez understood the grim realities in the territories, yet never lost sight of what was needed to lay the foundations of a new nation. While the Caracas elites dismissed anyone not to their liking, and dozens of cynical actors simply looked out for themselves, Páez fought to create something enduring while knowing the final puzzle would require plenty of unsavory deals.

Some historians tend to focus on the "civilization versus barbarism story" in this episode. For them, "good guy Vargas" was pushed aside by the kind of violent generals that would impede Venezuelan progress for 150 years. In this narrative, Páez has been cast at best as the least objectionable of a lot of brutish military men. Often, he is portrayed as the embodiment of their weak-principled mendacity.

Historian Arráiz Lucca has argued that "the culture of caudillos would immediately emerge to confront the republican synderesis, looking to impose its own grammar, wielding a sword for that purpose ..."[5] The assumption is that Vargas' presidency had a robust grammar of its own to govern the devastated territories.

Other writers like Manuel Caballero remain stuck on simplistic paradigms when trying to understand what happened to Vargas: "They're military men, and for that reason, their source of power, or their aspiration to attain it, rests on their weapons."[6]

Only political historian Diego Bautista Urbaneja finds irony in the Creole project behind Vargas: "A candid perspective according to which barely four years after Bolívar's death the independence heroes should give way to the owner class."[7]

What is clear about this historical period is that mere laws and rules were meaningless as tools or as an ideology of power in fragmented and violent territories ravaged by hunger and illness. Words, a flag, a president's throne, and a trophy capital could never add up to a functioning country.

This is difficult to understand then or now because we refuse to acknowledge the profound consequences of the wars. Just twenty-four years before, in 1810, there had been a strong colonial government with Crown administrators enforcing public laws over a highly regimented slave society. A large private-public enterprise ran the economy. While rebellions and the colony's poverty of resources had threatened the Crown's preeminent position for centuries, its institutions continued to grow in complexity and reach.

What president Vargas and his more recent supporters will not address is why the colonial legacy of statecraft could not continue after the independence wars. Even in France most royal state institutions and practices survived the bloody French revolution of 1789 to flourish well into the 1830s and 1840s.

The devastated Venezuelan territories after independence could not connect with colonial bureaucrats or their institutions because the racial and ethnic forces driving the wars had obliterated that world.

The French Revolution had been about middle-class lawyers like Danton and Robespierre taking over a machinery of government they understood better than the aristocrats whose heads they were chopping off.[8] Boves, Páez, and those who destroyed the formal caste system in Venezuela had no stake in the institutions they vanished. The bureaucratic machine required to run the colonial government was gone, its members dead or exiled after the frenzy of killing. While France's vast civil society of small artisans and peasants thrived in the economic boom brought about by the Napoleonic plunder of European countries, Bolívar's War to the Death and Boves' terror raids had targeted light-skinned shopkeepers, landowners, and small businesspeople for assassination. The scorched earth tactics of both Royalist and Independence armies and the general mayhem of civil insurrection annihilated the fabric of the empire over the territories.

A third of the population had perished during the Wars of Independence.[9] The country's only true legacies, the poverty of physical resources and the lack of population, had come back after the destruction and death brought about by the interminable violence. This is the more realistic context in which Páez forged a new grammar to navigate power in the territories.

Return of the Warrior

According to his own account, General Páez was finally enjoying some peace of mind at his ranch after two decades of war, and four years as president, when a posse of riders arrived with all sorts of news from Caracas.[10] Vargas had been deposed and exiled, Generals Mariño and Carujo controlled the city, and most interestingly, the troops participating in the putsch had been told that he, Páez, was the leader of the pro-military revolt. At the same time, he was presented with a letter from Vargas and his Council of State, giving "General Páez supreme military authority to fight the reformists and restore the Republic."[11]

And that is how on July 15th of 1835 Páez left his ranch for Caracas with fifty riders.[12] He led four dozen men as the nominal head of the coup d'état, and of the forces that were supposed to suppress it. His only action before leaving was to pledge allegiance to the constitution of 1830, the one he had passed as the country's first president. Later events would make clear that few knew where Páez stood.

What is obvious from the general's double duty, for and against the coup, is the extent to which even by 1834 there was no machinery of government, standing army, or not enough of either one that could be taken over. There was no *état* for a proper *coup*.

Underneath the manifestos, orders, and institutional mise-en-scène, General Páez was acting on his own behalf, freelancing as it were, rather than acting as the representative of something concrete. Venezuela was then more of a hope or an idea than an actual country.

Following the well-worn road out of the Llanos he had taken many times (and Boves before him), he crossed to San Juan de Los Morros, aimed directly at the city of Maracay, and detoured west toward Valencia. He gathered a few more riders for his small contingent but still had nothing like an army at his command.

Yet before him stood one of the largest cities, now under the control of General Laurencio Silva, who had come from Caracas with enough troops to be taken seriously.[13] A veteran of countless battles all over South America during the Wars of Independence, and married to Simón Bolívar's niece, Silva was a substantial figure in the Venezuela of 1835.

Páez did not stand a chance, yet he stood there, smiling and ready to negotiate. According to Páez's own memoirs, Silva sent emissaries to clarify who he was fighting for, to which he allegedly responded that he was the "chief of the constitutional army ready to reestablish order."[14] Apparently surprised that Páez was not the head of the rebellion, Silva agreed to sit down right away and sort everything out. No one seems to know what transpired, but the end result was a decree issued by Páez in his capacity as head of the Republican Army declaring he would guarantee the life, property, and military rank of every soldier and officer under Silva. He further committed to advocate their grievances before Congress.[15]

And with that, Silva and his real army now joined Páez's non-army to chase down another reformist General, Pedro Alcántara, who originally sought to intercept Páez but was now running back toward Caracas. Finally catching up with him, and after several maneuvers which left no doubt a big battle would ensue, Páez started yelling over his men to try and convince Alcántara to give up his arms. Soon enough Alcántara joined Páez, who now had enough of a real force to march on Caracas. Not a shot had been fired, yet Páez was already heading one of the most significant rebellious contingents on the way to suppressing the rebellion.[16]

In the meantime, Generals Mariño and Carujo, the original plotters, were well positioned in the capital city and under no illusions about Páez, or so it seems. They wanted power, had come to get it, and would soon face a strong opponent. But as the newly reinforced Páez approached, they chose to run: Mariño toward his native east, and Carujo to the old Puerto Cabello fort.

Páez entered an empty Caracas on July 25, 1835. After securing the capital, he gave chase to Mariño, following him all the way to the far east town of Petare before letting go.[17] Perhaps the entire conspiracy was now clear to him. First, he brought back deposed President Vargas as soon as possible and visibly sat him on the throne: a proper president, to be seen but not heard. Carujo had removed him, and now Páez had brought him back. It did not seem important who sat on the presidential seat, but rather whose authority determined who would sit on it. His second move, much more relevant, sought to unravel the true hidden hand behind the conspiracy.

Mariño's run to the east and Carujo's control of Puerto Cabello did not appear to be thoughtless retreats, but a plan with a purpose. Mariño was dashing to Barcelona to gain control of the main port on the east, allowing him to establish a Barcelona-Puerto Cabello sea lane to ferry troops between east and west easily. If successfully established, the sea lane would be much faster than a land connection. Páez could keep Caracas and the Llanos, but the main coastal cities from Maracaibo to Cumaná, and all coffee trade, would be lost to him.

For Mariño to take Barcelona would make no sense unless the East and every available soldier there were already behind him, which meant the Reforms Revolution started and ended with one José Tadeo Monagas. Another general from the independence wars, Monagas had parlayed his modest leadership then into a de facto rule of that whole part of the Venezuelan territories colloquially known as Oriente.

While Venezuela was born in the cities of Cumaná and Barcelona, in the east, a rising Caracas had cut off their direct contact with the world, reducing them to a secondary status that is as true today as it was at the beginning of the 19th century. José Tadeo Monagas had already tangled with Páez several times, most importantly in 1831.

Back at the beginning of the Republic, Páez had orchestrated the separation of Venezuela from the Great Colombian project, merging the interests of the Caracas elites with the power of his Llanero troops and his control of the country's geographic center. The generals from Oriente could see what they would lose in this newly independent Venezuela of 1830. Monagas had declared the independence of all the lands east of the Rio Unare and pledged his support to Bolívar's Great Colombia in faraway Bogotá. Still fresh from the Wars of Independence, Páez had gathered an army, marched straight toward Maturin, and forced Monagas to do a deal of some kind, details of which will probably never be known. The Venezuelan Republic, along the original boundaries of the Spanish Captaincy General, would have its start.

By the time Carujo dislodged Vargas from the presidency, the perception of power in the country had changed. The incipient coffee trade helped by free trade had given Caracas and the central region financial might, and the prospect of a wealthier future in the form of foreign loans and

investments in the coffee economy. The unintended consequence had been that regional caudillos no longer wanted
to secede. The central valleys and the capital city were now
a prize, and everyone had seen Páez come from the faraway
Llanos and take it. At the very least, caudillos throughout the
country demanded a share. In later years they would want all
of it.

It was clear to Páez that Monagas and his front men
Mariño and Carujo were—at a minimum—after a renego-
tiation of the 1831 deal over how power in Venezuela would
be parsed. More likely they were gambling for enough
supremacy so they would now dictate terms.

Seduction and Revenge

Páez's next move after bringing back Vargas was comical:
he wrote Monagas naming him head of the non-existent
Venezuelan armies in the east, and charging him with
putting down the rebellion (i.e. going after his proxy Mariño
on behalf of Caracas).[18] In a previous short letter, Páez had
already laid the groundwork:

> "... there is hearsay that troublemakers have their gaze
> fixed on Oriente and are thinking of digging their
> trenches there. I hasten to write you about this, so
> that you can lend me some help in the great mission
> to reestablish the constitutional order. Those that see
> themselves lost already, will want to compromise you
> and will look for your support; but I know you well
> and I'm hoping this time you will accompany me in
> saving the Fatherland."[19]

The double-entendres in this letter were designed for a world in which everything could be negotiated. The original rebellion had named Páez head of a military revolt designed to destroy the political order he had set up. Then Páez had written giving Monagas a role squashing the rebellion he had instigated just as things started to turn against him. These were classic invitations to the negotiating table, even before the action started: a style of politics necessitated by the fact that no one had enough power (money and soldiers) to overcome anyone else. Once Spain's financial and bureaucratic resources and its rigid social order were out of the way, no single entity or group was mighty enough to fill in the gap.

Meanwhile, Vargas, his supporters, and countless contemporary historians have questioned how laws could be so easily ignored in favor of raw power. But idealistic legal frameworks were meaningless without the money for people to feed themselves, resources to finance a state, and time for mechanisms to make laws widely accepted and therefore enforceable. The country was overrun by banditry, violence, and disease, none of which any laws would help fix.

Vargas started to voice his opposition to Páez for his pardon-and-negotiate policies, advocating the Caracas elite's favored imprison-and-execute program instead. The symbolic president demanded solemn trials and proper executions for the rebels. These gestures were supposed to give his side legitimacy, and therefore more power. Vargas and his allies imagined that a tough stance would tip the balance in their favor. That mere words would alter the parity between forces that had created the political impasse in the first place.

Given the military equivalences between both camps, Páez had no choice but to seduce Monagas into negotiation if he hoped to prevail. For Monagas, the situation was analogous. While the eastern chieftain would not openly commit to his own rebellion, he also refused to acknowledge Páez's letters, which kept getting longer and longer. In one of them Páez plays the ignored suitor, "Three letters I've sent you about the events of the 8th and of their consequences …"[20] He then continues with stories of how his spies were telling him that Mariño was fighting with Carujo.

The melodramatic scenarios by Páez always aimed to excuse Mariño, the most important and best connected of Monaga's front men, while shifting blame to Carujo: "It's shameful that Carujo managed to intimidate these old chiefs, compromising them into a complete ruin. I'm told, and I have no doubt, that there is no other voice but that of Carujo, that Carujo reigns supreme and that all obey him."[21]

In a few months, the July letter's implicit offers played out exactly as promised. By November Páez had accumulated enough support to force Monagas to the table. There everyone except Carujo was pardoned, promises of advocacy of the Reformist issues were made, and unknown payments or promises of a more substantial nature were surely negotiated and fully accepted.

Having settled the East, Páez turned toward Puerto Cabello and Carujo. The wily Llanero arrived at the western port town on Christmas Eve, expecting his opponent's men to be drunk from the festivities and impulsive for battle. In a few hours Carujo was mortally shot (he would die in Valencia a few days later) and the Reformist Revolution left in a coma. The fort itself would surrender in March, by which time Páez had gained the upper hand.

Back during the Independence Wars, Bolívar had never gained total control of his nominal allies in the east, and now Páez faced the same situation. And just as Bolívar had to accept Mariño's power but had also shown his strength by executing Mariño's ally, Piar, Páez had gone against Carujo and killed him.

In April of 1836, President Vargas quit just nine months after Páez had brought him back from exile and weeks after Puerto Cabello had finally surrendered. The constant give and take, the lack of formality in the negotiations, or perhaps their effectiveness, proved to be too much for the venerable doctor, a nominal head of a state over which he had no power.

Andrés Narvarte, a more pragmatic light-skinned lawyer who had been the vice president all along, became head of the state while Páez continued sorting out the puzzle of consolidating power without many resources in a deeply fragmented country.

The extent to which Páez's behind-the-scenes reign turned into a permanent negotiation to hold a weak center would become clear in a matter of months, when another serious rebellion erupted.

It was early 1837, and the threat came from Páez's backyard in the Apure Plains, and more dangerous still, from his close collaborators.

The delicate balance by which Páez had controlled Caracas, negotiated an accommodation with Monagas and Mariño in the east, while keeping western cities and territories in line, was based on the assumption that the heart of Venezuela and its most deadly military force, the Llaneros, were absolutely loyal to him.

All Politics is Local

José Francisco and Juan Pablo Farfán were everything President Vargas and the Caracas elites feared, and through a feat of mental gymnastics, managed to pretend were not central to Venezuelan society. The brothers were the type of ruthless, violent gang-like leaders that flourish anytime there is not enough of a state, even enough of a country, to impose its peace. Their grievance lay in the impositions of a liberal proto-state that needed them to control their regions and towns, yet wanted to impose its mores and its taxes. In the Farfáns' view, the latter always worked to the benefit of legalistic Caraqueños obsessed with the social and geographical hierarchies inherited from the Spanish Empire. While the Farfáns wanted to reassert their position or renegotiate their deal with Páez, or as Páez himself suspected, were in the pay of Monagas to undercut his return to power, what they claimed is telling. They wanted legal immunity and privileges (*fueros*) for veterans of the independence wars, an end to land taxes, and a "federal" republic centered in Bolívar's Grand Colombia (i.e. a capital in faraway Bogotá rather than nearby Caracas).[22]

When the Farfán brothers, the very men who were supposed to watch his back, decided to rebel, Páez had no choice but to get himself at the head of an army and face them. The way he fought them makes it clear that it would have to be him, or them.

Readers of French theorists Deleuze and Guattari will recognize in the Farfán rebellion a formerly nomad army, uneasily settled, pushing back against the bureaucratic impulse of a nascent state their lightning violence had created in the first place.[23] Páez himself was the first to describe the brothers in these terms:

"They were true Bedouins of the plains: men of gigantic height, athletic build, valor bordering on the ferocious and obedient only to naked force. They had served at first in the ranks of royalist Yánez. But when I had offered to give the rank of captain to any plainsman who brought me forty fighters, they showed up with several of their men and from then on rode with me in Apure. If I had been strict with my troop, I would have had to punish these brothers severely because they often deserted for a time with their men to go on plundering raids, and then would reappear with inadmissible excuses. In those times, tolerance was a virtue recommended by prudence and demanded above all by the need to count on brave men. Just before the Battle of Mucuritas, the Farfán brothers disappeared on one of these escapades, and I finally threatened to lance them through if they did not get out of my sight with all their people. That is why they did not share in the glory of Mucuritas. Later on, I took them in again, and it has been seen how valuable they proved to be in the capture of Puerto Cabello in 1823."[24]

The nomad warrior is fundamentally uninterested in laws, ideas of national allegiance rooted in territorial borders, and the fixed abstractions required for the building of countries. Nomad warriors believe in the speed with which they can project their power, and cover territories they do not recognize as distinct from each other.[25] Harnessing this kind of fury, Boves destroyed Bolívar's rigid forces, and Páez himself chased out the biggest army the Spanish Empire had ever sent to their colonies. But it is a fury that knows no bounds and can hardly stop, making the transition from plunder to settling an almost impossible one.

Páez knew the Farfán brothers had never been loyal to his colors and would never be. Their power could only be harnessed by war. Páez's Llaneros won battle after battle because their uncontainable bursts of violence confused, and then decimated Spanish troops that had been victorious against Napoleon. But after independence, it was Páez who needed to contain the violence if he was going to rule. As he chronicles his own nation-building there is a clear awareness of the delicate balance that had to be achieved:

"After the triumphs of Independence, the cattle of the Province of Apure had been distributed among the valiant warriors of the army whose lances doomed Spanish despotism there. By distributing herds, our country repaid their services and gave them a stake in the prosperity of the territory which they had conquered with heroism and defended with unfailing courage. Cornelio Muñoz, intrepid captain of my former guard, had property there, so did Rafael

Ortega, my constant companion in hardship and glory, whose recent death still grieved me at the time of these events ..."[26]

But cattle and some territory would never be enough for the most lethal of his warriors. They felt entitled to all the spoils, as the Farfáns told Páez directly after their first rebellion:

"For my part, I sent several letters to the rebel leaders, reminding them of their patriotic duty. In reply, they tried to convince me that what they demanded was no more than I had promised to the people of Apure during the war of Independence, that a free Venezuela would not levy obligations of any kind on its people. 'Your demands are unjust, quite unjust,' I wrote back to them. 'In no American republic are levies lower than in Venezuela; its treasury is gathered at the custom houses; the interior provinces suffer no more levies than those required for their upkeep and their progress; they need schools to educate the young and roads to increase their wealth, and this should be done with each province's own funds. Their abject misery would never end if they refused to contribute to such important works ...' "[27]

According to Páez's own words, the rebels finally accepted the clemency offered them in July of 1836, but only to rebel again in an apparent late alliance with the Reformists. They were "proclaiming reunification with Colombia, the reform of the Constitution, the reestablishing of special rights for military officers and clergy, the institution of trial by jury, the abolition of all taxes on rural property, a decree of amnesty for various conspirators fleeing justice, and finally the proclamation of General Mariño (instigator of all this) as Supreme Chief."[28]

The gauntlet had been thrown down. The Farfáns would have nothing to do with Páez's early liberal project, its costs, or its legal formulations. To which the caudillo could only respond by assembling his troops and setting out to suppress his former men personally. No individual or institution existed that could do the job.

> "I moved my troops to San Fernando as well, and on arrival, sent Captain Mirabal's infantry and Major Calderin's cavalry to reconnoiter. The enemy had crossed the river and withdrawn about a mile from the city just before my arrival. My men's horses were exhausted, so at nightfall, I had the advance parties return so that the entire force would be able to resume the pursuit together. When the moon rose, I had the men take their horses across the river, and we set out at eight in the morning."[29]

Few armies anywhere on the planet could take their horses through the 600-feet-wide, crocodile-infested Apure River without a bridge and emerge on the opposite bank ready for battle. Yet, the Llanero general could see that even this contingent was not mobile enough, perhaps not lethal enough, to get the job done. During the next few hours,

Páez's large army quickly morphed into a posse of light-ning-fast killers. As had happened time and again during the wars against the Spanish Empire, Páez had to lighten the load of a modern army to be able to fight and win in the name of a modern country that did not really exist:

> "Having ascertained the rebels had passed through Rabanal at six in the morning and realizing it would be impossible to give them chase with the forces at my disposal, I decided to get ahead with the men who had the best mounts, and leave the rest of the force as a rearguard at the helm of Muñoz. With sixty of them and at full trot, I chased the rebels with three times as much men as we. At the place called Yuca, five leagues from San Fernando, I found out they were not far away, and doubling down on our march I found the rearguard half a league away from the town of Payara."[30]

The forty-year-old former president, already having won all the glories of the independence wars, did not think twice about doing something that could easily cost him his life in a world that did not know penicillin. He personally led the charge against the rearguard, and then fought his way out of Payara: "leaving the settlement I saw the enemy was formed in three cavalry columns with a reserve unit on foot, all armed on the plain before the West Wind."[31]

The brutal hand-to-hand melee that followed is described like a bloody battle from the Napoleonic era. Yet how many times do we find the great generals of those armies in the thick of violence, even in the most self-serving autobiographies.

> "Locked in combat only comparable to the one at Queseras del Medio; singular combat in which everyone defends the palm of ground they can reach with their lance. Either one died or laid down the enemy. Juan Pablo Farfán came in person to knock me out of combat but was instantaneously felled, and killed, by the robust lance of my servant Rafael Salinas. At the end, the rebels ceded the field, and the government troops were not any less fired up in the chase of those who had left, than they had been in the heat of the fight."[32]

The other Farfán fled to Colombia, but Páez had already won a critical skirmish precisely when he needed to cement his authority throughout the land. The battle earned him the moniker "Lion of Payara," and most importantly, the prestige needed among his Llanero troops to renew their pledge of loyalty for another ten years. The battle sealed his successful rearrangement of all the political and military factors needed to hold on to power over the Venezuelan territories until 1847.

The Llaneros had his military back, which in the absence of a standing army was the *sine qua non* of power in the territories. Not enough to stretch his forces over the entire place, but enough to force the local chieftains east and west into feudal-like arrangements that recognized his authority. Each local caudillo had wide latitude in his region to administer private justice with his private army. In exchange, they provided enough peace for coffee agriculture to prosper, and for the shipments to reach the Puerto Cabello port. This gave Páez the leverage necessary to deal with the Caraqueño elites that ran the Atlantic trade and the legal framework required to launch a small economy. It gave him enough profit to have the biggest army, bigger than all other armed forces throughout the country.

He rode the coffee boom of the 1830s and even the 1840s—the value of coffee exports nearly quadrupled between 1830 and 1840—without ever losing his appetite for the cajoling, negotiating, and prosecuting of war that the early version of the country required.

Few others would have as much authority over the Venezuelan territories again until the next century, when World War I's trenches transformed coffee and chocolate from superficial pleasures into requisitioned necessities, and again when the new fuel engine transformed crude oil into a prized commodity. At that point General Gómez would have the resources to bring about the first fully functioning, central state over the Venezuelan territories since the Spanish colonial administrators had left.

As oil continued to flow, new political actors expanded Gómez's foundation into a gigantic, impersonal, and central-izing welfare state. When Chávez and Chavismo dismantled it over the course of twenty years, the country found itself where it had started.

The New and Ancient Ties of 2019

One day historians will compile the documentary evidence from the Chavista governments. They will look at economic and population data, statistics from daily life, government appropriations, headcounts, memoranda, other communications, and media and opinion poll trends to shed light on the country's changes between 1999 and 2019. We will then know the timing, degree, and scope of the transformations during that time.

For now, we see the unmistakable outline of a mutation. By 2019 the wreckage of the old society was everywhere. An old bureaucratic state and its monopoly over violence had been transformed. So were notions of public law. Sophisticated non-state actors and local gangs effectively controlled areas of the biggest cities and the countryside, jails, some coastal waters, trade routes for humans and drugs, mining areas, and massive money-laundering operations, among many contested spaces.[33, 34] The Chavista government and its armed forces arose above all other actors but were not strong enough to destroy them.

The workings of this world have been very confusing. We do not even have good concepts with which to describe them. Journalists, politicians, and even academics could not decide if the state of 2019 was controlled by a weak or a strong mafia-like cabal; if it was a rogue state capable of projecting its power, or an unpopular authoritarian dictatorship that would soon fall. The limited analytical toolset has been hindered by the prevalent assumption that a hobbled state cannot function.

Chavismo's command of the iconography of power created even more confusion. By 2019, the country was fragmented and power was dispersed among different actors, but the opposite message was skillfully promoted day and night. Various generals constantly posted photos and videos of a well-fed army in crisp uniforms on their personal social media accounts: military inspections of the electrical grid, highways, telecommunication centers; live-fire military exercises with moving tanks and armored carriers; the Defense Minister himself speaking at garrisons, training sites, ships, military airports, or directly at the camera with steady-cam shots out of the TV series *The West Wing*.

The highly produced theater of state included seemingly live video of the president and his wife driving incognito around Caracas, a king-in-disguise for the social media age. Choreographed popular assemblies reinforced the perception of general peace. The president would suit up to receive foreign dignitaries at the presidential palace. An effort to spruce up the more visible areas of the country's cities got underway.

For an increasingly large audience, the narrative of a nation in the grip of a strong central state made sense.

The mixed signals were encouraged by policy changes that affected the tiny middle-class bubbles in Caracas and other cities. The fact that luxury consumer goods were flooding a few stores contradicted the narrative of fragmentation and chaos. An opening of expensive imports coincided with more Instagram postings of happy gatherings. There was a perception that criminal violence in some regions of the city had subsided.

Many in the opposition implicitly accepted the government's message every time they appealed to old language describing 1950s authoritarian dictatorships. In their speeches, an all-powerful "regime" overseen by an "usurper" reigned over the land.[35]

But the seeming new stability of late 2019 was a manufactured message following ancient political principles. Weak rulers and uncertain new dynasties from time immemorial had projected their earthly and supernatural powers. Medieval kings with little authority perfected, among other rituals, the royal touch, which supposedly cured people suffering from illnesses. The symbolic power of thaumaturgy extended a ruler's precarious position with precious social and political credit.[36] Skillfully manipulated, the perception of power could be leveraged into the real thing. The Chavista production of social media powerfully updated this kind of magic.

Yet for most people in cities and rural areas, the effects of the humanitarian crisis deepened. Even if tiny islands were forming an archipelago of "normalcy" here and there, most of the country continued to suffer and the exodus of refugees did not stop.

Such a distribution of wealth and power over the land resembled, more than that of any other period, the aftermath of the independence wars. The descriptions of the violent countryside, the relationship between a bubble in post-colonial Caracas and severe poverty in the rest of the territories, the way most of the population barely subsisted and died young in post-independence Venezuela found echoes in 2019.

Daily life for most people in the country bore the marks of the Chavista ethno-nationalist fantasy. Venezuela was now defined as an inward-looking nation rooted in the land. A place where "cosmopolitan" political ideas of freedom and mobility would never work. The Chavista machinery of local councils and communes had promoted a belief in an originary right to the land even through the worse months of the Humanitarian Crisis. By 2019 they had fixed people's identities to their neighborhoods and homes.

Individuals were no longer considered citizens of an impersonal state that did not care about their origins or where they lived. People were now defined by their membership in neighborhood committees, Círculos Bolivarianos, and *colectivos*. In addition, every person had to acknowledge their social standing before the criminal gangs and other armed actors in their lives. The *pran* required fidelity and respect, and everyone in his orbit was categorized within specific circles of trust. In this ancient and ritualized world, some people had a higher standing than others. Every person's survival and that of their families depended on these local ties. This happened in neighborhood after neighborhood all over the country.

The myriad and conflicted layers of power tying down the life of most Venezuelans can be described, yet it is difficult to categorize them. Concepts such as fascism, authoritarianism, totalitarianism, and other 20th century models of power cannot help us understand the decentralized, purposely chaotic, yet socially hierarchical Chavista project.

The proliferation of sophisticated non-state actors, bandits, sea pirates, warring security forces, and local *prans* seemed at odds with efforts to regiment the lives of the poor: the exchange of food for loyalty, the technological control implicit in the fatherland's ID *(carnet de la Patria)*,[37] the targeted persecution of any violence related to political rebellion, etc. But the fragmentation of violence worked alongside the new social strictures.

The parallels with the early 1800s are everywhere. Former slaves who had freed themselves during the independence wars or were manumitted in their aftermath became sharecroppers. They were forced to pay for their right to stay on the land with work, product, and fidelity. Pardo peasants whose movements and opportunities would have been curtailed by the colonial caste system were now free to go, yet most stayed in place. Some were forced into forms of peonage that paid them with food and shelter. Those peons who were still able to come and go were paid with *fichasvales*, tokens that could only be cashed at the plantation store (*tiendas de raya*) for tools, food, shelter, and debt. The latter accumulated from year to year, effectively tying the debtor to his place of work for life.[38]

New laws and old customs allowed local "authorities" to draft indigenous workers for various purposes arbitrarily. When the government officially banned slavery, many who had been imprisoned all their lives stayed on their plantations in some form of serfdom. They had no other choice or possible destination.[39]

As the 19th century progressed, a ritualized set of private permissions, penalties, rewards, and obligations determined the lives of former slaves and free Pardo peasants turned into serfs.

The feudalization of life ran alongside unending waves of violence. Various armed actors fought each other for nearly one hundred years over lands and people. Caudillos and petty lords fought each other for the right to press more peasants into serfdom. While the nightmare went on for a majority throughout the 19th century, Caracas started thinking of its

European future. A minority within the city could pretend they were living in the great liberal century of industry and progress.

By 2019, a minority in Caracas and other big cities also imagined they lived above it all. Their smartphones and growing access to luxury goods and brand-new restaurants made them feel closer than ever to the great urban centers of the world. At the same time, Chavismo made every possible attempt to turn most other citizens into serfs.

To receive food in a government CLAP box people had to give up the nominal freedoms of citizenship: movement, speech, individual choice, and anonymity.[40] They had to swear allegiance to their local committee. A symbolic line of authority rose to the president. The fatherland's ID *(carnet de la Patria)* was the medal symbolizing that homage and the technical instrument fixing individuals to their literal commune.[41]

But there was no all-controlling regime. *Prans* imposed a private form of justice on their turfs. Their rule was as violent and arbitrary as the rights chieftains had exercised in the 19th century. *Prans* acted as proxies for the state in some instances but followed their private interests in many matters. Their ability to impose judgment on people of the areas they controlled was unquestioned. But their power was far from supreme. They, too, had to acknowledge and pay homage to those who had more power than they did.

For the serfs and semi-free peasants of the 1800s, violence extended far from their chieftain. Bandits, organized armed bands, and remnants of the independence armies roamed the countryside and killed at will. In the Venezuela of 2019,

commando units from FAES, the *colectivos*, and National
Guards roamed the land with virtual impunity.

By the late 2010s organizations associated with the
state had filled the country's prisons. This was not done as
punishment in the context of state justice. People were not
jailed for breaking public laws. For security forces bent on
consolidating their own power, prisons were a tool. The threat
of prison could secure a trade route for humans, gold, or drugs.
Sometimes, a gang was targeted by security forces on behalf of
another gang; sometimes, it was done to send a message in
a negotiation. Once inside prisons, inmates had privileges and
rights extended by the clans that controlled them.

The diffused and highly codified distribution of power
recalling ancient times engulfed the entire country. President
Maduro, in power since 2013, was forced to govern along
with several military-political overlords and the agents of
a foreign nation. As had been the case with the regional
chieftains and lords of the 1800s, these powerful, wealthy,
and influential leaders derived their legitimacy from different
histories, connections, and allegiances.

One had gained his standing as a tank commander in
the seminal rebellion of February 4, 1992; two others were
children of the left's martyred saint; another headed an essentially autonomous army; the fifth one had tribal connections
to influential fiefdoms in the Levant, and through them to
faraway Persia. The Cuban legation's agents hovered nearby.
Everyone in this court of rivals wanted more power but were
stopped by each other's independent standing. Their collective
ability to overcome spectacular odds must be attributed, at
least in part, to the workings of so many checks and balances.

The world of formal, visible money was just as fragmented and yet functional. Some of Caracas' wealthiest mansions belonged to a bourgeoisie popularly known as *enchufados*. They dealt with currency complications, traded what they could, and moved within and around a constant ebb of violence and the whims and calculations of the political-military overlords.

All of this while an economic and legal war by the United States was driving the nominal state's international commerce and its financial transactions into the global underground of the dark web, rogue states, cartels, and criminal syndicates.

It is difficult to underestimate the massive challenges posed by the US Justice, Treasury, and State departments for Maduro and the overlords. That they were able to survive until at least 2019 also speaks to the profound misunderstanding on the part of the Venezuelan opposition. The actors seeking "regime change" imagined a perfectly coherent, visible, and quantifiable enemy they could easily topple. They never grasped that fragmentation, chaos, and utter poverty worked against their aims. Acting as if in a different country, the opposition lived to crash into a wall over and over again.

The Future

Overcoming the tragedies and contradictions of Venezuela seems, as of this writing, a titanic enterprise. Three things are required to move forward: doing away with an inward-looking Chavismo while acknowledging its grievances and legacies, navigating a fragmented field of power where no actor will peacefully give up their stake, and building something tangible on the wreckage of what was destroyed. Each of these puzzles appears to be unsolvable.

The aftermath of the independence wars was also a social tragedy and an economic disaster. The political and military landscape was booby-trapped at every turn. Against all odds, José Antonio Páez managed to broker two decades of tenuous peace, open the door to world investment and commerce after three centuries of Spanish mercantilism, and buy time to lay the foundations of a brand-new nation. Páez has been harshly judged through the lens of today's certainties and comforts, which misses the complexity of the challenges he confronted. What little he accomplished made a difference in his time and down to our days.

How he did it remains one of the lessons in Venezuela's history that can illuminate a path through the treacherous decades to come.

Endnotes

Preface

1   One of this book's core arguments is that there was no single war of independence against Spain but rather a series of distinct conflicts between ethnic, racial, and regional groups. The first chapter presents the general argument while the third, "Ethnic and Racial Wars, 1498-1821," chronicles the distinct wars between 1810 and 1823 as well as their demographic and historical roots. The book contends that instead of referring to a "Venezuelan War of Independence" it is more accurate to speak of "Wars of Independence."

Implosion: 1999–2019

1   See endnote 1 in the Preface.

2   Historian Federico Brito Figueroa asserts that census figures in 1810, the year the war broke out, placed the colony's population at 898,043, while those of 1822 put it at 616,545, in which case 282,498 perished from all causes during the conflict. He also quotes geographer Agustin Codazzi, who claimed in 1841 that 200,000 soldiers and civilians had died in the violent conflict, and another 60,000 had died from plagues and the earthquake of 1812. Federico Brito Figueroa, "La población y la estructura social de Venezuela en las primeras décadas del siglo XIX," **Bulletin Hispanique**, Tome LXIX, No 3-4, (Bourdeux, July-December 1967). Codazzi, Agustín, **Resumen de la geografía de Venezuela**, (París, Imprenta de H. Fournier y Compañía, 1841), 245.

3   German naturalist Alexander Von Humboldt calculated that Caracas had 50,000 inhabitants by 1810. By 1820 the population stood at 20,000. "Annual Report of the Director of the International Bureau of the American Republics," House of Representatives, Government Printing Office, (Washington D.C., 1904), 99.

4   Jennifer L. McCoy and Heather D. Heckel, "Venezuela, History," Encyclopaedia Britannica, 2020, https://www.britannica.com/place/Venezuela

5   Michael Clodfelter, **Warfare and Armed Conflicts: A Statistical Encyclopedia of Casualty and Other Figures, 1492-2015**, 4th Ed. (McFarland Incorporated, 2017), 312, https://www.google.com/books/edition/Warfare_and_Armed_Conflicts/8urEDgAAQBAJ?hl=en&gbpv=0

6	Vivian Sequera, "Venezuelans report big weight losses in 2017 as hunger hits," Reuters, (February 21, 2018).

7	Susana Raffalli, "En Venezuela los niños son el eslabón más débil de la crisis alimentaria," entrevista a Susana Raffalli, Civilis Derechos Humanos, April 4, 2018, https://www.civilisac.org/emergencia-humanitaria-compleja/ venezuela-los-ninos-eslabon-mas-debil-la-crisis-alimentaria

8	Juan Forero, "Hyperinflation Shatters Venezuelan Manufacturing," Wall Street Journal, (March 5, 2019); Sheyla Urdaneta, Anatoly Kurmanaev, and Isayen Herrera, "Venezuela, Once an Oil Giant, Reaches the End of an Era," New York Times, (October 7, 2020).

9	2018 inflation was 929,790%. Ryan Dube, "Venezuela's Central Bank Releases Data on Dire Economy," Wall Street Journal, (May 28, 2019).

10	Already by 2011 "the Bolivarian Republic of Venezuela was the most prominent country of origin for direct cocaine shipments to Europe, with the cocaine coming mainly from Colombia." United Nations Office on Drugs and Crime, "The Transatlantic Cocaine Market," (2011). https://www.unodc.org/ documents/data-and-analysis/Studies/Transatlantic_cocaine_market.pdf

11	Jim Wyss, "Caracas was the most dangerous capital city in the world last year, study says," Miami Herald, (March 8, 2018).

12	Tom Phillips, "Venezuela's 'staggering' exodus reaches 4 million, UN refugee agency says," Guardian, (June 7, 2019).

13	Igor Hernández and Francisco Monaldi, "Weathering Collapse: An Assessment of the Financial and Operational Situation of the Venezuelan Oil Industry," Working Papers, Harvard University Center for International Development, (November 2016), https://growthlab.cid.harvard.edu/files/ growthlab/files/venezuela_oil_cidwp_327.pdf

14	Federico Brito Figueroa, Historia Económica y Social de Venezuela: Una Estructura para su Estudio, Universidad Central de Venezuela, Ediciones de la Biblioteca, (1979), tomo 1, 160.

15	The standard scholarly assumption is there were as many as 500,000 people living in the area comprising today's Venezuela. However, more recent research is starting to revise this number upwards. Massimo Livi Bacci, "Venezuela's Melting Pot: 1500-1800," Revista Brasileira de Estudos de População, (September 2017), Vol. 34, No. 2, 199.

16	Agustín Basave Benítez, México mestizo: análisis del nacionalismo mexicano en torno a la mestizofilia de Andrés Molina Enríquez, Fondo de Cultura

Ecónomica, 1992, 17. For more detail on the execution of the Queen's instructions by Governor Obando in the Spanish American colonies see Carlos Nouel, Historia eclesiástica de la Arquidiósesis de Santo Domingo, Primada de América, T.I. Santo Domingo, Editora Santo Domingo, 1979, 24. Cited by Esteban Mira Caballos, "Algunas Precisiones en torno al gobierno de Frey Nicolás de Ovando en al Española (1502-1509)," Revista de Estudios Extremeños. Badajoz: Diputación Provincial. Institución de Servicios Culturales, 1996, 83.

17   Gabriel Jackson, The Making of Medieval Spain, Harcourt Brace Jovanovich, 1972, 25.

18   Federico Brito Figueroa, El Problema de la tierra y esclavos en la historia de Venezuela, Caracas, Universidad Central de Venezuela, Ediciones de la Biblioteca, 1985, 93-131.

19   Federico Brito Figueroa, La Estructura Económica de Venezuela Colonial, Facultad de Economía, Universidad Central de Venezuela, 1963, 355.

20   Ibid.

21   Federico Brito Figueroa, "Venezuela colonial: las rebeliones de esclavos y la Revolución Francesa." Caravelle, No. 54, 1990, 267.

22   Chi-Yi Chen, Michel Picouet, Dinámica de la población: caso de Venezuela. Edición UCAB-ORSTOM, 1979, 19.

23   Anonymous, Caste painting with all 16 combinations. Museo Nacional del Virreinato, Tepotzotlán, Mexico, https://commons.wikimedia.org/wiki/File:-Casta_painting_all.jpg

24   The Zambo caste designated those thought to be of indigenous and African descent.

25   Historically and geographically the term "Pardo" has been fluid. Many legal and popular texts of the time distinguish Pardos from Mulattos, the latter being those of Black and white ancestry. In other documents Pardos are described as necessarily having African ancestry, and no Amerindian blood. Contemporary historians Castellano Rueda and Caballero Escocia write of Venezuelan Pardos as having "a genetic heritage and pheno-typical content notably charged with Afrincannes," a very broad description corresponding to some writings of the time. In their examination of historical documents, they nonetheless conclude the category was very flexible and came to include anyone of brown skin and mixed-race. Brito Figueroa does not make a distinction in most of his assessments of population numbers. Castellano Rueda, Caballero Escorcia, La lucha por la igualdad: los pardos

en la independencia de Venezuela 1808-1812, Caracas, Archivo Nacional de la Nación, Centro Nacional de Historia, (2010), 36-43. Brito Figueroa, Historia Económica, (1979), tomo 1, 160.

26   Rosenblat, La población indígena y el mestizaje en América. Buenos Aires, Editorial Novo, (1954), Tomo 158-60 and 87-90, cited by Brito Figueroa, Historia Económica, (1979), tomo 1, 134.

27   Brito Figueroa, Historia Económica, (1979), tomo 1, 160.

28   Ibid.

29   Laureano Vallenilla Lanz, "Cesarismo demócratico," in Cesarismo demócratico y otros textos, (Caracas, Biblioteca Ayacucho, 1991), 40. (Author's translation.).

30   Ibid.

31   See Castellano Rueda and Caballero Escorcia, La lucha por la igualdad, 36-73.

32   Brito Figueroa, "Venezuela colonial," Caravelle, (1990), 270.

33   Laureano Vallenilla Sanz, "Cesarismo," (1991), 21. (Author's translation.).

34   Juan Uslar, Historia de la Rebelión Popular de 1814, (Edime, Madrid, 1962), p. 8.

35   Ibid.

36   Arturo Uslar Pietri (Juan Uslar's brother) has emphasized the destruction of all colonial institutions and the exile or death of most Spanish in the war's aftermath. Arturo Uslar Pietri, "Valores Humanos: La Inteligencia Venezolana," (YouTube, posted by PNTDXTR, August 12 2013), https://www.youtube.com/watch?v=VLSz94NJSH8

37   Philippe Girard, Haiti: The Tumultuous History—From Pearl of the Caribbean to Broken Nation, (St Martin's Griffin, 2010), 23.

38   Ibid., 65-66.

39   Ibid., 65.

40   Susan Berlung, "The 'Musiues' in Venezuela: immigration goals and reality, 1936-1961," Doctoral Dissertation, (University of Massachusetts at Amherst, Scholar Works @ Umass Amherst, 1980), 86.

41   The census does not break down the Caracas metropolitan area from other parts of Miranda state. The population of the Caracas metropolitan area was estimated to be 975,000 by 1961, while the census counted

246,000 foreign-born residents in the Federal District and Miranda. Berlung, "The 'Musiues' in Venezuela," Table 31, 205.

42 Manuel Beroes, "Historia Caracas," **Diccionario de Historia de Venezuela.** Fundación Empresas Polar, https://bibliofep.fundacionempresaspolar.org/ dhv/entradas/c/caracas/#temporaryDirectBibliography

43 Gerardo José Siso Quintero, "La población de Venezuela: evolución, crecimiento y distribución geográfica," **Terra Nueva Etapa**, Vol. XXVIII, issue 43, (January—June 2012, Universidad Central de Venezuela Caracas), 109-140.

44 Guillermo Luque, **Momentos de la Educación y la Pedagogía Venezolanas**, Historia Oral, Fondo Editorial de Humanidades, UCV, (Caracas, 2001), 163.

45 Arnoldo Gabaldon and Alberto Berti, "The first large area in the tropical zone to report malaria eradication: North-Central Venezuela," **American Journal Tropical Medicine Hygiene**, (1954 September); Vol. 3, No. 5, 793-807.

46 Judith Ewell, **Venezuela: A Century of Change**, (Stanford University Press, Stanford, 1984), 18.

47 Ibid., 112.

48 Raul Gallegos, **Crude Nation: How Oil Riches Ruined Venezuela**, (University of Nebraska Press, Lincoln, 2016), 72.

49 Encyclopaedia Britannica, "Ethnicity," (2023), https://www.britannica.com/topic/ethnicity

50 Alfredo Brillembourg, Hubert Klumpner, "Rules of Engagement: Caracas and the Informal City," in **Rethinking the Informal City: Critical Perspectives from Latin America**, ed. Felipe Hernández et al., (Berghahn Books, United Kingdom, 2012), 123-124.

51 Ibid.

52 Nora Castañeda and Raúl Cubas, "Extreme Poverty Has Doubled," (Centro de Estudios de la Mujer. Universidad Central de Venezuela, PROVEA, 2001, Caracas), Social Watch, https://www.socialwatch.org/node/10732

53 Robert Weiss and Nigel South, eds, **Comparing Prison Systems: Towards a Comparative and International Penology**, (Routledge, New York, 2013), 118.

54 Alejandro Rebolledo, **Pin Pan Pun**, Codex Novellus, 2018, 99. "De repente volteas un día y te das cuenta de que lo que hay a tu alrededor no se parece a las películas que ves en la tele, que esto no es California, que lo que hay es un poco de ranchos, gente que oye merengue y desayuna gatos..." (Author's Translation.).

55   Thomas T. Vogel Jr., "Ex-Coup Leader Hugo Chavez Rattles Venezuelan Investors," The Wall Street Journal, (April 27, 1998).

56   Interview with Andrés Caleca, president of the National Electoral Council between 1998 and 2001, (November 27, 2019).

57   Ibid.

58   "Storytelling the Revolution: Narrative and Latin American Revolutionary Politics 1959-2016." Symposium, New York University King Juan Carlos Center, (New York, April 22, 2016).

59   Ibid.

60   Ibid.

61   "Movimientos y Partidos Políticos," Nueva Sociedad, Fundación Friedrich Ebert N° 40 / Enero-Febrero 1979, https://nuso.org/articulo/partido-accion-democratica-postulados-doctrinarios/

62   José Vasconcelos, The Cosmic Race / La raza cósmica, (Johns Hopkins University Press, 1997).

63   "Many people have commented on the special characteristics of his Spanish, his use in both speaking and writing of colloquial Venezuelan words and phrases of provincial origin ..." Robert Alexander, Rómulo Betancourt and the Transformation of Venezuela, (Transaction Books, 1982), 20.

64   Arturo Uslar Pietri, Lanzas coloradas y cuentos selectos, (Argentina: Biblioteca Ayacucho, 1979).

65   Rómulo Gallegos, Doña Barbara, Doral, Stockcero, (2009).

66   Augusto Mijares, La interpretación pesimista de la sociología hispanoamericana, (Coop. de artes gráficas, 1938. Digitized by the University of Michigan, August 11, 2006), https://books.google.com/books?id=MNoEAAAAMAAJ&source=gbs_book_other_versions

67   Arturo Uslar Pietri, Lanzas Coloradas y cuentos selectos, 1979, 79. Author's translation ("...lo sabía indeciso y tímido (...) El [el dueño de la plantación] se creía fuerte y no lo era; se creía revolucionario y no lo era; se creía inteligente y no lo era; se creía amo y no lo era.").

68   Jeffrey Dixon and Meredith Sarkees, A Guide to Intra-state Wars: An Examination of Civil Wars, 1816-2014, Congressional Quarterly Press, Sage Publications, Thousand Oaks, California, 2016, 149.

69 See his remarks in Arturo Uslar Pietri, "La inteligencia de Venezuela," Valores Humanos. YouTube, posted by Juan José Briceño Nava, (January 21, 2014). https://www.youtube.com/watch?v=5WeA8u48r8U

70 For the tradition of liberal historians focusing on the intellectuals who tried to build a civil, sophisticated country in the 19th century, see Elías Pino Iturrieta, País archipiélago: Venezuela 1830-1858, (Editorial Alfa, Caracas, 2016).

71 The nominal price of oil started dropping in 1980 and would not return to its peak again until the end of 2004 (except for the 1990 Gulf War hiccup). https://www.macrotrends.net/1369/crude-oil-price-history-chart

72 Elena Holodny, "155 years of oil prices–in one chart," World Economic Forum, (December 16, 2016). https://www.weforum.org/agenda/2016/12/155-years-of-oil-prices-in-one-chart/

73 Dieter Nohlen, ed, Elections in the Americas: A Data Handbook, Volume 2: South America, (Oxford University Press), 2005, 555-566.

74 Venezuela Population 1950-2020, Macrotrends.net. Based on United Nations–World Population Prospects. https://www.macrotrends.net/countries/VEN/venezuela/population

75 Dieter Nohlen, ed., Elections in the Americas, 555-566.

76 Elena Holodny, "155 years of oil prices–in one chart."

77 Vote tally sourced from the International Foundation for Election Systems (IFES), CNN, http://edition.cnn.com/WORLD/election.watch/americas/venezuela.html

78 Federico Brito Figueroa, Tiempo de Ezequiel Zamora, Universidad Central de Venezuela, Ediciones de la Biblioteca, (Caracas, 1981), 405. A more detailed reading of Zamora's correspondence and proclamations reveals the tone, words, and expressions that Chavez often used before 1998 and during his presidency. Zamora was the self-proclaimed "jefe del pueblo soberano," and used the expression "pueblo soberano" to highlight that his revolution emanated directly from the people, without mediation from minority castes. Chavez used the shorthand "el soberano" to root and legitimize many of his decisions, particularly those that gave him power over all representative bodies and over organized civil society. Zamora often called the army "people in arms."

79 Brito Figueroa, Zamora, (1981), 393.

80 Rory Carroll, Sybilla Brodzinsky, "Chavez sends 10 battalions to Colombian border after killing of Farc commander," The Guardian, (March 3, 2008).

81   "New interim leader sworn in, interim govt dissolves Congress,"
      YouTube. Posted by AP Archives, (July 21, 2015),
      https://www.youtube.com/watch?v=JzNLx8Rbf-s

82   José Ignacio Hernández, "La Lista Tascón y la persecución política:
      a propósito de la sentencia de la Corte Interamericana," Prodavinci.com,
      (June 4, 2018), https://prodavinci.com/la-lista-tascon-y-la-persecucion-
      politica-a-proposito-de-la-sentencia-de-la-corte-interamericana/

83   Chang-Tai Hsieh, Edward Miguel, Daniel Ortega, and Francisco Rodriguez,
      "The Price of Political Opposition: Evidence from Venezuela's Maisanta,"
      American Economic Journal: Applied Economics, 3. (April 2011), 196–214,
      http://www.aeaweb.org/articles.php?doi=10.1257/app.3.2.196 f

84   Juan Forero, "Chávez Is Declared the Winner in Venezuela Referendum,"
      New York Times, (August 16, 2004).

85   The Carter Center, Observing the Venezuela Presidential Recall Referendum:
      Comprehensive Report, Atlanta, 2005.

86   Adjusted for inflation, the May 1980 peak for benchmark crude would not be
      reached again until 2007, but by June 2004 the price was already breaking
      a mark not seen since the 1990 oil shock associated with Iraq's invasion of
      Kuwait. Elena Holodny, "155 years of oil prices – in one chart."

87   The exact calculation of Venezuela's oil exports is obscured by secret
      contracts of oil futures to China, under-reporting of exports to OPEC, and the
      general lack of transparency of the Chavez PDVSA era. In 2019 dollars the
      figure of sales between 2004 and 2013 hovers around US$750 billion, and
      could conceivably reach the trillion dollar mark, https://www.americasquar-
      terly.org/fulltextarticle/venezuelas-oil-tale/, https://www.ceicdata.com/en/
      indicator/venezuela/crude-oil-exports, https://www.reuters.com/article/
      us-venezuela-pdvsa-military-specialrepor/special-report-oil-output-goes-awol-in-
      venezuela-as-soldiers-run-pdvsa-idUSKCN1OP0RZ

88   Mark Weisbrot, "Poverty Reduction in Venezuela," Revista: Harvard Review
      of Latin America, (Fall 2008), https://revista.drclas.harvard.edu/book/
      poverty-reduction-venezuela

89   Jonathan Jakubowicz, Las Aventuras de Juan Planchard, (Epicentral Studios,
      2016).

90   Jakubowicz, Juan Planchart, (2016). Kindle location 344 of 5829. "Todos
      nos debemos al Che. Sin el Che todavía estaríamos trabajando para los
      gringos, cobrando sueldos de mierda, enriqueciendo a algún portugués
      o judío capitalista sin ninguna posibilidad de ascenso social. El Che nos dio

libertad y, pase lo que pase, siempre debemos recordarlo.¡Patria o muerte, venceremos!" (Author's translation.).

Economics in the Magical Century, 1922-1998

1   Alberto S. Finol and Z.A. Sancevic, "Chapter 7 Subsidence in Venezuela," in eds G.V. Chilingarian, E.C. Donaldson, T.F. Yen, Developments in Petroleum Science, Elsevier, Vol. 41, (1995), 342, http://www.sciencedirect.com/ science/article/pii/S0376736106800543

2   Average crude prices by the U.S. Labor Bureau of Statistics, adjusted to 2019 dollars by Inflationdata.com, https://inflationdata.com/articles/inflation-adjusted-prices/historical-crude-oil-prices-table/ 2019 Venezuelan crude oil and lease condensate numbers by U.S. Energy Information Administration, https://www.eia.gov/todayinenergy/detail. php?id=39532. 1974 crude oil production numbers by Trading Economics based on OPEC data, https://tradingeconomics.com/venezuela/ crude-oil-production

3   See Annual Average Domestic Crude Prices in Inflationdata.com, https://inflationdata.com/articles/inflation-adjusted-prices/historical-crude-oil-prices-table/

4   Asdrúbal Baptista, Bases cuantitativas de la economía venezolana 1830-2008. (Caracas: Artesano Group Editores, 2011), 80-81.

5   See oil crude price chart at InflationData.com, https://inflationdata.com/ articles/inflation-adjusted-prices/historical-crude-oil-prices-table/

6   The World Bank, "GDP growth (annual %) – Venezuela, RB," https://data.worldbank.org/indicator/NY.GDP.MKTP.KD.ZG?locations=VE

7   Harold A. Trinkunas, Crafting Civilian Control of the Military in Venezuela: A Comparative Perspective, Kindle Edition, (The University of North Carolina Press, 2011), 184.

8   Trinkunas, Crafting Civilian Control, (2011), 184-185.

9   Daniel García Marco, BBC, "Un fracaso militar, un éxito político": 2 visiones opuestas del golpe de Estado fallido en Venezuela que creó la figura de Hugo Chávez hace 25 años, (February 5, 2017), https://www.bbc.com/mundo/noticias-america-latina-38863571

10   Interview with Ignacio Betancourt, former private secretary to President Pérez, in Miami Beach, (March 2017).

11 "Chávez – 4 de febrero de 1992," YouTube, posted by Davidtubeven,
    (April 29, 2007). https://youtu.be/dV1fKQscgSQ

12 Garcia Girón, Letter of February 18, 1612. Cited in Brito Figueroa, Historia
    Económica, (1979), 135.

13 Baptista, Bases cuantitativas, (2011), 777-778.

14 Arturo Almandoz Marte, "Caracas," (Oxford Bibliographies, July
    30, 2014), https://www.oxfordbibliographies.com/view/document/
    obo-9780199766581/obo-9780199766581-0165.xml

15 Andrea Wulf, The Invention of Nature: Alexander von Humboldt's New World.
    (Vintage, 2016), 74-79.

16 Cristobal Colón, Diario de Abordo, editor Luis Arranz. (Edaf, 2011), 93.

17 Ibid., 101.

18 Ibid., 109.

19 Adam Smith, Wealth of Nations, Cosimo Classics, (2007), 248.

20 Pedro Palma, La Política Cambiaria en Venezuela, Ediciones IESA, (2020), 15.

21 Ibid., 14.

22 Ibid., 15.

23 Raul Gallegos, Crude Nation: How Riches Ruined Venezuela, (Potomac Books,
    2019), 60-61.

24 Ibid.

25 Christine Ebrahimzadeh, "Dutch Disease: Wealth Managed Unwisely,"
    imf.org, International Monetary Fund, (February 2020),
    https://www.imf.org/external/pubs/ft/fandd/basics/dutch.htm

26 Arturo Uslar Pietri, "Sembrando el Petróleo," Diario Ahora, (July 14, 1936).
    Reproduced by Digo.Palabra.Txt, https://digopalabratxt.com/2017/05/16/
    sembrar-el-petroleo-por-arturo-uslar-pietri-caracas-1906-2001/

27 Ibid.

28 Ibid.

29 Elena Ianchovichina and Harun Onder, "Dutch disease: An economic illness
    easy to catch, difficult to cure," (Brookings Institute, October 31, 2017),
    https://www.brookings.edu/blog/future-development/2017/10/31/
    dutch-disease-an-economic-illness-easy-to-catch-difficult-to-cure/

30   Jeffrey D. Sachs and Andrew M. Warner, **Natural Resource Abundance and Economic Growth.** National Bureau of Economic Research Working Paper Series, (1995), 4.

31   Ibid.

32   Also see Aaron Tornell and Philip R. Lane, "The Voracity Effect," **The American Economic Review,** Vol. 89, No. 1, (March 1999).

33   Ibid.

34   "Crude Oil Prices – 70 Year Historical Chart," Macrotrends.com, https://www.macrotrends.net/1369/crude-oil-price-history-chart

35   Baptista, **Bases cuantitativas,** 2011, 80-81.

36   The debate between CEPAL-inspired economics and the latter Washington Consensus is so polarized that the intellectual contributions of each approach are consistently ignored by the other. For a historical summary from the Washington perspective see Sebastian Edwards, "Forty Years of Latin America's Economic Development: From the Alliance for Progress to the Washington Consensus," **National Bureau of Economic Research,** Working Paper 15190, (Cambridge, MA, 2009). http://www.nber.org/papers/w15190. For a summary from the **desarrollista** perspective see Joseph L. Love, "The Rise and Decline of Economic Structuralism in Latin America: New Dimensions," **Latin American Research Review,** The Latin American Studies Association, Vol. 40, No. 3, 2005, 100-125, https://www.jstor.org/stable/3662824

37   Celso Furtado, **The Economic Growth of Brazil: A Survey from Colonial to Modern Times,** (The University of California Press, 1971), 225-230.

38   Furtado was keenly aware of the conundrum facing Venezuela. One of his concerns was how the imbalance provoked by oil blocked the generation of highly productive employment for the population at large: "no fundo do problema está o fato de que quanto mais capitalizada é uma atividade produtiva, mais participação tem nos lucros que a elevada produtividade do setor petroleiro oferece ao conjunto da economia por meio do intercâmbio externo. Cria-se assim um círculo vicioso, pois a excessiva capitalização das atividades produtivas implica lenta absorção da força de trabalho em ocupações de produtividade mais elevada, desenvolvimento lento do mercado interno e, portanto, oportunidades mais escassas para novos investimentos" (Furtado, 2008, 70). He also remarked on the folly of a Venezuelan free market economy on the back of oil exports, particularly in relation to currency overvaluation: "Se se permitisse o jogo espontâneo das forças do

mercado, a Venezuela tenderia a ser transformar numa economia principal-mente monoprodutora, com grande parte da sua população desempregada ou subempregada e com uma moeda ainda mais sobrevalorizada; os recursos provenientes do setor petroleiro seriam transferidos para os consumidores através de um forte subsídio cambial oculto; os salários monetários exces-sivamente elevados tornariam impraticável qualquer investimento destinado a substituir importações; a falta de investimentos nesse importante setor reduziria a necessidade de investimentos em infra-estrutura; os recursos financieros disponíveis tenderiam a emigrar e o desenvolvimento geral do pais seria muito lento ou nulo (Furtado, 2008, 54). Celso Furtado, **Ensaios Sobre AVenezuela:Subdesenvolvimentocomabundânciadedivisas.ArquivosCelso** Furtado, Contraponto, 2008.

39   Interview with Raúl Delgado, CEO of Venezuelan shoe manufacturer Neutroni, (Miami Beach, 2017).

40   Reuters Staff, "Timeline: Mexico's Cemex shares hit multi-year low," Reuters, (October 4, 2011), https://www.reuters.com/article/ us-cemex-timeline-idUSTRE7937HI20111004

41   Miguel Rodríguez, "El verdadero origen de la deuda," **Revista Sic**, (Caracas), 47, 469.

42   Ibid.

43   According to a World Bank internal memorandum, "real private investment decreased continuously in Venezuela from 1977 to 1982." Latin America and the Caribbean Regional Office, Country Economic Report on Venezuela, Policy Choices and Economic Growth (In Two Parts) Part II, World Bank (March 3, 1988), 12, http://documents1.worldbank.org/curated/ pt/200321468309391820/text/multi0page.txt

44   Federal Funds Rate – 62 Year Historical Chart, Macrotrends.com, https:// www.macrotrends.net/2015/fed-funds-rate-historical-chart, Crude Oil Prices–70 Year Historical Chart, Macrotrends.com, https://www.macrotrends. net/1369/crude-oil-price-history-chart.

45   Ibid.

46   Stephen Kinzer, "Venezuela Resisting IMF Rein," **The New York Times**, (July 25, 1983), https://www.nytimes.com/1983/07/25/business/ venezuela-resisting-imf-rein.html

47   Ibid.

48   Palma, **Política Cambiaria**, (2020), 69-70.

49 Walter Little and Antonio Herrera, "Political Corruption in Venezuela," in
    Political Corruption in Europe and Latin America, eds. Walter Little, Eduardo
    Posada-Carbo, (Palgrave Macmillan, 1996), 270-274.

50 Macrotrends.com, sourced in UN Population Prospects, https://www.macro-
    trends.net/countries/VEN/venezuela/population

51 Gisela Blanco Gómez, "Pobreza y Desempleo en Venezuela," Cuadernos de
    la Escuela de Salud Pública, Escuela de Medicina, Universidad Central de
    Venezuela, Vol. 4, No. 92, (Julio-Diciembre 2016), http://saber.ucv.ve/ojs/
    index.php/rev_edsp/article/download/12732/12443

52 Roberto Briceño León, "Tres fases de la violencia homicida
    en Venezuela," Ciênc. saúde coletiva [online], (2012),
    Vol. 17, No. 12, 3233-3242, <http://www.scielo.br/scielo.
    php?script=sci_arttext&pid=S1413-81232012001200008&lng=en&nrm=iso

53 Edwards, "Forty Years," Bureau, (2009), 26-27.
    http://www.nber.org/papers/w15190.

54 Historical Archive, Inter-parliamentary Union, Venezuela (Bolivarian Republic
    of), Asamblea Nacional (National Assembly), 1988 Election Results,
    http://archive.ipu.org/parline-e/reports/2347_arc.htm

55 Dan Fastenberg, "Carlos Andrés Pérez," Time, (Monday, January 10, 2011),
    http://content.time.com/time/magazine/article/0,9171,2040189,00.html

56 Reuters, "Venezuela Pact with IMF," The New York Times,
    (February 23, 1989).

57 Moisés Naím, Paper Tigers and Minotaurs: The Politics of Venezuela's
    Economic Reforms, Carnegie Endowment for International Peace, (1993),
    p. 50.

58 Ibid.

59 Ibid., 31-33.

60 El Caracazo Case, Judgment of November 11, 1999, Inter-Am. Ct. H.R.
    (Ser. C) No. 58 (1999), in University of Minnesota Human Rights Library,
    http://hrlibrary.umn.edu/iachr/C/58-ing.html

61 Ibid.

62 Alba Morgade, "Qué fue 'la masacre del Caracazo' hace 30 años y qué nos
    dice de la situación actual en Venezuela," BBC News Mundo, (February 27,
    2019), https://www.bbc.com/mundo/noticias-america-latina-47379668

63 El Nacional, "El Caracazo: las imágenes más impactantes que divulgó El Nacional," (El Nacional, February 27, 2020), https://www.elnacional.com/venezuela/el-caracazo-las-imagenes-mas-impactantes-que-divulgo-el-nacional/

64 As a proportion of all payments made by Venezuela abroad, interest on the debt went down from 34.9% in 1988 to 20.5% in 1991. Juan C. Navarro and Roberto Rigobón, "La economía política del ajuste estructural y de la reforma del sector público en Venezuela," Coyuntura Económica, Vol. XXII, No. 3, (Fedesarrollo, Bogotá, 1992), 139, https://www.repository.fedesarrollo.org.co/handle/11445/2311

65 Navarro and Rigobón, "Economía Política," (1992), 142.

66 World Bank, "GDP growth," https://data.worldbank.org/indicator/NY.GDP.MKTP.KD.ZG?locations=VE

67 Navarro and Rigobón, "Economía Política," (1992), 139.

68 Ibid., 144.

69 Ibid.

70 Naím, Minotaurs, (1993), 120-121.

71 Ibid.

72 Navarro and Rigobón, "Economía Política," (1992), 139.

Ethnic and Racial Wars, 1498-1821

1 Juan Uslar mentions General José Trinidad Morán's estimate of 20,000 refugees. Juan Uslar, Historia De La Rebelión Popular De 1814, Edime, Caracas, 1962, 145.

2 Jose Francisco Heredia, Memoria sobre las Revoluciones de Venezuela, Edit. Garnfer. (Paris, 1895), 201. Cited by Uslar, Rebelión, (1962), 145. "El camino que llaman de Sabana Grande o Chacao estuvo todo el día cubierto de una columna de todas clases y edades que huían despavoridas a pie y cargando cada cual con lo que podía..." (Author's translation.).

3 Tito Salas, "Emigración a Oriente," (1913), Casa de Bolívar, Wikimedia Commons, https://commons.wikimedia.org/wiki/File:%C3%89xododeCaracasen 1814.jpg.

4 Uslar, Rebelión, (1962), 138 and 145.

5 Ibid., 161.

6   Ibid., 160-161.

7   Ibid.

8   The episode is recounted by Uslar citing Ducoudray-Holstein's Histoire de
     Bolivar, and Enrique Bernardo Nuñez's La ciudad de los techos rojos, (1947),
     121. Uslar, Rebelión, (1960, 161).

9   For a history of Castile's "comunero movement" see Joseph Perez, Comuneros,
     La Esfera Libros, (2016).

10   For a detailed study of the changing Creole-Crown dynamics in Mexico's XVII
     century see Cayetana Alvarez de Toledo, Juan De Palafox: Obispo y Virrey,
     Marcial Pons Ediciones de Historia, 1° ed. edition, (2011).

11   John V. Lombardi, Venezuela: The Search for Order, the Dream of Progress,
     (Oxford University Press, 1982), 81-82.

12   Ibid., 77.

13   Ibid., 94-95.

14   Ibid., 98-99.

15   José Vicente González, Biografía del general José Félix Ribas, primer teniente
     de Bolívar en 1813 y 1814, Madrid, Editorial América, 54. "...con doscientos
     treinta soldados entre españoles y coreanos, un cura de nombre Torellas, un
     cirujano, diez mil cartuchos, un obús de a cuatro y diez quintales de galletas."
     (Author's translation.).

16   Names inscribed under the Arc de Triomphe, Wikipedia,
     https://en.wikipedia.org/wiki/Names_inscribed_under_the_Arc_de_Triomphe

17   Uslar, Rebelión, (1962), 18.

18   Ibid.

19   John Lynch, Simon Bolívar: A Life, (Yale University Press, 2006), Kindle Edition,
     location 1006.

20   The rise of those enslaved was probably more relevant to the early battles of
     independence than other military calculations. When Francisco de Miranda
     realized that Bolívar had lost the Puerto Cabello garrison, he doubted he
     could successfully fight Domingo Monteverde's troops to the west of his
     position. But more important still, he could not ignore a full-fledged slave
     revolt on his eastern flank. The Curiepe Valley rebellion of July 13, 1811 sent
     escaped slaves in the direction of Miranda's army. This was probably the
     biggest threat to his military position. The central valley's landowners, principal
     source of soldiers and financial support for the independence cause, were

now focused on both the actual slave rebellion, as well as further rebellions rumored to be imminent. In an alternative version of events mentioned by Juan Uslar and citing the memoirs of French eye-witness H. Poudenx, Miranda's order to march forward and attack Monteverde was reversed by Congress in fear of slave rebellions that would bring "bloody scenes by the week's end." Either way, the real factors driving the war's outcome are evident.

21 Federico Brito Figueroa's life-long oeuvre brought the Annal school to Venezuelan historiography. His academic research stands as the foundational work on the country's social and economic history from the XVI through the XIX centuries, as well as the history of slavery.

22 Federico Brito Figueroa, "Venezuela colonial: las rebeliones de esclavos y la Revolución Francesa," Caravelle, n°54, 1990. L'Amérique latine face à la Révolution française, 273. "No hubo una región que no fuera afectada por alguna rebelión or insurgencia armada, bien esclavos, negros libres, indios encomendados, tributarios o libres, peones o 'poblaciónn de color libre.'" "Hubo extensas áreas del territorio venezolano que en todo momento estuvieron dominadas por los negros cimarrones." (Author's translation.).

23 Pedro Simón, Demetrio Ramos Pérez, R. J. Lovera De-Sola, Noticias historiales de Venezuela, (Biblioteca Ayacucho, 1992), Vol. 2, 344.

24 Ibid.

25 Brito Figueroa, História Económica, (1979), Tomo 1, 128.

26 Simón, Ramos Pérez, et al., Noticias, (1992), Vol. 2, 344.

27 Ibid., 68-71.

28 Ibid.

29 Ibid.

30 The Editors of the Encyclopaedia Britannica, "Battle of Carabobo," Encyclopaedia Britannica, (17 June 2020), https://www.britannica.com/event/Battle-of-Carabobo

31 Lombardi, Venezuela, 71.

32 Brito Figueroa, "Venezuela colonial," 280.

33 Brito Figueroa, "Venezuela colonial," 267.

34 Ibid.

35 Ibid.

36 Manuel Guevara Baro, Venezuela en el tiempo: Cronología desde la
    Conquista hasta la fundación de la República, (Libros El Nacional, 2007), 20.

37 Wim Klooster and Gert Oostindie, Curaçao in the Age of Revolutions,
    1795-1800, (Brill, 2011), 89-90.

38 Ibid.

39 Federico Brito Figueroa, La Estructura Económica de Venezuela Colonial,
    Facultad de Economía, (Universidad Central de Venezuela, 1963), 351.

40 Ibid.

41 Between 1771 and 1774 a full-fledged guerrilla war led by Negro Guillermo
    kept the Tuy Valleys, south of Caracas, in a state of permanent alert. The best
    chronicled insurrection took place in 1795 near Coro, the territories' first
    seat of power. Jose Leonardo Chirinos led the revolt under the banner of the
    'French Law' of equality and was directly inspired by the Haitian revolution of
    former slave Toussaint Louverture. Unable to take the city, the rebel army fled
    to the nearby mountains where they sought the support of indigenous groups.
    In time Chirinos was betrayed and turned over to the Spanish authorities and
    Creole slaveowners, who hanged him in the main square in Caracas. His body
    was cut up for public display and the severed head returned to Coro. See Brito
    Figueroa, "Venezuela colonial," 283-287.

42 Federico Brito Figueroa, El Problema de la tierra y esclavos en la historia de
    Venezuela, (Caracas, Universidad Central de Venezuela, Ediciones de la
    Biblioteca, 1985), 93-131.

43 Ibid.

44 Simón Bolívar, "El Manifiesto de Cartagena 1812," Los Estandartes de la
    Independencia, ed. Gustavo A. Vaamonde, (Fundación Empresas Polar, 2014).

45 Simón Bolívar, "Decreto de Guerra a Muerte," Escritos fundamentales, ed.
    Germán Carrera Damas, (Monte Avila Editores, 1982), 107.

46 According to the UN's Office on Genocide Prevention, the deliberate targeting
    of a "national group" with the "intent to destroy, in whole or in part, a national
    group as such," by "killing members of the group" would be considered
    genocide. Case law has "associated intent with the existence of a State or
    organizational plan or policy." In addition, "victims of genocide are deliberately
    targeted – not randomly – because of their real or perceived membership in one
    of the four groups protected" (national origin being one of the four). In terms of
    the death decree, it is particularly relevant that "genocide can also be committed
    against only a part of the group, as long as that part is identifiable (including

within a geographically limited area) and 'substantial.'" United Nations Office on Genocide Prevention and the Responsibility to Protect, "Genocide: Background," United Nations, https://www.un.org/en/genocideprevention/genocide.shtm

47 Lombardi, Venezuela, 129.

48 Uslar, Rebelión, 1962, 78. "La paz parecía estar asegurada en el centro de la República. Todo parecía en calma. Pero la realidad no era así. En el campo la situación era distinta, el gobierno del Rey era mirado con cariño, ya que los isleños no habían cometido los desmanes que habían hecho en las ciudades, y más bien se consideraba como protectores de los intereses populares contra la tiranía de sus señores. Los negros de Barlovento, siempre fieles a su consigna revolucionaria, se levantaron en armas contra la República de los blancos, sus amos, lanzando gritos de viva el Rey. Bolívar envió a José Felix Ribas a pacificarlos, cosa que logró éste en poco tiempo por carecer de armas los insurrectos, y al mes de haber comenzado su campaña todo estaba en manos de los patriotas. Al propio tiempo que en Barlovento los esclavos tomaban las armas contra los blancos, en Los Llanos empezaban a surgir bandas armadas con lanzas y picas, comandadas por jefes oscuros y sin relieve, que se dirigían por los pueblos patriotas asesinando a sus habitantes y proclamando al Rey, a la vez que satisfacían el hambre de reivindicaciones sociales degollando a los blancos y repartiéndose las riquezas que robaban." (Author's translation.).

49 See the classic Magnus Mörner, Race Mixture in the History of Latin America, (Little, Brown and Company, 1967), and the more recent Joanne Rappaport, The Disappearing Mestizo: Configuring Difference in the Colonial New Kingdom of Granada, (Duke University Press Books, 2014), and Ben Vison III, Before Mestizaje: The Frontiers of Race and Caste in Colonial Mexico, (Cambridge University Press, 2018).

50 Roberto Marín-Guzmán, "Ethnic Groups and Social Classes in Muslim Spain," Islamic Studies, Vol. 30, No. 1/2, Special Issue on Muslim Heritage in Spain (Spring-Summer 1991), 51, 52-54.

51 Gabriel Jackson, The Making of Medieval Spain, (Harcourt Brace Jovanovich, 1972), 25.

52 Magnus Mörner, Race Mixture in the History of Latin America, 54.

53 For a visual description of Aztec social structure see "Aztec and Maya Law: An Online Exhibit and Bibliography," Tarlton Law Library, University of Texas, https://tarlton.law.utexas.edu/aztec-and-maya-law/intro

54 For a visual representation of Inca social structures produced under the United Nations Civilizations Legacy Executive mandate, see Inca Group, "Inca Civilization," (U.N.C.L.E., 2020), http://wludh.ca/dh100/2015/CSAm/Inca/social-structure/

55 Agustín Basave Benítez, México mestizo: análisis del nacionalismo mexicano en torno a la mestizofilia de Andrés Molina Enríquez, (Fondo de Cultura Ecónomica, 1992), 17. For more detail on the execution of the Queen's instructions by Governor Obando in the Spanish American colonies see Carlos Nouel, Historia eclesiástica de la Arquidiósesis de Santo Domingo, Primada de América, T.I. Santo Domingo, Editora Santo Domingo, (1979), 24. Cited by Esteban Mira Caballos, "Algunas Preciosiones en torno al gobierno de Frey Nicolás de Ovando en al Española (1502-1509)," Revista de Estudios Extremeños. Badajoz: Diputación Provincial. (Institución de Servicios Culturales, 1996), 83.

56 Brito Figueroa, História, (1979), Tomo 1, 164-165.

57 Brito Figueroa, La Estructura Económica, (1963), 382.

58 Ibid.

59 "Slave, Free Black, and White Population, 1780-1830," History 407 The Founding of the American Nation (course materials), (University of Maryland Baltimore County, Spring 2010), https://userpages.umbc.edu/~bouton/History407/SlaveStats.htm

60 Brito Figueroa, La Estructura Económica, 1963, 382.

61 Santos Rodulfo Cortés, Documento No. 19, El Régimen de 'Gracias al Sacar' en Venezuela durante el período hispánico. Tomo 1, Anexo Documental, (Caracas, Biblioteca de la Académica Nacional de la Historia, 1978), 1-5, in Rocío Castellanos Rueda, Boris Cabellero Escorcia, La Lucha por la Igualdad: Los Pardos en el Proceso de Independencia de Venezuela, 1808-1812, (Caracas, Archivo General de la Nación, Centro Nacional de Historia, 2010), 57.

62 Ibid.

63 For an extensive argument on the growing fluidity of castes see Joanne Rappaport, The Disappearing Mestizo: Configuring Difference in the Colonial New Kingdom of Granada, (Duke University Press Books, 2014).

64 Cortés, Documento No 19, Tomo 2, 45-48, in Castellanos Rueda, Caballero Escorcia, La Lucha por la Igualdad, 58-59. "...es espantoso a los vecinos y naturales de América porque solo ellos conocen desde que nacen o por el transcurso de muchos años de trato en ella, la inmensa distancia que separa

a los Blancos y Pardos; la ventaja y superioridad de aquéllos y la baxeza y subordinación de éstos." (Author's translation.).

65   Ibid. "para que entren a influir en el gobierno público unos hombres de infame y torpe linaje, faltos de educación, fáciles de moverse a los más horrendos excesos y de cuya fiereza propia de sus mismos principios y trato, solo pueden esperarse movimientos escandalosos y subversivos del orden establecido por las sabias Leyes que hasta ahora nos han regido..." (Author's translation.).

66   Ibid., 193,"...si la carrera de las letras les abre las puertas a los honores y empleos, y las luces y conocimientos desenrollan la perniciosa semilla de sus ideas de igualdad y predominio, si el empeño de acopiar libros y formar bibliotecas, empeño consiguiente a la profesión literaria, pone entre sus manos algunas de las monstruosas producciones subversivas de las máximas de nuestro gobierno destructoras de todo orden social y enemigas de toda dominación...si estos libros que halagan tanto su amor propio, que exaltan con tanto atrevimiento los derechos del hombre y que alimentan el orgullo del bajo pueblo los hace reflexionar sobre su pasada esclavitud, sobre su actual abatimiento y sobre la supresión de unas inmunidades que pretenden debérseles justicia...con unas máximas tan seductoras comunicarían a sus hermanos el contagio con tanta mayor facilidad..." (Author's translation.).

67   Ibid., 73.

68   Brito Figueroa, **História**, (1979), Tomo 1, 160.

69   Ibid.

70   Uslar, **Rebelión**, 1962, 82-89.

71   Ibid.

72   Ibid.

73   Ibid.

74   Brito Figueroa, **Historia**, (1979), Tomo 1, 196.

75   Uslar, **Rebelión**, (1962), 82-89.

76   Ibid., 107-108.

77   Ibid., 155-156.

78   José Ambrosio Llamozas, "Memorial Presentado al Rey como Vicario General del Ejercito de Barlovento en las Provincias de Venezuela," **Boletin de la Academia General de Historia**, Caracas, No 71. Cited by Brito, **Historia**, (1979), 196-197. "El Comandante General Boves desde el principio

de la campaña manifestó el sistema que había propuesto del cual jamás se separó: fundabase en la destrucción de todos los blancos, conservando, halagando y contemplando a las demás castas (...) repartiendo las casas y los bienes de los muertos y de los desterrados entre los pardos y dándoles papeletas de propiedad." (Author's translation.).

79   Memoirs of Archbishop Narciso Coll y Prat, August 25, 1812. Cited by Thibaud Clément, Repúblicas en armas: Los ejércitos bolivarianos en la guerra de Independencia en Colombia y Venezuela. (Bogota, Institut français d'études andines, Editorial Planeta, 2003), 109. "...entabló una igualdad de hecho entre los oficiales blancos que seguían en su ejército y la feroz multitud de negros y zambos libres y esclavos que sacó de los Llanos." (Author's translation.).

80   Morillo's letter is cited by Laureano Vallenilla Lanz, Cesarismo democrático y otros textos, (Biblioteca Ayacucho, Caracas, 1991), 25. "Varias veces he informado a V.E. de la inclemencia de este clima y de estos llanos para las tropas europeas, cuyo rigor se hace sentir tan duramente en la salud del soldado... Los continuos pasos de ríos y caños, atravesando días enteros pantanos y lodazales, con el agua a la cintura, unido al escaso y miserable alimento del soldado en los arenales ardientes del Llano, ha ocasionado muchos enfermos de gravedad, y son muchos también los heridos por las 'rayas' y mordeduras por los pescados llamados 'caribes'..." (Author's translation.).

81   For an argument on the relationship between political culture and army structure in ancient Greece see Gregory F. Viggiano, "The Hoplite Revolution and the Rise of the Polis, Men of Bronze: Hoplite Warfare in Ancient Greece, Princeton University Press, 2013. For an analysis of Viking social structure and warfare see Anders Winroth, The Age of the Vikings, (Princeton University Press, 2016). For the unique tactical features of Napoleon's citizen-soldier army see Martin Van Creveld, Command in War, (Harvard University Press, 1987).

82   Lynch, Bolívar, (2006), Kindle Edition, location 1325.

83   Uslar, Rebelión, (1962), 128.

84   Ibid., 184.

85   Simón Bolívar, "Discurso de Angostura, pronunciado por el General Bolívar el 15 de Febrero de 1819, al Segundo Congreso General de Venezuela," transcribed from the original in the Archivo del Libertador, Volumen 100-B, folios 1–32, Letra de Jacinto Martel, Documento 3589,

http://www.archivodellibertador.gob.ve/escritos/buscador/spip. php?article9987

86   Ibid. "La diversidad de origen requiere un pulso infinitamente firme, un tacto infinitamente delicado para manejar esta sociedad eterogenea cuyo complicado artificio se disloca, se divide, se disuelve con la más ligera alteración." (Author's translation.).

87   Ibid. "Tengamos presente que nuestro Pueblo no es el europeo, ni el Americano del Norte: que mas bien es un compuesto de Africa y América que una emanación de la Europa; pues que hasta la España misma, deja de ser Europea por su sangre Africana, por sus Instituciones y por su carácter. Es imposible asignar con propiedad, á qué familia humana pertenecemos. La mayor parte del indígena se ha aniquilado, el Europeo se ha mezclado con el Americano y con el Africano, y este se ha mezclado con el Indio y con el Europeo..." (Author's translation.).

88   Ibid. "Nuestros Padres, diferentes en orígen y en sangre, son extrangeros, y todos difieren visiblemente en la epidermis: esta desemejanza trae un reto de la mayor trascendencia." (Author's translation.).

89   Ibid. "La sangre de nuestros ciudadanos, es diferente, mezclémosla para unirla..." (Author's translation.).

Dismantling the System, 2004-2019

1   Uslar Pietri, "Sembrando,"(1936), (Author's translation.).

2   Bolívar, "Angostura," Archivo del Libertador, (Author's translation.).

3   The 18th Brumaire of Louis Bonaparte haunts writers down the centuries because few books surpass the poetic lucidity of its political analysis. Borrowing its memorable phrases, even as the book warns of farcical repetitions, is hard to avoid.

4   Juan Uslar, Historia Política de Venezuela, (Editorial Mediterraneo, 1975).

5   François Furet offers the most compelling analysis of how Rousseau's "general will" was deployed by Jacobins to annihilate individual freedoms. "Society is thus conceived of in terms of the nation: the multiplicity of individuals and of private interests is immediately cancelled out and reaggregated by the existence of a historical contract harking back to the nation's origins." These words would just as well describe Chavez's successful vanquishing of the liberal justice project through the recuperation of "originary rights." Furet's rereading of Tocqueville in his history of the revolution, and his analysis

of Rousseauian politics in his interpretation of those events, remain critical to decode the Chavista revolution. François Furet, The French Revolution 1770-1814, (Blackwell Publishers, 1988), and François Furet, Interpreting the French Revolution, (Cambridge University Press, 1997).

6   A Convention resembling a modern parliament stood at the center of the French Revolution's early days. The Jacobin faction loudly fought the center-right, rallying around Lafayette and the center-left's Girondins, led by Danton. But Robespierre, the Jacobin leader, understood that his path to power lay in exiting the endless debates. He became the head of an all-powerful Committee of Public Safety charged with enforcing the revolution's security. His new executive power was increasingly legitimized by revolutionary clubs sprouting all over the country. The clubs, essentially neighborhood committees of the faithful, formed a symbolic pyramid rising from the people, "the streets," all the way up to Robespierre as guarantor of the revolution's safety. For a while, the Jacobins played in both worlds. Their discourse and power emanated from the clubs, while the legal justification for their rule still came from the Convention. As the revolutionary imaginary increasingly found its legitimacy in a national origin embodied by "the streets," a new logic appeared on the horizon. A frenzy of revolutionary authenticity took over politics. Not long after, many of the Convention's leaders and all imagined and actual dissenters were detained and decapitated at the scaffold. The general will, the one nation without differences, sent the transactional Convention and its pluralistic promise into a symbolic limbo.

7   George Rudé, Robespierre: Portrait of a Revolutionary Democrat, (London: Collins, 1975), 108.

8   The widespread use of the word "monkey" in Venezuelan society was the subject of extensive commentary by artist Enrique Enríquez in several performances, art works, and a book. Enrique Enríquez, Iván Larraguibel, Vanessa Gutiérrez, Mono ve, mono hace: memorias de viaje de un ejemplar venezolano, (Caracas, Litterae Editores, 1995).

9   Memes depicting Hugo Chavez as a primate can be found on Twitter and in general Google searches to this day. https://www.google.com/search?q=hugo+chavez+mono&tbm=isch&ved=2ahUKEwj0t8OD7u-v2AhW1l2oFHdLpB94Q2-cCegQIABAA&oq=hugo+chavez+mono&gs_lcp=CgNpbWcQA1C-CFi-CGDuEGgAcAB4AIABWYgBrgGSAQEy-mAEAoAEBqgELZ3dzLXdpei1pbWfAAQE&sclient=img&ei=vkNDYvTg-G7WvqtsP0tOf8A0&bih=677&biw=1536

10   See end note 86 in the first chapter of this book.

11   "Hugo Chavez bajo la lluvia el 4 de octubre de 2012," YouTube, posted by
     Luigino Bracci Roa, https://www.youtube.com/watch?v=TGXh9V1AqYQ

12   Reinaldo Silva, "El espíritu de nuestras tribus ancestrales, al grito de "Ana
     Karina Rote," Aporrea (March 21, 2019), https://www.aporrea.org/
     actualidad/a277242.html

13   United States of America v. Francisco Convit Guruceada. United States District
     Court Southern District of Florida, July 24, 2018. Court Docket Number:
     18-CR-20685-KMW.

14   Jakubowicz, Juan Planchard, 2016. Kindle location 61 of 5829. "Esa es la
     manera a través de la cual se enriqueció todo el que quiso y supo hacerlo.
     Cero riesgos. Todo pa'l bolsillo, todo bolivarianamente legal. Es una especie
     de asalto al país, pero un asalto por voluntad popular deja de ser un asalto y
     se convierte en una filosofía colectiva..." (Author's translation.).

15   Roy Carroll, Comandante: Hugo Chávez's Venezuela, (Penguin Books, 2013).

16   Ibid., Kindle location 2791 of 4265.

17   Alexandra Ulmer and Marianna Párraga, "Special Report: Oil output goes
     AWOL in Venezuela as soldiers run PDVSA," Reuters, (December 26, 2018),
     https://www.reuters.com/article/us-venezuela-pdvsa-military-specialrepor/
     special-report-oil-output-goes-awol-in-venezuela-as-soldiers-run-pdvsa-idUSKC-
     N1OP0RZ

18   Robert Rapier, "How Venezuela Ruined its Oil Industry," Forbes, (May 7, 2017).

19   Marianna Párraga, "Venezuelan oil exports fell by a third in 2019 as U.S.
     sanctions bit: data," Reuters, (January 7, 2020).

20   Carroll, Comandante, 2013. Kindle Location 2676 of 4265.

21   Instituto Nacional de Estadística, "En el 2003 se creó la Misión Barrio
     Adentro – 16 de Abril," (April 16, 2018), http://www.ine.gov.ve/index.
     php?option=com_content&view=article&id=1129%3Aen-el-2003-se-creo
     -la-mision-barrio-adentro-16-de-abril&catid=154%3Aefemerides&Itemid=5#:~:-
     text=El%2016%20de%20abril%20de,atenci%C3%B3n%20
     m%C3%A9dica%20preventiva%20y%20gratuita

22   Ibid.

23   Carlos Alvarado (Ministerio de Salud), César Arismendi (Ministerio de Salud),
     Francisco Armada (Ministerio de Salud), Gustavo Bergonzoli (Organización
     Panamericana de la Salud), Radamés Borroto (Misión Médica Cubana),
     Pedro Luis Castellanos (Organización Panamericana de la Salud), et al.,

"Derecho a la salud e inclusión social en Venezuela," Pan American Health Organization, World Health Organization, (Caracas, July 2006).

24 Ibid., 29-31.

25 Carles Muntaner, MD, PhD, Francisco Armada, MD, PhD, Haejoo Chung, RPh, PhD, Rosicar Mata, Leslie Williams-Brennan, Bsc, BScN, RN, and Joan Benach, MD, PhD, "Venezuela's Barrio Adentro: Participatory Democracy, South-South Cooperation and Health Care for All," Social Medicine, Vol. 4 No. 4, (November 2008), 237, https://pdfs.semantic-scholar.org/6ef6/3c749c1fc0b1d16a52dc3a6c5753fff678dc.pdf?_ga=2.203600208.1333617764.1592674434-1082690709.1592674434

26 Alvarado, Arismendi, et al., "Derecho a la salud e inclusión social en Venezuela," 26-27.

27 Muntaner, Armada, et al., "Venezuela's Barrio Adentro: Participatory Democracy, South-South Cooperation and Health Care for All," 238.

28 Alí Rodríguez Araque, Seminario Nacional: Política Social ¿Un Nuevo Paradigma?. FEGS, (Caracas 11,12 y 13 de mayo de 2004). Quoted in Las Misiones Sociales en Venezuela, Yolanda D'Elia and Luis Francisco Cabezas, ILDIS, (May 2008). "Las misiones no son otra cosa que el germen de una nueva institucionalidad; ante un gran obstaculo como es ese Estado burocrático, ineficiente e ineficaz, pues van surgiendo, al lado de el, formas paralelas." (Author's translation.).

29 Alvarado, Arismendi, et al., "Derecho a la salud e inclusión social en Venezuela," 42.

30 Muntaner, Armada, et al., "Venezuela's Barrio Adentro: Participatory Democracy, South-South Cooperation and Health Care for All," 238.

31 Ibid., 239-240.

32 "Hospital Cardiológico Infantil Latinoamericano Dr. Gilberto Rodríguez Ochoa," YouTube, posted by Brasilego NaNet, (May 1, 2013), https://youtu.be/_loCm-vTz5s

33 Javier Segura del Pozo, "Misión Barrio Adentro (1° parte: origen y desar-rollo)," in Salud Pública y algo más, Blog Madrimasd.org, 9 enero, 2012, http://www.madrimasd.org/blogs/salud_publica/2012/01/09/132990

34 Ibid.

35 "Gran Misión Barrio Adentro," Transparency Venezuela, January 2015, Misiones Transparentes, 11, https://transparencia.org.ve/wp-content/uploads/2016/04/5.-Barrio-Adentro.pdf

36   Holly K. Sonneland, "Update: Venezuela Is Running Short of Everything by Holly K. Sonneland," America's Society/Council of the Americas, (March 24, 2016), https://www.as-coa.org/articles/update-venezuela-running-short-everything

37   Alberto E. Paniz-Mondolfi, Adriana Tami, Maria E. Grillet, Marilianna Márquez, Juan Hernández-Villena, María A. Escalona-Rodríguez, Gabriela M. Blohm, Isis Mejías, Huníades Urbina-Medina, Alejandro Rísquez, Julio Castro, Ana Carvajal, Carlos Walter, María G. López, Philipp Schwabl, Luis Hernández-Castro, Michael A. Miles, Peter J. Hotez, John Lednicky, J. Glenn Morris, James Crainey, Sergio Luz, Juan D. Ramírez, Emilia Sordillo, Martin Llewellyn, Merari Canache, María Araque, and José Oletta, "Resurgence of Vaccine-Preventable Diseases in Venezuela as a Regional Public Health Threat in the Americas," **EID Journal**, Centers for Disease Control, Vol. 25, No. 4, April 2019.

38   Ibid.

39   "Venezuela's Humanitarian Emergency: Large-Scale UN Response Needed to Address Health and Food Crises," **Human Rights Watch**, (April 4, 2019), https://www.hrw.org/report/2019/04/04/venezuelas-humanitarian-emergency/large-scale-un-response-needed-address-health#

40   Sarah Boseley and Emma Graham-Harrison, "Venezuela crisis threatens disease epidemic across continent–experts," **Guardian**, (21 February 2019).

41   Kirk Semple, "'We're Losing the Fight': Tuberculosis Batters a Venezuela in Crisis," **The New York Times**, (March 20, 2018).

42   "Venezuela's Humanitarian Emergency," **Human Rights Watch**, (April 4, 2019), https://www.hrw.org/report/2019/04/04/venezuelas-humanitari-an-emergency/large-scale-un-response-needed-address-health#:~:text=(Washington%2C%20DC%2C%20April%204,secretary%2Dgeneral%2C%20researchers%20from%20Johns

43   Ibid.

44   Melody Schreiber, "Researchers are Surprised by the Magnitude of Venezuela's Health Crisis," National Public Radio, (April 5, 2019).

45   "Venezuela's Humanitarian Emergency," **Human Rights Watch**, (2019).

46   Boseley, Graham-Harrison, "Venezuela crisis threatens disease epidemic across continent," **Guardian**.

47   "Venezuela's Humanitarian Emergency," **Human Rights Watch**, (2019).

48   Melody Schreiber, "Researchers are Surprised," (2019).

49   Sean Griffing, Leopoldo Villegas, Venkatachalam Udhayakumar, "Malaria Control and Elimination, Venezuela, 1800s-1970s." **Emerging Infectious Diseases**, Centers of Disease Control, (20, October 2014), 1700.

50   "Gran Misión Barrio Adentro," **Transparency**, 13.

51   Griffing, Villegas, Udhayakumar, "Malaria Control."

52   Boseley, Graham-Harrison, "Venezuela crisis threatens disease epidemic across continent."

53   Ibid., 1698.

54   Ibid., 1699.

55   Gideon Long, "Venezuela crisis: malaria spreads as economy implodes," **Financial Times**, (April 24, 2019).

56   See Luis Gerardo Gabaldón, Seguridad ciudadana, confianza pública y policía en Venezuela, **Revista Venezolana de Economía y Ciencias Sociales**, Vol. 13, No. 3, (Caracas: December 2007).

57   Nikolas Kozlooff, **Hugo Chavez**. Griffin, Kindle Edition, (2007), 97, location 2222. Citing Marta Harnecker, **Venezuela: Militares junto al pueblo**, El Viejo Topo, (2004), 13, 24.

58   Cristóbal Valencia Ramírez, "Venezuela's Bolivarian Revolution: Who Are the Chavistas?," **Latin American Perspectives**, 85, (2020), from http://www.jstor. org/stable/30040243, Vol. 32, No. 3, Venezuelan Exceptionalism Revisited: New Perspectives on Politics and Society (May, 2005).

59   Patricia Torres and Nicholas Casey, "Armed Civilian Bands in Venezuela Prop Up Unpopular President," **The New York Times**, (April 22, 2017).

60   "Radiografía de los colectivos chavistas: qué bandas armadas controlan cada zona de Venezuela y quiénes son sus líderes," **Infobae**, (11 de Enero 2020), https://www.infobae.com/america/venezuela/2020/01/11/radiografia-de-los-colectivos-chavistas-que-bandas-armadas-controlan-cada-zona-de-venezue-la-y-quienes-son-sus-lideres/

61   Max Fisher, Amanda Taub, "How Venezuela Stumbled to the Brink of Collapse," **The New York Times**, (May 14, 2017).

62   International Crisis Group, "Violence and Politics in Venezuela Report," **International Crisis Group**, (August 17, 2011), https://www.crisisgroup.org/ latin-america-caribbean/andes/venezuela/violence-and-politics-venezuela

63 Patrick Oppmann, "The Venezuelan radio host leading an armed 'colectivo' in support of Maduro," **CNN**, (May 24, 2019), https://www.cnn.com/2019/05/24/americas/venezuela-colectivos-oppman-intl/index.html

64 Daniel Wallis, "Venezuela violence puts focus on militant 'colectivo' groups," **Reuters**, (February 13, 2014).

65 G. Lorena Meléndez, "Gobierno tolera negocios de paramilitares para no perder a sus pistoleros," **Provea**, (August 10, 2017), https://www.derechos.org.ve/paramilitares-investigacion/gobierno-tolera-negocios-de-paramilitares-para-no-perder-a-sus-pistoleros

66 Jeremy McDermott, "Venezuela, el nuevo centro latinoamericano del crimen," **The New York Times**, (July 17, 2018).

67 Unidad de Investigación, "Venezuela, crimen sin fronteras," **El País**, (Septiembre 2017), https://consejoderedaccion.org/noticias/venezuela-crimen-sin-fronteras

68 Antulio Rosales, "Statization and denationalization dynamics in Venezuela's artisanal and small scale-large-scale mining interface," **Resources Policy**, Vol. 63, (October 2019), https://www.sciencedirect.com/science/article/pii/S0301420718306718

69 Girish Gupta, "Cárceles Venezuela, un coctel de armas, droga y mafias," **Reuters**, (September 26, 2011).

70 Venezuela Investigative Unit, "Venezuela Prisons: 'Pranes' and 'Revolutionary' Criminality," **Insight Crime**, (September 2017), https://www.insightcrime.org/wp-content/uploads/2017/09/Venezuela-Prisons-Pranes-Revolutionary-Criminality.pdf

71 Redacción, "Juez Casado: Protección de Wilmito está en manos del alto gobierno chavista," **El Carabobeño**, (March 1, 2017), https://www.el-carabobeno.com/juez-casado-proteccion-wilmito-esta-manos-del-alto-gobierno-chavista/

72 Melisa Silva Franco, "La última 'balada' de 'El conejo' chavista," **El Mundo**, (February 4, 2016), https://www.elmundo.es/cronica/2016/02/04/56abaee7ca4741c3368b45d0.html

73 Investigative Unit, "Venezuela Prisons," **Insight Crime**, (2017).

74 "Carcel Venezuela Margarita despidiendo a el ex pran el conejo," YouTube, posted by FrankTv Olivier, (October 23, 2016), https://youtu.be/HUBJPp6iLh8

75 Redacción, "Juez Casado," **El Carabobeño**, (2016).

76 Investigative Unit, "Venezuela Prisons," Insight Crime, (2017).

77 Venezuela Investigative Unit, "The Devolution of State Power: 'The Pranes,'" Insight Crime, (May 20, 2018).

78 Sebastián Liste, "On the Inside of a Venezuelan Prison Controlled by Inmates," Exhibition Sebastián Liste, International Festival of Photojournalism, 2020, https://www.visapourlimage.com/en.

79 World Prison Brief, World Prison Data, Venezuela, https://www.prisonstudies.org/

80 Andres Schipani, "Venezuela's Jackson Gutierrez makes films that are gangland hits," Financial Times, (January 31, 2016).

81 Jackson Gutierrez YouTube Channel, YouTube, JacksonGutierrez, https://www.youtube.com/channel/UC0f6jhh0mA4k-fTs0X5zjVQ

82 Human Development Reports, "Homicide rate (per 100,000 people)," United Nations Development Programme, http://hdr.undp.org/en/indicators/61006

83 Dorothy Kronick, "How to Count Our Dead," Caracas Chronicles, (July 1, 2016). https://www.caracaschronicles.com/2016/07/01/our-dead/

84 Ibid.

85 Observatorio Venezolano de Violencia, "Informe Anual de Violencia," Observatorio Venezolano de Violencia, https://observatoriodeviolencia.org.ve/informes/informe-anual-de-violencia/

86 Although the advisory and executive roles of Cuban security forces have not been completely documented, they are widely understood to have been profound and sustained at least until this writing. See Angus Berwick, "Special Report: How Cuba taught Venezuela to quash military dissent," Reuters, (August 22, 2019), and Adam Taylor, "How many Cuban troops are there in Venezuela? The U.S. says over 20,000. Cuba says zero," The Washington Post, (May 2, 2019).

87 Guillermo D. Olmo, "Venezuela: la FAES, la polémica policía de élite creada por Nicolás Maduro a la que se acusa de ser un 'grupo de exterminio,'" BBC.com, (December 11, 2019).

88 Ana Vanessa Herrero, Nicholas Casey, "Maduro Turns to Special Police Force to Crush Dissent," The New York Times, (June 30, 2019), https://www.nytimes.com/2019/01/30/world/americas/venezuela-maduro-protests-faes.html

89 Felipe Romero (2019). [Photo of a FAES commando with full uniform in the street]. Infobae, August 6, 2019. https://www.infobae.com/america/

venezuela/2019/08/06/la-ong-justicia-venezolana-denuncio-que-el-regimen-de-nicolas-maduro-mantiene-a-211-militares-como-presos-politicos/

90   Nick Cumming-Bruce, "Venezuela Forces Killed Thousands, Then Covered It Up, U.N. Says," The New York Times, (July 4, 2019).

91   María Pilar García-Guadilla, Ana Mallen, "Venezuela: Democracia participativa, socialismo del siglo XXI y polarización," LasaForum, Vol. XLIV, Issue 4, (Fall 2013).

92   Asamblea Nacional N° 434, "Ley de Consejos Comunales," La Asamblea Nacional de la República Bolivariana de Venezuela, Dirección de los Servicios de Secretaria, (2006), https://www.acnur.org/fileadmin/Documentos/BDL/2008/6641.pdf

93   Ibid.

94   Provea, Una mirada a los Consejos Comunales esde la perspectiva de los derechos humanos,(Caracas: Provea, 2007), 17, http://www.derechos.org.ve/pw/wp-content/uploads/consejos-comunales1.pdf

95   Adam Gill, "Interview: Michael Albert on the Communal Councils in Venezuela," London Progressive Journal, (November 21, 2008), https://londonprogressivejournal.com/2008/11/21/interview-michael-albert-on-the-communal-councils-in-venezuela/

96   Misiones Transparentes, "Cinco Grandes Misiones en Venezuela," Transparencia Venezuela, (December 2014), https://transparencia.org.ve/wp-content/uploads/2016/04/1.-Cinco-Grandes-Misiones-Dic.pdf

97   Alvarado, Arismendi, et al., "Derecho a la salud e inclusión social en Venezuela," 26-27.

98   Asamblea Nacional N° 899, "Ley Orgánica de las Comunas," La Asamblea Nacional de la República Bolivariana de Venezuela, (December 2010), http://www4.cne.gob.ve/onpc/web/documentos/Leyes/Ley_Organica_de_las_Comunas.pdf

99   "Antecedentes," Ministerio del Poder Popular para las Comunas y los Movimientos Sociales, Gobierno Bolivariano de Venezuela, https://www.mpcomunas.gob.ve/2017/01/19/mision-vision-y-antecedente/

100 Provea, Una mirada a los Consejos Comunales, Provea, 19.

101 Alfredo Cilento, "Discurso De Incorporación a La ANIH De Alfredo Cilento Sarli y Respuesta De Arnoldo Gabaldón," Academia Nacional De La Ingeniería y El Hábitat, (2016), https://www.academia.edu/37805170/Discurso_de_incorporaci%C3%B3n_a_la_ANIH_de_Alfredo_Cilento_

Sarli_y_respuesta_de_Arnoldo_Gabald%C3%B3nHttp://Www.acading.org. ve/Info/Publicaciones/Boletines/boletin31.Php Boletin 31 (2016).

102 Comando Central Bolivariano, Reorganización para Profundizar la Ofensiva Revolucionaria. **Partido Socialista Unido de Venezuela**, Boletín 50, (February 23, 2017), https://www.yumpu.com/es/document/read/57038656/ reorganizacion-para-profundizar-la-ofensiva-revolucionaria-bolivariano-agenda

103 Vivian Sequera, "Venezuelans report big weight losses in 2017 as hunger hits," **Reuters**, (February 21, 2018).

104 Kozloff, **Chavez**. Griffin, Kindle Edition, 78, location 1759. Citing Harnecker, **Venezuela**, El Viejo Topo, (2004).

105 CMI Working Paper | 2016, "A Civil-Military Alliance: The Venezuelan Armed Forces before and during the Chávez era," Iselin Åsedotter Strønen (2016) Bergen: Chr. Michelsen Institute (CMI Working Paper WP 2016:4), https:// www.cmi.no/publications/5808-a-civil-military-alliance

106 Brian Ellsworth, Mayela Armas, "The Maduro mystery: Why the armed forces still stand by Venezuela's beleaguered president," Reuters, (July 28, 2019).

107 Ibid.

108 Ibid.

109 KonZapata, Roberto Deniz, "Maduro ficha a un defensor de la 'guerra económica' como ministro de Economía," **AmericaEconomía**, (January 8, 2016), https://americaeconomica.com/noticia/22236/noticia/maduro-ficha-a-un-defensor-de-la-guerra-economica-como-ministro-de-economia.html

110 "Maduro dice Chávez se le apareció en forma de pajarito chiquitico y lo bendijo," YouTube, posted by ÚltimasNoticiasDiario, (April 2, 2013), https:// www.youtube.com/watch?v=487Mp7Un7Eg

111 El Nacional, "Delcy Rodríguez: No existe crisis humanitaria en Venezuela," **El Nacional**, (August 31, 2018), https://www.elnacional.com/gobierno/ delcy-rodriguez-existe-crisis-humanitaria-venezuela_250038/

112 See the second endnote of the first chapter in this book.

Epilogue: Politics Without a State, 1834–1837

1   José Antonio Páez, **Autobiografía del General José Antonio Páez**, Tomo I, (Caracas, Tipografía de Espinal e Hijos, 1889), 10, Google Books: https://books.google.com.mx/

books?id=AXgCAAAAYAAJ&printsec=frontcover&dq=editions:O-CLC20340611&lr=

2   Anonymous, **Recollections of a Service of Three Years During the War-of-Extermination in the Republics of Venezuela and Colombia**, Volume 1, (Hunt and Clarke, 1828), 175, Google books: https://www.google.com/books/edition/_/TW81AAAAIAAJ?hl=en&sa=X&ved=2ahUKEwix85_mjf_xAhXGmq0KHR1GCKYQre8FMA56BAgJEAk

3   Juan Uslar mentions General José Trinidad Morán's estimate of 20,000 refugees, Juan Uslar, **Historia De La Rebelión Popular De 1814**, Edime, (Caracas, 1962), 145.

4   While the ultimate source for the quote cannot be found, it lives on in dozens of internet outlets, starting with the article on José María Vargas in Wikiquote. com, https://es.wikiquote.org/wiki/Jos%C3%A9_Mar%C3%ADa_Vargas "El mundo le pertenece a los valientes, Dr. Vargas." "No, el mundo es del hombre justo. Es el hombre de bien, y no del valiente, el que siempre ha vivido y vivirá feliz sobre la tierra y seguro sobre su conciencia." (Author's translation.).

5   Rafael Arráiz Lucca, **Historia Política de Venezuela** (1498 a nuestros días), Editorial Universidad del Rosario, (Bogota, 2013), 262, "el caudillismo emergería de inmediato enfrentando la sindéresis republicana, buscando imponer su propia gramática, empuñando para ello una espada..." (Author's translation.).

6   Manuel Caballero, **La Peste Militar: Escritos Polémicos 1992-2007**, Editorial Alfa, (2007), 142, Cited by Ana Teresa Torres, **La Herencia De La Tribu. Del Mito De La Independencia a La Revolución Bolivariana**, Editorial Alfa, (2009), Kindle Edition, location 483, "Son militares, y por lo tanto la fuente de su poder, o de su aspiracion a tenerlo, eran las armas." (Author's translation.).

7   Diego Bautista Urbaneja, **Bolívar, El Pueblo y el Poder**. Fundación Para La Cultura, (2004), 91. Cited by Ana Teresa Torres, **La Herencia De La Tribu. Del Mito De La Independencia a La Revolución Bolivariana**, Editorial Alfa, (2009), Kindle Edition, location 454, "...el intento correspondiente a una visión risueña de las cosas, según la cual sólo cuatro años después de la muerte de Bolívar ya los procederes debían dar paso a los propietarios..." (Author's translation.).

8   See Alexis de Tocqueville, **Tocqueville: The Ancien Régime and the French Revolution**, Jon Elster, ed., (Cambridge University Press, 2011).

9   Historian Federico Brito Figueroa asserts that census figures in 1810, the year the war broke out, placed the colony's population at 898,043, while those of 1822 put it at 616,545, in which case 281,498 perished from all causes

during the conflict. He also quotes geographer Agustin Codazzi, who claimed in 1841 that 200,000 soldiers and civilians had died in the violent conflict, and another 60,000 had died from plagues and the earthquake of 1812. In both counts the country had lost a third of its population in a decade of war. Federico Brito Figueroa, "La población y la estructura social de Venezuela en las primeras décadas del siglo XIX," Bulletin Hispanique, Tome LXIX, No 3-4, (Bourdeux, July-December 1967). Codazzi, Agustín, Resumen de la geografía de Venezuela, (París, Imprenta de H. Fournier y Compañía, 1841, 245).

10 Autobiografía del General José Antonio Páez, Tomo II, (Caracas, 1890, 294). Google Books: https://books.google.com/books?id=aXgCAAAAYAA-J&printsec=frontcover&source=gbs_ge_summary_r&cad=0#v=onep-age&q&f=true294

11 Ibid.

12 Ibid., 297.

13 Ibid., 298.

14 Ibid.

15 Ibid., 298-299.

16 Ibid., 299.

17 Ibid., 302.

18 Ibid., 318.

19 Ibid., 316.

20 Ibid., 317.

21 Ibid., 318.

22 Ibid., 395-396.

23 Gilles Deleuze and Félix Guattari, A Thousand Plateaus, translated by Brian Massumi, (University of Minnesota Press, 1987), 351-378.

24 Paez, Autobiografia, (1888), 395-396.

25 Deleuze, and Guattari, A Thousand, (1987), 351-378.

26 Paez, Autobiografia, 1888, 395-396.

27 Ibid., 397.

28 Ibid.

29 Ibid., 398.

30   Ibid., 399.

31   Ibid., 400.

32   Ibid.

33   BBC, "Venezuelan pirates—the new scourge of the Caribbean," BBC News, (January 28, 2019). https://www.bbc.com/news/stories-47003108. Vasco Cotovio, Isa Soares, and William Bonnett, "A trail of 'bloody gold' leads to Venezuela's government," CNN.com, (August 23, 2019). Jeremy McDermott, "Venezuela, the New Regional Crime Hub," The New York Times, (July 15, 201). Office to Monitor and Combat Trafficking in Persons, "2019 Trafficking in Persons Report: Venezuela," US State Department. https://www.state.gov/reports/2019-trafficking-in-persons-report-2/venezuela/

34   While these sources date from 2021, the trends here described were clearly present by 2018 and 2019, if not before. Isayen Herrera, Anatoly Kurmanaev, "Gangs Erode Maduro's Grip on Caracas," The New York Times, (May 30, 2021), Anatoly Kurmanaev, "Terrorist Group Steps into Venezuela as Lawlessness Grows," The New York Times, (April 26, 2021).

35   D.I., "Guaidó llama a nuevas movilizaciones hasta la salida del "usurpador Maduro," El Confidencial, (January 25, 2019).

36   See Marc Bloch, The Royal Touch, (Routledge, 2015).

37   Angus Berwick, "How ZTE helps Venezuela create Chinese-style social control," Reuters, A Reuters Special Report, (November 14, 2018).

38   Brito Figueroa, Historia, (1979), 253.

39   Ibid.

40   Although some of this reporting refers to later years, the Patria System was started in 2018 and was firmly in place by 2019. Florantonia Singer, "El Sistema Patria, una nueva estructura de control social en Venezuela," El País, (April 20, 2021).

41   Berwick, "ZTE," (2018).

In the aftermath of tragedies precipitated by human folly, imagining a future requires a cold, hard look at what happened. But we must also honor our victims as well as those we never knew:

Alberto Lizarralde, who, as early as I can remember, made sure I understood his own beloved country could easily unravel and yet could not see the storm through.

Trina Maradey Fernández, whose stories of how modern Venezuela came together are as unforgettable as her stoicism at the beginning of the end of the only world she ever knew.

Fr. Steven Wood, who taught me about compassion when I was not yet ten years old, and still at his good work four decades later, fell to the ravages of sadistic violence gripping his adoptive country.

To the millions of anonymous victims, those killed, those who fled or are still fleeing, and those who stayed and barely survived the dreams of revolution.

CREDITS

Editors: Caroline Greeven, Nikola Krestonosich Celis,
Allison McKechnie, Louise Stahl.
Cover Design: Christian Báez.
Cover Art: Tony Vázquez.
Book Interior Design: Michael Grossman.
Author Photo: Jaime Navarro.
Proofreader: Louise Stahl.
Readers: Ximena Fuentes, Sonia Gil Montero,
Rafael Osío Cabrices, Edgar Ramírez, Tony Vázquez.

Photo by Jaime Navarro

Carlos Lizarralde writes about
the long-term structures of Latin
American history to question our
conventional wisdom about the
present times.

He pursued a doctorate in
Comparative Literature at the
University of Massachusetts at
Amherst, and studied politics
and literary theory at Hampshire
College.
He divides his time between
Miami Beach and Mexico City.

Printed in Dunstable, United Kingdom